AWKWARD

A DETOUR

AWKWARD

A DETOUR

Mary Cappello

BELLEVUE LITERARY PRESS
New York

First published in the United States in 2007 by
Bellevue Literary Press
New York

FOR INFORMATION ADDRESS:
Bellevue Literary Press
NYU School of Medicine
550 First Avenue
OBV 640
New York, NY 10016

This book was published with the generous support of
Bellevue Literary Press's founding donor the Arnold Simon Family Trust
and the Bernard & Irene Schwartz Foundation.

Cataloging-in-Publication Data is available from the Library of Congress.

Book design and type formatting by Bernard Schleifer
Manufactured in the United States of America
ISBN-13 978-1-934137-01-7
FIRST EDITION
1 3 5 7 9 8 6 4 2

For Karen Carr,
fellow writer, gardener,
reader, friend

"Can you understand," asked my father, "the deep meaning of that weakness, that passion for coloured tissue, for papier-mâché, for distemper, for oakum and sawdust? This is," he continued with a pained smile, "the proof of our love for matter as such, for its fluffiness or porosity, for its unique mystical consistency. Demiurge, that great master and artist, made matter invisible, made it disappear under the surface of life. We, on the contrary, love its creaking, its resistance, its clumsiness. We like to see behind each gesture, behind each move, its inertia, its heavy effort, its bearlike awkwardness."

—BRUNO SCHULZ, *"Treatise on the Tailor's Dummies or the Second Book of Genesis"*

THE WORLD AND I

This is not exactly what I mean
Any more than the sun is the sun.
But how to mean more closely
If the sun shines but approximately?
What a world of awkwardness!
What hostile implements of sense!
Perhaps this is as close a meaning
As perhaps becomes such knowing.
Else I think the world and I
Must live together as strangers and die—
A sour love, each doubtful whether
Was ever a thing to love the other.
No, better for both to be nearly sure
Each of each—exactly where
Exactly I and exactly the world
Fail to meet by a moment, and a word.

—LAURA RIDING, *Selected Poems in Five Sets*

Can we make progress if we do not enter into regions far from equilibrium?

—GILLES DELEUZE, *"He Stuttered"*

CONTENTS

I

BREATHING

TOUCHING

BREACHING

BARING

2

FACING

FALLING

STALLING

3

SURGING

DETOURING

4

DELVING

I

BREATHING

spasmodic

ONE DAY I READ in order to know *things*, another day, to know *the truth*. I read to be aided in my lust—to be seduced to feel, to be lured out. I read not to be alone. I want for my day to be split open by a tidal wave of strange imaginings when I read, for something, anything, to break through. A book gains a place on my shelf for the way it forces me to remember. A sentence becomes locked in my heart for the way it helps me to forget. I admit to enjoying that "good feeling" of being in the midst of something higher and better when I read, but lately I long for a literature that can throw a wrench into the works. A mucking up of the machinery is called for, and instantly I wonder how it came to be a wrench that won that telling phrase rather than a screwdriver or a hammer, because a wrench seems so right now, so necessary to messing things up and forcing the plant to shut down. Had someone been tightening by way of repairing a delicate part when, distracted, they "lost their grip" and dropped the tool into a spring of well-greased gears, or did overzealousness for work bring the whole works to a standstill? Some anger slipped through, slipping into the work; the worker tightened too well and too hard until the wrench flew. Perhaps no accident at all incited the phrase but a worker's quite conscious rebellion. Some momentous act must have lent the world a new sense of the "wrench," but now it is yours and mine to use, and use well and more often until wrench has nothing to do with a tool for tightening bolts and everything to do with injury (an ankle, say), and suddenness (a tightening in the stomach), anguish even (you grip your gut), and distorted meanings (desperately you wrest matter from nothingness). The further the wrench travels from the feeling of cold metal in my hand, the closer it comes to becoming a word: see it now standing at the far end of all that happens to us daily for which we *have* no words. The worker has vanished.

You write the book you want to read.

Something has to give.

I try to forget my computer. I compose a novel using crayons and no sharpener. I experience a waxen feel and acknowledge unplumbed resources. If I write with my arm in a monkey grip, if I compose awkwardly—forget grace—the truth will out. I will not allow myself certain phrases: no sentences can begin with the word "today," or "now," as if to plead originality, distinctness, departure, or difference. There are to be no arms raised in greeting, no morning dew, no illuminations clear as rock candy and just as liquid, dissolvable; no melting, no account of how "I began to understand." No lilting, or claims of possibility, no coulds, how I *could* do this or that, no refrains but interruptions, and certainly no more than one reference to how I continue to avoid my reflection in the mirror, how "it begins in the body," or my memory of swing sets. I've been chattering without knowing all the while that my interlocutor is deaf. Or that my interlocutor is my deaf self. I've been listening without hearing a thing my companion has said. Are these the conditions for awkward situations or just the norm? Poet: plaintive illuminator, exposer of secrets, paragon of self-pity who sometimes said what it *was* and sometimes said what it was *like*. Now. Today. Through the window gazing at the swing set.

But what if writing sought to describe all that has a claim on me that isn't pretty? Give me a literature of the spasm. Let sentences plunge, a pear plashing through branches gleaming gold, a gift from the gods. No. Let them ooze like a mangled, rotten, half-bitten possibly poisonous hapless thing landing with a splat onto a well-intended platter. Make a paragraph out of overstuffed drawers, the stuff of attempted purges, all you've pushed out of sight without discarding, the drawer overflowing, the drawer that refused to be neatened, that is refuse, what is refused but can't be gotten rid of. Fashion a voice that can break the spell. Where I thought the ground was smooth, I now feel its graininess poking up into my heels, scraping my arches, piercing toes, the sound of a person pushing a locomotive up the street, beneath my window, the trundling of an overloaded trash can on wheels.

I will seek out awkwardness over and against revelation, even if I find myself beginning again, against my better judgment, with a dream.

backward

Inside any relationship to knowledge, any labyrinth of truth, any interlocutory space, there are entryways and exits that refuse to play their promised role. The choice of a back door could be evasive and it could be revelatory.

Most people don't display a welcome mat before their back-doors. The front door opens for guests to enter its well-pruned threshold, the face the home's owner wants to present to the world. The back door, ever subordinated, is so much more interesting in what it might reveal. Guests enter through the front door, whereas the backdoor might be reserved for deliverymen, workmen tramping past moldering socks and into the house's bowels, its cellar, or engine room, the dwelling's unconscious. The backdoor can come to be the choice of children on their way out to play or burglars on their way in. Once, locked out of the house, my father in a fit of desperation broke one of the panes of glass in the backdoor with his bare fist. We filed in, and, after one of us fetched a dishtowel to wrap around his bleeding hand, he went to the hospital. A bird was stuck in the basement of our house, and an unusually tall police-man had to crouch, quite as caught as the bird, to get through the backdoor. My brother and I fought so fiercely over a badminton game one day that my mother rushed out the backdoor and in a fury took each racquet in her hand and broke it over her knee. Standing high on the pedals of my tricycle at three, I galumphed into the handlebar's hard metal, meeting the space between my legs. The pain and blood sped me like an automatic motor through the backdoor and up the stairs to my mother. Relatives bustled in all a blur through the front door, Santa Claus climbed in by the roof (though our house was without a chimney), while the back-door was the entryway for the unnameable.

The backdoor to my mother's father's house, that immigrant threshold, on the other hand, was a benign and sensuous egress. A sunporch stood adjacent to the kitchen, with windows that splashed to either side of it, one side opening into the kitchen. The porous scent of laundry hanging to dry acted as a sieve for the other scents of ripening fruit and boiling sauces in the kitchen. Feeling my way through the sheets and blessed scents, I grasp the latch on the whining screen door, push and fall back before the paradise that is my grandfather's homemade garden.

"What *is* this beautiful place?"

"France," he replies. He doesn't say "Italy."

This beautiful ghostly place.

untoward

Backward, forward, awkward, fourteenth century from "awk," backhanded, obsolete since 1600, from Old Norse, *ofugr*, "turned backwards" + adverbial suffix "-weard." Originally "in the wrong direction," "turned the wrong way." In Old High German, *abuh*. Back foremost, directed the other way, backhanded, from the lefthand. Awkward, then, seems to descend from backward and forward but cannot be contained by either. To understand awkward's departure from the norm, we would have to distinguish forward from backward, but unfortunately the difference is not at all clear cut. To me. Which is perhaps why I would like to herald a universe of the awkward, to hail the awkwardness of awkward, word with two w's, cousin to wayward.

What, for example, does forward motion have really to do with its metaphorical referent? Progress, development, optimism, time: we move forward into the future, we move backward into the past even though everyone knows that the past is not behind but ever with us (it has produced us, it is "inside" us) *even as* the past is gone, not behind us but without us. I have to look, to search, to think to make the past present to myself; I have to look forward to incite the past. The past is before me, and here the language both serves and stumps me when "before" can mean in front of me and "before" can mean preceding me. If something follows me, does it come after me or is it in pursuit of me? What time puts in front of me, space puts behind me. Sometimes you have to go backward in order to go forward, it is said, but why the primacy on forward, and how did forward come to mean pushy, stubborn, immovable after all? If our faces and our eyes let forward motion win the day, then maybe awkwardness depends on a revaluation of the senses. Imagine being able to say, encouragingly, "Place your best foot awkward," rather than forward, or, with adamancy, "You need to move awkward!"

There is a door behind you. There is a door in front of you. There is a door beside you. Which do you choose? A door atop? A door below? Awkward undoes the compass, it un-coordinates the map.

Awkward can also mean "untoward," a strange word this: not toward. If not toward, then how or where, and why? To be untoward is to be hard to manage, to be unseemly, and again, like a belch in the middle of the sermon, perverse, where "toward" means docile, compliant, tractable, educable.

Let us turn away. Let us turn awkwardly and see where we arrive. Toward an alternative system of ardor and gist, of ebullience and drift, of being and bearing. Toward speaking with the breath held. Un-toward.

cumbersome

I don't like the sensation—who does?—of what might be the most fundamental awkwardness on earth: the gap between the sheer *fact* of being alive and not knowing how to live; the space between life as a given and life as a series of acts of will; the gulf between biology and mind. Imagine the forgotten ancestors or the people recently deceased catapulted into sheer sound beyond the speed of light, not really members of anything anymore, no longer individuated but taken up into a vast subtlety, the music of the spheres. The awkwardness of individuality makes me fantasize such a release from the self into a music out of bounds; otherwise, I picture the dead as benign souls with greater sight than our own who can glimpse our struggle but who cannot reach us to help.

cumbersome   The gap between life and living life, between being alive but never being certain of what that could possibly mean, between the irreconcilability of solidity and transparency, makes for an essentially *purgatorial* existence. If we're lapsed Catholics, it leaves us with the option of reaching for heaven, retreating to hell, or choosing instead to dwell, a decision that reduces itself for me to being compelled periodically to *purge* not my sins, but my things.

The worst reminder of the frequency with which this need exerts itself combined with the inexhaustibility of the act came in the form of an old list of things to do that I found during a recent purge. The purge felt new, it felt final, as in, *finally* I am carrying out this much needed purge, but the old list of things to do reminded me that I'd hoed this row before, and I laughed out loud at the recurrence of that emphatic phrase on the page: "purge entire house!"

While some people opt to keep *everything* and more, I like to pretend to be able to choose what has a hold on me and what doesn't, what I'll hold onto and what will hold me, and thus to control the contours of what will keep me safe. The need to purge my living space became more acute after living and teaching in Russia and Italy for a year, and it is always indicative of a crossroads, desired or imposed. You should never own more than you yourself can carry, otherwise you could be doomed to awkwardness, heavy and dependent. Thus my decision one day systematically to dump drawers and boxes and piles of folders containing decades-old teaching, research, and writing notes. Hauling huge bins into my study, I ruthlessly dumped what felt like the steerage that kept my identity afloat. Papers like those I'd trashed retain the impress of the body, they represent hours of labor, and the place a person held in time, which is maybe why for weeks thereafter I couldn't enter my study without experiencing sudden bouts of shortness of breath. It was as though I were facing my own little death, doing the job of evacuating remains rather than leaving it to others. The shortness of breath, I later decided, wasn't indicative of drowning because of having let go, but was the body's reaction to there being *more* not less oxygen available to me. I guess I came to see it as a temporary flailing.

Paper, the shed lining of trees, abounds in my living space. The question is where to put it, what to save, and why? Here's a copy of

the letter I wrote the hospital staff in 1986 in honor of the nurses   *cumbersome*
who cared for me so fully following major surgery; the first post-
card I received from a gay male writer who later died of AIDS, "so
happy to make your acquaintance"; the ticket stub from a film I
didn't want to forget called *What Time Is It There?*; the audible
awkwardnesses of twenty-year-olds, their papers knee-deep, and my
comments to help them correct or learn to love their awkwardness,
equally dense, scattered about my rooms; the rip of a sheet from the
pad that alarmed the cat as though a razor had sliced through the
air; notes on bits of snatches of fragments of Post-its, one-liners and
taut images; an envelope scrawled with ancient dissertation notes
(what is that doing here?)—a formula for understanding authorship
and idleness; manuscripts and manumissions; litter-box lining and
all the news that's fit to print; the cash register receipt for the orange
juice and grilled-cheese sandwich that I ate in the Heathrow airport
the morning after my mother's middle-of-the-night phone call to tell
me that Sid had died of a heart attack; a folder in a file cabinet
marked "Sid Remembrances"; a half-torn and yellowed sheet describing the basic principles of Tai Chi: "clearly distinguish between yin
and yang, heavy and light, empty and full at all times."

Sid, my mother's partner of fifteen years and my beloved father
and friend, was suddenly lost to us one terrifically hot July day, on a
day a lot like this one in which I force an encounter with my "stuff."
The folder of "Sid Remembrances" gives me the most pause. It's
obvious that I'm not going to discard it, but the awkwardness of the
reduction of life to documents in a file folder is bald and piercing.
There are two such folders marked "Sid"—one is filed among similar
folders labeled "Marge's Obituary," "Dana's Memorial service,"
"Memorials to Constance," in a drawer with M.A. and Ph.D. exam
questions, grant applications, the minutes to department meetings,
and university review materials. The second Sid folder appears in a
drawer among files marked "Other People's Writing." What could
possibly be the logic of such placements? Filed this way, these papers
seem appallingly inappropriate; their intimate contact with life erased,
they reappear as personnel files of the missing. Is there a proper place
for such documents, or is the problem one of the falsity of a documentary, period, the need to save and place these papers even though the
people they represent remain displaced and unsaveable?

cumbersome   I'm supposed to be clearing a space, but I'm not: I'm sifting and
pausing, I'm leafing and pulling papers through holes in a meshing.
I'm embroidering and searching for a pattern, I'm crying to read a
copy of a letter of sympathy addressed to my mother by a friend of
mine who is a writer, perfect in its poetry and in its heart.

In a folder marked "Texts after Sid's Death," I find a newspaper
that I saved on the first anniversary of his death and an article that,
two weeks before his death, Sid had clipped from the paper to give to
me, a kind of human interest story on Philadelphia's Poe House and
one exuberant Park Ranger's enthusiasms for Poe. Sid had glued the
article to a stiff paper backing, the better to preserve the brittle page.
Emulsion mixed with newsprint left patches of Sid's fingerprints in the
center paragraphs and in the margins of lines. In the folder marked,
"Sid Remembrances," there's a letter Sid sent to me and my partner
written in that same week, two weeks before his death, just as Jean
and I were boarding a plane for England, in which he agrees to take
me up on a project to record what he called his "aperçus": "On my
alleged 'aperçus,' if you do in fact rate any of my past statements with
durability value as a 'quotable' please not [sic] it down somewhere in
hard print for my sake. You can be my amanuensis, if it is worth the
bother. . . ." The letter goes on to describe a cassette that Sid has made
to accompany his homespun Yiddish primer and his theory that "a
serious student, who wants to learn, should by my judgment, pick up
the language the same way an infant learns the language with mother's milk—by experiencing 'Mamalushen' or mother tongue in total
immersion, hearing complete sentences from the beginning, spoken
by an authentic ethnic voice."

I'm dumbstruck now mostly by a document I could not have
anticipated, this awkward grid that bears some relation to Sid: his
death certificate. I don't even know how it came into my possession,
until I recall that the airline agency that found me a seat on a plane
at the last minute needed proof of the deceased.

*Name of "decedent": Sidney Shupak. Sex: M. Social Security
Number. Date of Death: July 26, 1997. County of. Race of. Decedent's
Usual Occupation. Kind of Business: Pickles. Marital Status.
College: 1–4, or 5 + 3. Residence. Father's Name. Mother's Name.
Informant's Name. Method of Disposition. Place. Signature of Funeral
Service Licensee. License #. Place. Immediate Cause of Death. Other*

Significant Contributing Conditions. Manner of Death: Check One: cumbersome
Natural, Accident, Suicide, Homicide, Pending Investigation, Could
Not Be Determined. Place and Time of Injury. Injury at Work?
Certifier. Pronouncing Physician. Medical Examiner.

Is the awkwardness of a death certificate obvious? I don't think
so. What's awkward about it is that it can't be expected, the fact of
it, of finding it in a folder, a stumbling block in the process of a
clearing of the decks. It's awkward for the way it makes you wonder how you will come to fit within its squares; awkward for how
it makes death by "natural causes" something to aspire to. It's awkward in its redaction of a person to a list of wheres and whens. It's
full of information, and it's full of gaps. The death certificate makes
me awkward as it plays its certitude against my confusion. It claims
to know what happened to Sidney, whereas I do not.

Here's the documented life (see certificate). And the lived life,
where is that? The lived life is apparently much less certifiable.

Here's a bureaucratic awkwardness; here's ontological awkwardness. Which, if you had the choice, would you prefer to get to
know, sitting alone, inside a room?

What was awkward about Sidney was also what was beautiful
about Sidney, all that was attributable to him and to no one else.
There was his voice—deep, bass, rollicking, so low down it met you
like a bluesy comfort or a growl . . . which led him to speak in movie
theaters in what he called a "stage whisper," which made the seats
around him vibrate when he tried not to talk, which led to awkward
stares, shushes, and "will you PLEASE shut up!" There was his
force of being, or his impatience. He was a burly man who fixed
things in a jiffy, prepared simple but elaborate meals for groups of
people well into old age, which he never seemed to reach, and this
untoward energy led him to break things. Sid was an autodidact,
which made for fiery and learned conversations and debate. And the
awkwardness of his never having had his knowledge certified with
a degree, or his paintings hung in a museum, though his music was
performed in local theaters. Sid was at one time a communist, and
that led him to side with the factory workers when they were striking. Consequently, he was cut out of the family's pickle-business for-
tune. Sid identified with his mother, the pushcart pickler who saved
the family when the father fell prey to an accident. Sid was the only

one in the family who actually made the pickles, who saved his mother's recipes, and wore her aprons around his wide-as-a-punch-bowl waist.

Can I choose this awkwardness and discard this other one? Or do rival awkwardnesses necessarily coexist?

Can I clearly distinguish between heavy and light, empty and full at all times? A friend's sympathy letter seems light *and* full; the death certificate seems empty *and* heavy. And full. And empty. It's trying so hard with its serial numbers, and seals, its approvals and affirmations, its clockwork and authenticating signatures, its decipherable grid, to be correct in its assertion that this person was not buried alive.

precarious

I remember talking with a woman I knew who had finally come through several years of Chronic Fatigue Syndrome into health. The vague and depleting forces of the illness had kept her from socializing for long periods of time, but now she had encouraged a walk together through the woods that rose behind her house. When I asked her how she was feeling, she replied, "I'm content." I looked at her, searching her eyes, her demeanor, her gait more closely to see what "content" might look like. "Wow!" I thought, "she feels 'content.' I can't imagine saying that for myself." "Content" is *beyond* happy; content is contained; content is asking nothing but being met nevertheless. Content doesn't require outward form—it is fullness incarnate, stillness, stasis. I noticed she looked both tired and bright. Content is accepting. Awkward must be on the other side of content, which would suggest that awkward is the place where we reside most of the time even though it assumes an unusual or cock-eyed state. Of course there are degrees and types of discomfort, there are gradations of feeling ill at ease, and some people feel more "right" with the world more of the time than others. If to be content is to have found a zone of comfort, to be awkward is in some sense to remain unconsoled, possibly inconsolable. Contentment says a subject has found a place to live, but it also features life ground to a halt, whereas the awkward one lives the struggle of refusing to fit

and the fear of falling, of falling out of life as we all pretended to   *precarious*
know it, entirely.

Awkward is gangly and out of place, it is the person unschooled
in social graces. It invokes decorum but also the body as though certain *natural* rules, lost on some people, make them appear askew.
Awkwardness's other might be grace, though awkward isn't as far
along on a continuum of difference as grotesquerie. Guilt could be
involved, and the fear that something will be revealed about you,
some truth will be laid bare that is usually kept under wraps and the
burden of concealment makes you feel awkward, or appear awkward, which of course are totally different conditions. How do you
feel today? Sad, happy, angry, bored . . . awkward? Phrenologically,
awkward would have to appear in a different part of the brain than
those others, for maybe the feeling requires the presence of another
person, or at least the presence of an observing ego.

Awkwardness so regularly threatens us that we've invented the
situation comedy to help us cope. Each week, new and unimaginable awkward situations are devised for our favorite characters
either to happen into or themselves introduce. The favorite comedian
is she who most brilliantly, unabashedly, and with a knowing innocence inhabits her awkwardness: Ricky borrows a mink coat for an
act at the club, but Lucy thinks it's for her and won't take it off.
Lucy is hiding fresh chicken eggs in her shirt, eggs that she had
intended to plant among the chickens she's invested in but that have
failed to lay any eggs. Ricky insists on dancing with her, and she
dances the dance of awkward avoidance of her partner until the
inevitable crash of torso into torso leaves her soggily discovered,
guilty and dripping with goo. Slapstick, at its best, turns awkwardness to grace: Charlie Chaplin falls without fearing, falls without
harm. The table is collapsing beneath him, his tie is caught in a door,
his belt loop caught on a handle: he's bound to trip up and slip, to
induce a crash, innocently to transform order into chaos. Slapstick
is choreographed awkwardness. Order isn't destroyed but undone.

As an ontological state, to be awkward is to be clumsy, unnatural, embarrassed, shy. It is a sign—"awk"—posted by an old-fashioned
English teacher in the margin of your prose. It is a reminder of impending disorder, the object awkwardly placed or awkwardly posed that
throws off the arrangement. It is precariousness, and danger.

opposed

> This posture and this manner suit
> Not that I have ease in them
> But that I have a horror
> And so stand well upright—
> Lest, should I sit and, flesh-conversing, eat,
> I choke upon a piece of my own tongue-meat.
> —LAURA RIDING, *"Grace"*

It is easy to find awkwardness everywhere we look, but never grace. Grace is the rare and shocking moment of exultation that picks itself out from among the ruins and flies. But what would awkwardness have to be, how would we have to define it for it to strike us with the sudden wonder that grace commands? Awkwardness as rare and amazing possibility. As a condition of being to which one might aspire.

Is a literary style or use of language awkward if the work sounds as though it has been translated, poorly, from one language into another, or is that the mark of great literature: the beautiful insistence of inhabiting language other-wise?

In the realm of morality or theology, grace is a virtue. It can be striven for and achieved, but it's not reducible to nor to be confused with Eliza Doolitle learning the decorum she presumably lacks—the social graces. Grace, no, is a *state*. A state of utter beatitude, linked with purity, marked by transcendence, perhaps, of the gory route through torture it took to get there. Where saints are concerned, an investment in awkwardness leads to a state of grace. A belief in another world that runs counter to the world one is in makes for an awkward existence in the present, rewarded by grace in the hereafter.

Grace and dance, especially if ballet (which of course requires contortions so awkward to the body's natural tendencies that most people can't endure or would never attempt them). Grace and sport, grace and nature—feline grace, especially, which is about stretching and silent paws on floorboards, agility, and furry poise, not as slow as a turtle but not as fast and ungainly as a horse, but, then again, graceful horses: ease of movement, balance of parts in spite of the *opposed* animal's size.

Grace can function as a proper name: never awkwardness.

Chewing too long on the emptiness of grace can cause dizziness, whereas awkwardness is an elbow in the ribcage, the acute pain, felt and remembered, of being called a jackass by your father in front of your friends, the feel of shit sliding uncontrolled through your asshole and into your underwear during a church service and the stench making the nun beside you swoon, the sting in the center of your back, a verbal smack so strong you can feel it take your breath away because the nun overheard you telling the girl from the orphanage whom you were supposed to be tutoring in math that she was dumb, and even the fact that numbers had names without being things, this was profoundly awkward so you tried not to think of it because it made you feel crazy.

We were temporarily deposited onto a shore to read the horizon line: this was grace. We ate four marinated artichokes, gray-green, bulbous, and thorny. We drank a vanilla-chestnut cognac tranquilizer; a blond child cried playfully, "auita-mi!" ("help me!"). I returned to a window not to buy, only to look at the same garnet ring. You are who you are where you are, you are yourself and someone else, someone you are becoming. When bread has the consistency of cotton candy. We run, they walk; we whisper, they shout. How long can the foam last on a latte macchiato? The feeling in the train of wanting it to go on and on and on and on. White fleece, a flock of warmth, and iceberg lettuce. To sleep by a candle and a bowl of fruit. To become in one's body and being like a clock, balanced, moving, choosing to desire or attend to one kind of act over another at different "times" of day. She was paused, three steps up on the stairs, heavy bags, so I carried them for her to her door. Wind in the form of gales sends moisture down the chimney. Platinum day. Why not consider a fish out of water a happy, speckled, flying thing? A woman in a bright red parka rows a boat in circles in the Villa Borghese pond; my head lolls on your lap, watching her, while you read to me from Henry James. In the glorious, gorgeous cemetery in Rome, a cat frolics with only three legs; in this most tranquil of places, a bird teases another cat with one eye; in this place where nothing teems, I stoop to touch the tombstone of a child, I want to *untraceable* get closer to the words carved there, MUSIK, CUORE (heart), I want to take the quiet and the sweet sorrow in through my pores, but a piece of the tombstone, to my horror, literally comes off in my hands. Reverie broken, my eyes widen. "Shit!," I try to reattach it. This was awkwardness, not blessedness like grace and I expected that it meant that I'd been cursed.

untraceable

Imagine the fuchsia-colored legs of a moth clinging to the cracked and gnarled trunk of a tree in New York City's Central Park. Its antennae mimic what's left on a branch after a flower has fallen, or the feathery offshoots of mimosa sprung along a tropical bank. Its wings, in color, shape, and size, mimic nothing. They are brilliant green veined with white, rimmed by a black mantle underscored on either side by symmetrically false eyelets; they sport an elaborate gossamer dorsal; they span an amazing four inches or more. A mythological headline might suffice: "Fantastical creature emerges from the foam and blue-green firmament glimpsed by a whale as it breaks water's surface." It's not the kind of gorgeous wonder one expects to find on the front page of the *New York Times*, but there it was on the anniversary of Sid's death in 1998. I was visiting Philadelphia, visiting my mother, and fighting the feeling of Sid's absence from us, so I have to admit that I read, sentimentally and personally, the front page full-color image of the nearly extinct moth that park rangers hoped to propagate. I read it as a message meant for me, something like the consolation of nature, and while I wouldn't go so far as to say that I thought of the moth as Sidney's soul come back to greet me, I did think of it as kin to his spectacular presence and decided to treat this newspaper as an anniversary keepsake of good tidings. In just this way we had read the blooming of my mother's sansevieria on the day of Sid's funeral as a confirmation of his buoyancy, a cause for celebration rather than tears. (Have you ever seen one of those common houseplants bloom? I certainly hadn't.)

Now, in my rummaging, I'm reading that newspaper as an historical record of a particular day in July.

I'm browsing adjacent headlines—France's upset of Brazil in the

World Cup, the death of three innocent Catholic youth in a fire in *untraceable*
Ulster, the drowning of a twelve-year-old Bronx boy at Orchard
Beach—until the awkwardness of juxtapositions of all the news
that's fit to print seems everywhere and all the more apparent. The
article on the park rangers' attempts to protect endangered species
informs us smilingly of how ". . . this year rangers will reintroduce
screech owls, bobwhite quails, and short-tailed weasels, among others . . . columbine, pink-lady slipper and even prickly pear cactus"
into the park. They will work tirelessly to bring back the luna moth,
"probably done in by some combination of large-scale DDT spray-
ing in the 1960s along with urbanization and possibly the bright
city lights." The article is illustrated with whimsical artist's render-
ings of the screech owl, head anthropomorphically cocked to listen,
and the woodchuck, hands raised to an inquiring nose . . . perched
just above a box containing the headline to another story: "An
Immigrant Mourns Brother Who Was Buried Alive."

Alarmed that I missed this story in my original encounter with
the news, no longer distracted by my need for a consolatory keepsake, I begin to read about Luis Gomez, a thirty-two-year-old illegal
Ecuadorian immigrant who had been buried alive in a six foot hole
on a construction site where he worked. "A co-worker on a back-
hoe filled in the pit at a Tribeca construction site, apparently unaware
that Mr. Gomez was still underground." Gomez's brother "struggled to understand how workers could have been unaware that his
brother remained in the hole . . . 'I don't know how they couldn't
have seen him,'" he keeps repeating.

Luis Gomez was working to pay off the $7,000 it took to get
him to the United States. His brother, Lucas, would now have to pay
$6,000 to send his brother's body back to their hometown of
Cuenca. In case we doubt the unimaginable horror of his demise, we
can cite the Medical Examiner's pronouncement of death caused by
"asphyxia due to burial in earth."

I supposed that a check mark would appear on Gomez's death
certificate next to the question "Injured at Work?," until I realized
that without a social security number or birth certificate he probably would not be granted a death certificate in the U.S. The awkwardness of a death certificate was a privilege.

Is it possible that identity papers really have the power of conferring visibility, embodiment, presence on human beings, and that without our proper documents, we'll be mistaken for absent, taken for dead, not seen at all?

reversed

Today, in a cabinet, in a folder, I discover these slips of prose: two undated letters addressed to me as a child that I have never before read. And my heart swells and breaks around them to hear again the voice, to find the voice not heard, to encounter the trace of the living, loving being, the grace and beauty of a letter from a man advanced in years, an elder addressing a child, the letters never sent.

> *Dear Little Mary,*
> *Believe you me, I have had the best time with you on my third day of my vacation.*
> *Your wonderful speech in relating me your knowledge of things, showing/expressing me your great writing works, and explaining the life of Pinocchio was colossal. It is almost unbelievable! I am here in the front of my table before my chitar and mandolin, flowers in the center of the table/lain on the table, letters and blank/sheets schattered all ~~round~~ over. But your smile is with me and I am writing to you with all my heart and full of bliss.*
> *Dear little mary will you thank your darling mother and very kind daddy that have so kindly offered us to stay and have supper with them. And they took us home to. The food was extremely delicious and the visit with your Aunt Frances pleased me so much because you and your handsome brothers had a very good time.*
> *Please give my best wishes to your mother and Daddy, to your sweet brothers and giving you a big kiss I say bye bye I remain and may God bless you all ~~your~~ Grandfather*

The gift of my grandfather's letter is this startling and comforting picture of myself as a child. As child narrator, and child writer, child being listened to, child eager to share, enthusiastic innocent who doesn't know or doesn't want to know if grandfather already knows the story of Pinocchio. I see myself in a way I can never know

or recall on my own. It exceeds a photograph, videotape, memento, *reversed*
this letter of his, the generous flourish of his y's, scooped like a ladle,
the humility of his personal pronoun shaped like a small clasp or
hook; his pencil pressed into a slightly waxy paper, its feminine
hand, composing at the dining room table. The letter is a testament
to a smile glimpsed in spite of a crowd of competing details (the
significance of the "but"), or as if to say this smile is even more
important than all these things I cherish, through which I make a
life—flowers, paper, mandolin, guitar.

The letter says he saw and was moved to make.

It gives me back a moment followed by a movement.

I find him most particularly and exquisitely in his choice of the
word, "colossal," a word only he would choose—its Mediterranean
root sprung from one of the wonders of the Ancient world. Maybe
too he'd seen the word in a late 50s early 60s American newspaper,
alongside the exclamation "gee," in a description of a film just out
from MGM, in which case the child's utterance gets to merit a
superlative not used to it, and Italian ancient and American popular
culture get to cross.

I'm reveling in the uniqueness of my grandfather's presence, this
rare gentleness. I'm not revisiting a place that I know, exactly, but
going to a place I had one time inhabited and yet never quite been . . .
until a different, simultaneous trace, like the evidence of a code, appears.
There are other words here, quite apart from the letter, upside down
upon the page. Turning the slip of paper upright, I see the words that
my grandfather was teaching himself that day from the English dictionary. He had listed the English terms, and gave them, instead of
their English definitions, their Italian counterparts. At the top of the
page, flipside of this beautiful letter, the impossible, the weird con-
glomerate of sounds, the word "awkward" appears, followed in
reverse alphabetical order by "awhile" and "awe."

> *awkward—incomodo—guffo—brutto—spiacevolo*
> *awhile—per un instante—per qualche tempo—non ancora*
> *awe—sono colpito di terrore—paura*

There ends the list as my grandfather makes his way backward
through the dictionary, moving up rather than down, awkwardness
in two languages.

Wanting to know what awkwardness might have meant to him, I search out but fail to find "guffo" in my Italian/English dictionary. There's "gofo"—owl, or misanthrope, but no "guffo." I decide to consult friends who know the language better than I who suggest the word is "*goffo*," usually used to describe a person or a gesture as clumsy or inelegant. Different words in Italian refer to different types of awkwardness—of time, situation, or appearance. I love that the same word, "brutto," "ugly," can also mean "awkward," especially since Italians seem obsessed with exclaiming its opposite: "che bella!" Where I read "spiacevolo," I learn that my grandfather meant "spiacevol*e*"—a relative of the words pleasing (piace) and displeasing (dispiace): unpleasant, disagreeable, awkward. "Incomodo" yields the most complex meaning. If "comodo" meant convenient, handy, comfortable, easy, my grandfather's synonym for awkward wasn't "scomodo," a simple negation of "comodo," but "*in*comodo," which offered the added sense of the situation of one person being in another person's way: "essere d'incomodo a qualcuno," to be a nuisance to someone, to inconvenience someone, and "fare il terzo incomodo"—which, according to my dictionary means "to play gooseberry." No one seems to know this expression in English; the numerous ellipses at work in the encounter between Italian and English, even between American and British English, widen until one friend suggests it's "like being a third wheel"—but isn't the correct phrase "being a fifth wheel"? To be awkward, to be incomodo, was to play the part of fifth wheel (which is different again from playing second fiddle), to be present and absent at once, excluded and painfully aware. These phrases yielded another obsolete synonymous sense: "to hold the lantern," which is said of one assigned the role of disappearing so that something can happen between other people to whom one was originally attached. Holding the lantern and being a fifth wheel aren't quite the same though. In one case you're awkward because you're the unwanted but necessary chaperone, and in the other case you're awkward because you're just unwanted, or worse, unneeded.

supplementary

My grandfather's letters live in a space between definitions. They are trials, drafts, practice runs that never reach completion. What, after all, could it mean for a letter to meet its recipient accidentally thirty-five years after it was written? Saving the letters, he couldn't predict the hands they would fall into, the eyes they would meet, if any; he only knew that awkwardness prevented him from sending the letters out from his shop. My grandfather never fails to feel awkward about his command of the language; he never trusts it even when he achieves poetry in it.

Question: "What is the space between awkwardness and awe?" Answer: "Awhile." To be awkward is to be broken, unsure, self-conscious. To experience awe is to be overcome, terrified, but temporarily freed from the self, ecstatic, excessive, remarked, observed, beholding and beholden, encountering and encountered, sent.

Did my grandfather consider his letters so many supplements, so much ejected debris, inadequate to feeling? Fifth wheels, inconveniences, saved, buried, now exhumed? Here I turn to face to receive—to feel—another of his beautiful, awesome, awkward letters without him, or without a chance to respond except to an anonymous future reader. Written, rewritten, some sentences evoke a supplemental voice, like water answering rock:

Dear Mimi,

Forgive me for calling/addressing you so as I know that you are growing ~~to be a big~~ up to be a nice (inserted) girl and your name will be what it is "Mary" because you can now pronounce it properly (inserted) ~~as it should be~~. Your speech has improved lot, but to me you are the same little pretty doll(y) (inserted).

Dear granddaughter I cannot forget your smile when you saw us walking up the three steps of your home/up the first three steps of your blessed home. You looked at us awed/You looked at us in awe. I could see your happyness running through your heart/I could see your true happyness running through your fare heart. You remained at a standstill as if

*you had seen, alone before the horizon the greatest picture of
sunset!*

*I paused for few seconds looking at you and then I
approached and embraced you, kissing with all my love your
forehead, ~~and~~ as your eyes and face remained the same you wel-
comed us so dearly from the beginning til we left/til we said
good by to the end of our of my best fourth of July.*

*I shall not say anything of your wounded temple and the
dark eye that was caused by an accident which I had not known
but I shall thank you, your wonderful brothers and your dear
mother and Dad that treated us so majestically which we will
never forget—There was so much food, drinks and what not
that only to royalty is given. And of course all the fun we had it
is impressed in my heart which seems like a dream . . .*

I love the way that my grandfather inserts adjectives into this
letter. He angles them in so that they appear as birds perched,
heads tilted upward, they teeter not in the manner of delicate orna-
ments but as bold harbingers of truth. I look into this letter as into
a mirror in which bits of the tain show through. Look, Mimi, now
Mary, at this vision I have glimpsed, he seems to say, and he puts
the two of us before us as into a crystal ball. The mise en scène,
captured, stilled, makes me melt—the description of the gaze of the
child so pleased to see her grandparents, so in love with them that
she can barely believe her eyes and thus rather than run to them
remains at a standstill. I feel the intensity of that love until the letter reveals a different source of the paralysis or "awe"—until the
line, "I shall not say anything of your wounded temple," a funny
use of the negative, saying/not saying at once. Then I see that the
occasion of the letter was trauma, the aftereffects of my having fall-
en from the top step of a high diving board to cement when I was
seven years old.

Is it more awkward to say "until we left" or "until we said good-
bye"? More awkward to arrange "little" after "pretty" or "pretty"
after "little"? At what point should a girl stop calling herself Mimi
and begin to call herself Mary?

It chills me a little, it scares me to see in my grandfather's poetry
the vestiges of shock on my child face, maybe because I sometimes

feel that even as an adult I move through life a little stunned, and I *supplementary* trace my fall from innocence into experience back to that accident, my fall from grace? The picture of immobility that he paints strikes me as uncanny. I retained the same look on my face even after he kissed me. He perceives my spell, but his letter wants to replace it with relation. In place of the look of trauma—of having fallen out of the physical world and into my body, or out of my body and into the physical world—in place of that resulting awkwardness, **he** wants to see, to create love. Or did awkwardness, the missed step, constitute the *cause* after which a physical truth or bodily immutability was felt? No matter: he wants to move me from awkwardness to awe, to find love in awe, to replace the terror of awe with singular intimacy, a different order of dreaming.

My grandparents' figures on the horizon greet me like figures in a mirage: I'm glad and amazed that they exist too in the new world I awakened to post-accident. I see them through old/new eyes, as from within a different body. I am now in some way supplementary to myself, just in the way we all, with or without violent breaks, are split off from ourselves, alive in the seams. (We are our own fifth wheels.)

The body was awkward, and then it vanished. (A life could be described this way.) What had it become in its awkwardness? What would it become hereafter? The body acted upon the world queerly, inviting what it did not understand to become its companion. Was awkwardness equivalent to all of the mind's leftovers, all that any consciousness could not contain?

All that you know or feel that can't be owned, the awkward extras sensed but out of reach—is it better to bring those into alignment with *the real*, or to keep chasing them like a buoy in the beyond? Would translating my grandfather's letters be equivalent to smoothing over all that exceeds them, muting their inconsistencies, denying their awkwardness?

An anorexic friend says she wants out of the body, and I think I want *in* to the body but don't know how to get there. She wants in, too, I suppose, into a different body than the one prescribed. A male friend tells me he feels like his body isn't part of the world. A female friend tells me she often has the feeling of not knowing what to do with her hands at a dinner party—as though there is a place they are supposed to go, something they are supposed to do that she can't figure out—and it makes her feel beside herself and as though her hands and arms are hugely visible, at which point she would love nothing more than a volleyball to slam with her palms as mallets into the center of the table.

Loves to eat. Check. Sleeps well. Check. Enjoys a bath. Check. Multiple orgasms. Check. In what sense then do I feel disembodied? Distrusts surfaces. Check. Chairs. Occasionally and worse, the ground. Thus making for an awkward relation to the physical world. Exists, therefore, in spite of a suspicion of hereness and thereness: to be awkward was to be neither here nor there. Wishes for a steed. And a fearless trainer. Encourages others who conceive her as fearless. Trembling fingers result from excessive desire, the opposite of contentment, and thus unexpected bowel movements at inopportune times and an afternoon spent weeding, pulling up grass from the roots till fingers bleed in nooks and crannies. Desire *for* what? Desire attached, detached. Floating, you could be on cloud nine or terribly untethered. Mismatched. She finds the body in the writing. Ah, but only the voice is there. She retrieves the grandfather's body in his letter—brings the letter to her face, smells cigarette and lead, peach juice and muscatel, chicken bouillon. (Smells of nothing really after all these years in file cabinet; these are the smells she remembers and associates with him). Wants to eat the letter but then would no longer have it to read. Narcissists, they say, need to incorporate everything around them into themselves. They can't perceive distance or difference, they fundamentally refuse awkwardness. The degree of awkwardness you can tolerate may tell you just how much you can love—other people, living, the world.

I could thank my grandfather's letters for throwing me off course, but I don't really like awkwardness any more than the next person. I'm like the woman, a repressed mystery writer in a film, who sits poolside rather than plunge in for fear she might lose track of her body. (I prefer to get lost in a book, preferably one heavy as a paperweight sunk within my widening lap.) My seven-year-old niece Justine is splashing about in this same pool; her five-year-old brother is "making rain." In a video her mother gives me, my niece plays the violin. Unlabored, she smiles through a recital beside her teacher, and her legs, I notice, hold her, bent like young boughs, just like the bow. Each successive child on the video is older, and each

more awkward with the violin as though it's harder for their wandering minds to match the measured music, less likely for their bellies to breathe in steady intervals to move the bow across the strings.
If a musical instrument is an extension of the body into space, an
added dimension, these kids are stuck. My niece moves more like a
monkey; no matter the circumstance, if the spirit moves her, she
jumps into my lap and laces herself around my neck. She brings her
face so close to mine we merge. Then pulls it back and laughs. She
scrunches my lips with her fingers into impossible positions and
then requires that I try to talk. I teach her how to walk like Charlie
Chaplin and to carry out a Shemp-of-the-Three-Stooges skip. She
sucks on my neck and I show her the goosebumps that appear on
my arms. "You like poetry," she says and hands me a pouch made
of purple construction paper and green-red glitter as a gift. The
pouch holds a heart I'm told I can stick to my window at home as
a decorative appliqué, and a cutout square of white lined paper
folded into fours. The poem reads: "When I eat dinner I think of
getting thinner. But which one? Eat dinner or get thinner?" She has
illustrated her verse with question marks that morph into a smiley
face and geometric shapes that pass for food on a plate. I could
imagine my niece a happy questioner, see her feasting on rhymes
that mimic and mock one another. It's hard not to worry, though,
that this poem is her first articulation of a flight from awkwardness,
that, like so many girls, she'd rather disappear.

I have no granddaughter but a seven-year-old niece. She lives
across a continent from me, and so I only see her once a year. I
explain to her that when we're distant she's my inner smile. "I think
of you here," I say, "when I do my meditation," and point to my
forehead, "I picture your smiling face here." When I leave, she laces
her hands around my neck and kisses me there, just above my eyelids, in the center of my brow. "Do you know why I kissed ya'
there?" she asks. "Of course," I say, "my delight," I call her, "my
whippoorwill, my fellow vampire." This love so large, this love
without a name. How lucky I am to have been kissed twice in my
life this way, *kissing with all my love your forehead*, to be continuously brought back to my senses. On each visit, I teach Justine an
Italian word. "Arrivederci," I say, rapidly trilling my *r*'s, "Ah-rear-
va-dirtchee," she struggles, and laughs.

splayed

Awkwardness imagistically suggests pigeon toes, mismatched shoes, some extremity splayed; in an extreme instance, a feeling of not fitting properly into one's imagined place in the world, a disconnect between *who* and *where* because the self cannot be a meaningless everywhere-at-all-times figure (a spacelessness reserved for God, the nonhuman creator of the human) but must have, must begin with, a local habitation and a name. Why is there nothing more right, in terms of an image of awkwardness, than shoes worn on the wrong feet? And the uncanny feeling countered by laughter at oneself when one accidentally some day puts the wrong shoe on the right foot. The way the shoe draws the foot out from the body, toward a wall, the feeling of the shoe as a mechanism now that will draw its wearer to roam in particular, unfamiliar, and clownish ways. One wonders if a child could unselfconsciously run around with his shoes on the wrong feet—of course she could, it happens all the time—and it's not because the child lives in a zone of only partial awareness, a zone in which play in the abstract or pure action takes precedence over a consciousness of the body. Maybe those shoes wrongly worn do take her into untoward realms, or maybe the child's foot has a will beyond what binds it, or maybe the child more happily adapts to a new sensation.

To adapt to a new sensation all of the old sensations have to be stripped off like heavy clothing that stinks from its absorption of blood, sweat, and tears produced by the body's traipsing of well-worn trails. This is true for the adult but not yet for the child. The child hasn't decided yet which habits will define her, what *straying* will mean for her, the degree to which she will ever again in her life allow herself to wander, or to feel. (To feel *is* to wander, to seek without knowing what one will find.)

Shoes athwart—you'd have to keep drawing your feet back in against the current of a shoe drawing them out. You would finally feel the weight of those bodily objects, applied to the body, tied or buckled, slipped into or pulled onto the length of a knee and zippered.

What would be the point of pretending that one's shoes weren't *splayed* on backwards? Of walking normally, of toeing the straight line forward even as the shoes said "no," or "resist," or, oddly angled, announced themselves like the hole in the crotch of a bathing suit, or a shirt with its tag showing? Would pretense signal (merely) an indifference toward, or detachment from, the world of objects—an absentmindedness reserved for intellectuals, a return to childish abandon? Here was a set of divergent options and their differing stakes: 1) to proceed in spite of one's mismatched shoes; 2) to proceed because of them; 3) to proceed according to them; 4) not to proceed at all, but to stand stock still, peer down at them, and laugh.

TOUCHING

tongues

"You are beautiful; you are more than tactful, you are tenderly, magically tactile . . . I'm alone & think of you . . . I'd meet you at Dover—I'd do anything for you."
—Letter to Morton Fullerton from Henry James

There are certain things that can never go missing—a tongue, for example. You can't wake up and find it one day gone. Or touch. These are ever present, never to get lost. But of course a tongue can wander, and if it does, say, lurch backward in the mouth toward the throat, threatening to close the space to breathe through, or if it wags, blabbing, spilling guts or telling lies, if it loosens, might touch shift too, might the skin start to creep, crawl, or grow numb as if in flight from it? Mightn't the skin turn sheet-white as a surrendering flag, or spring flowerets to woo the tongue back to its place in the mouth? Or is touch designed to follow the tongue? Rather than recoil, to rejoice. The tongue is skin too. So what of it? No. The tongue is flesh. (There is a difference.) The tongue is not a finger but it can point (with words, I mean); it's on the tip of my tongue. A finger cannot taste, but it can write and it can etch. It can choose, bring, and gather, it can lift, reach, release. To be tactless is, lexically speaking, to be without touch, but also to be tasteless.

Winding the reel of the word "tact" back toward its roots, one arrives at *touch*. Opening a dictionary, I read down a column of words for tact, then point in astonishment at the etymology of the compact word, neat as a package, as full of surprise and sure as a tack in a buttocks: "tact," tactus, tangere, tactum, to touch.

Awkward: lacking dexterity in the use of the hands.   *tongues*
Tactful: to have the right words at one's fingertips.
Tactless: to rub people the wrong way.

As a form of awkwardness, tactlessness suggests impoliteness, a rude, unselfconscious, or ignorant, inconsiderate, and even irreparable use of language. But the origin of the word opens awkwardness onto still new territories of the body and of relations.

"Tact"—a use of the voice, of the tongue—hails from "tactum," to touch, but the tactful person isn't necessarily one who draws close. The touch in tact has to do with the deftness with which a speaker *handles a situation*, a nearly intuitive grasp, a knack for finding the right words to meet (to touch?) a circumstance. Tactfulness does not presume those words will touch the person whom they address. In fact, the touch of tact asserts a distance rather than an intimacy. Tactfulness protects its hearer and insulates its bearer. The touch in tactfulness points to the intimacy the tactful have with *language*: so close is the tactful person's relation to words that her use of language does not greet another person so directly as to prick him. In which case, I'd rather be the recipient of tactlessness than tact. I think I want to be touched.

But when I'm touched, I talk . . .

Not the anatomizing talk of a visit to the doctor or the dentist where they use talk to distract me from my body, where words are designed to absent the presence of a finger in an orifice, or to deny the discomfort that wells when that same cold finger palpates in search of disease. This was the worst form of tactless talking and tactless touching—where words serve merely as vehicles of distantiation, words directed in such a way to encourage me to leave my body, or leave the room while they examine it, to leave it up to them, to leave my body in their hands, while I dither in the zone of vacant chatter.

These situations assume that language occurs only in the mind and has nothing to do with the body. Does the doctor engage me in irrelevant conversation when he touches me to take my mind "off" my body, or does he affiliate talking with mentation, pure and simple and detached? He assumes, I think, what most of us do, that talk is of the mind and touch is corporeal, never the twain shall meet.

touch

Each person could answer for herself where talk resided or how it figured with regard to "tact"—at the hairdresser, in the sexual encounter, as the tailor pulls a tape measure against your inner thigh, as the salesman pulls your foot into a shoe or scoops a shoehorn against your heel, in combat, hand-to-hand so-called, do people talk? On a subway car so crowded you are forced to touch, or in solitude—I mean, are there occasions when you feel compelled to talk to yourself, and where is the body when that happens? Weren't there instances when touching was a ground for telling, and telling a form of touch? When talking in a touching context happens on a threshold of sensation. At a limen. When the stories another person tells literally impress one, or keep an intimacy from being dumb. When talking is a locale that people make together, a tactful space.

A muscle recoils, retracts, it tickles, or gives back, lets the hand enter, into a yawn. A voice locates: you know where another person is standing in relation to you even if you cannot see her. A voice reverberates larynx, belly, breath, and lip. Eyes closed, a palm turns upward as you talk. Facing down, today politics are on the tip of a tongue on the verge of a tear. Nothing intricate—just the raw fact of the death in war and the collective demand to ignore it, to live, live your daily life in all its stupidly doggy dailiness. If we remain stupid long enough, there will be no need to talk. Certainly not to go so far as feeling talking's stroke or sting, tongue's touch. Mothers talked to their babies when they touched them, or not, and thus established future relations to talk as embodied or abstract, talk as dangerous or secure.

fingers

Tactful, full of touch, touchy. I am the sort of person who plays with her hands, but I am not alone. I watched a famous philosopher knead her hands one into the other following dinner. She'd eaten more quickly than her hosts, who, appropriately awed by her, were careful to eat slowly in her midst. They ate so slowly, they hardly knew if it was food that they'd delivered from plate to mouth. She finished early, and so, as she sat thinking, she kneaded her hands almost as if she were continuing to chew along with us, or hoping to hurry us along, or more likely to assure herself of her presence, a place where she begins and ends.

I have a habit of fingering things, an awkward tactfulness, leftover, no doubt, a recalcitrant trace brought on by years of hands folded at the edge of my Catholic school desk. In a church service, I long for nothing more than to lose my hands inside a white-fur muff that otherwise hangs, lifeless, from an elastic band around my wrist. In my muff, my hands find a private home in which to play while all the while my lips pretend to pray. As an adult, I turn into confetti the tab attached to the string of a teabag, then feel the bits, little paper squares, miniature playing cards, again and again and again. Talking with a friend, there's a ritual I have of tearing paper, noiselessly, then feeling the pattern that remains. Crumbs are also useful in this way, as my fingers in conversation or in silence can pull them into a zone of togetherness, stick them to a finger, feel their sharp edges, then drop them onto the rim of a saucer. Napkins are handy for folding and unfolding, dropping onto a table and lifting, smoothing onto a lap or tucking, removing and folding, dumping then folding again the way a cat might play with a dead mouse. (I was aware of a friend's habit of twisting a paper napkin into a tourniquet so that by the end of a meal the paper appeared tortured and torn and wet.) Fingering doesn't only come to the fore during dinner parties but almost everywhere publicly else: I may not be able to lecture without pressing a finger forward into a paper clip, sometimes painfully letting a finger get caught inside a paper clip's hook. One hand can be used, or two, and by the end of it all the paper clip is reduced to useless bits. In a movie theater, the zipper to a purse can be zipped and unzipped, or the top of a pen click, click, clicked.

Often enough, I'm annoyed to observe fiddling in others. I feel uncomfortable, even want to recoil, before one friend's tendency to thumb the arms of a couch while she talks, or rhythmically to smooth it, as though she were doing something best kept behind closed doors. Her stroking, this furniture petting, seems entirely unrelated to anything currently at hand, and I don't know why she wants me to watch: is there something else she'd *rather* talk about, something she'd *rather* do?

Fiddling claims to bespeak a lack of serenity or poise: this tact-ful awkwardness. Its interlocutors assume it means a splintered atten-tion, an excess energy, distractedness, but why can't it also be read as the attempt to gather the energy of a conversation into a bouquet, or to keep the threads of a conversation present. Was it indicative then of a desperate salvaging, a desire to keep at hand the unsaid, all that each word sheds without flowering—my gathering, gathering, gather-ing of crumbs? Fingering is inelegant, yes, and a sign of lack of finish, for composure is *still*. And there can be hidden shame involved, a plethora of layers of embarrassment: a transgressive body aware and ashamed of its transgressiveness. Fingering some substance in the presence of others—because it wasn't something I'd venture to guess a person more regularly indulges in solitude, so-called obsessive compulsive disorders aside—is a form of molding that doesn't leave anything *made* in its wake. It performs a perpetual trial to modify the world to one's desire: see how the tab of a teabag becomes a minia-ture accordion playable only by finger-sized men.

Birds, I presume, don't express misgivings about the world as they find it, they find no need to modify the world. They accept it as a given; they learn to adapt or they die. Or maybe not: each molting leaves the bird with a new body, a chance to fly differently, and no two nests are alike but plied to shape an urge to hold the delicacy of eggshell so that this time, this time, and for once.

It's natural to stand upright in your body but what if today you feel the need to crawl? If, for once. If, for once. How would you fill in that blank if not for fingering?

ill-mannered

"Who are you? What kind of gloves do you wear? Whose hands do you shake? What do you take away with you from the mystery of contact?" The Russian theorist Mikhail Epstein posed these ques-tions in an essay, and I took them to heart toward a more primitive inquiry, like how do we achieve contact in the first place? And who is the you I am touching? How do I know it is you whom I touch? I shake the hands of my dentist and his assistant following a proce-dure. They look at me smilingly and oblige me the way they might the antics of a mental patient, dishonestly assuring me my weirdness is okay. It's a geeky intellectual thing to do: to extend the hand as though a business transaction has been sealed; to confirm the completion of a job well done; to assert that together we succeeded when really it was they who acted intrusively on me as I struggled to suppress discomfort knowing that my supine and upside-down position, my admission of instruments into an orifice of power and want and breath, my submission to fingers, hands, numbings, and titanium posts, and my letting them dig while the dentist gently whistled and the Muzak played on as a winter storm raged outside—I never felt so strongly the desire to flee into a winter storm—all happened in the name of my being able to chew my meal, a hunk of savory meat; the last time I ate veal scaloppini, a part of a molar fell, with a clink, onto my plate. Not knowing how else to thank them, really wanting to hit them, I offer to shake their hand. If I had been wearing a hat, I could tip it.

In scenarios of utmost intimacy, of unusually close contact, it's funny how tactless people can be. In the medical domain, they call it poor bedside manner as though it's an exception to a rule, a gaffe to be avoided, but most people come to accept it as par for the course. Settling none too easily into the oral surgeon's chair for a root canal, I tell the doctor what scares me—that I've developed some gum inflammation around the tooth he aims to treat. "There'll be a lot more inflammation than that after I get through with you," he chortles, then thrusts a *People* magazine into my hands saying, "Here, read this while we wait for that novocaine to do its work. I want to be sure that you're nice and numb before I start!"

tactless

I've come to accept the fact that most people maintain an unthinking relationship to words; everyone *uses* language, but you can't expect people who aren't in the word trade to use language sensitively, ethically, radically, or well. Maybe that's why I'm continuously surprised and subsequently tortured by my own tactlessness. I'm at an awards ceremony intended to celebrate the fruits of our students' labor as writers at the university. I've served as judge for *tactless*

the creative nonfiction contest and am eager to meet the student writers who have won, as well as to congratulate winners whom I've played a part in mentoring and whose work has earned a prize. One woman's name appears several years in a row. I've never worked with her, though she always promises to take a course, and I am awed by the way her work repeatedly rises to the top with each year's new slate of judges. Here's a sheerly great writer, I think, destined for great things, and I want to tell her that. I remember last year she had her small son with her, and between attempts to offer her effusive praise, I looked down on the small shy shuffling form beside her and said something wholly in-apropos, like "Maybe your mom will write something about *you* someday! Or, maybe you'll be a writer yourself!" This year, I immediately find the face of this writer in the buoyant, noisy, crowded room. She smiles and waves, and I yell "Congratulations!" She's taken first prize in the fiction competition and an honorable mention for a piece about her mother's battle with cancer. Her mother, all her life, had been the model of unflinching survivorhood, but now she appeared afraid, and the daughter had to face this—her mother's vulnerability. Across the heads of several people and a clanking bevy of voices and noise, I tilt my head toward the student, and ask "Did you lose your mother?" She can't hear me and probably can't imagine that this would be a question that a person in her right mind would attempt to yell across a crowded room, maybe especially at an awards ceremony. I leave my seat and move closer to her, even though the ceremony is about to begin. "Did you lose your mother?" I ask. "No," she says, "she's still alive." The essay, submitted to the contest weeks ago, described the mother in ICU in a septic state. Nonfiction often puts us in touch with the intimate realities of people's lives. Should I have asked "How's your mother?" and risked the writer telling me she was dead? Or ignored the subject matter of the essay altogether and simply said "Once again, you've produced a fine piece of writing," and that's what we're here to celebrate after all: tact, craft. I didn't think much about the supreme tactlessness of yelling across a crowded room "Did you lose your mother?" until later. There was so much more to observe, so much to be nervous about: a mutual inability to get beyond small talk with one new colleague for four consecutive years; another aging male colleague's decision to lean forward and kiss the female award recipients as they received their *tactless* awards; the fact that upon offering the briefest hug to one of my students who had won an award, she literally fled from the room. And how the act of her abrupt running made me feel that the hug was a deep and long embrace, how the announcement of awkwardness elongates time and makes the feeling of an untoward act linger, persist, abide.

I once knew a woman who was an obsessive reviewer of her own faux pas. She didn't seem in search of absolution but appeared to enjoy the confession and the self-aggrandizing fantasy that she was continuously transgressing the sensibilities of others. She was offensiveness incarnate, and it was hopeless to save her; she only bade you listen to the details of her latest embarrassment. "Oh, oh, oh," she would whimper, and the pores on her forehead would open with sweat, she would bite her nails, and in a sing-song voice, as though admitting self-irony, exclaim "Ohhh, woe is me!"

Following the awards ceremony, I suffered my own share of writhing, a wringing of hands to the tune of the memory of my insensitive blurt. And then something strange happened. We were trying to leave, we were cleaning up the last dregs of coffee and cake crumbs, but my colleague who kissed the girls remained. He was sitting at a table alone, eating cheese squares and cream puffs. "Somebody has to eat it," he said when I asked him what he was doing. I was wondering why he was staying, why he wasn't leaving. Clearly we were cleaning up. Was he feeling the anticlimax of such events, did he want the party to go on, was he lonely and hopeful that something touching would emerge from this, a sweet inside his belly? I felt I understood, but my own impulse was to head home to my flagellation booth. On my way out the door, I spotted a credit card that obviously had fallen from someone's pocket unbeknownst to them. As I picked it up, the name of the outstanding writer whose mother was ill blinked back at me, as though a guardian angel had put a means of reparation in my path—I could help rather than harm her—as though a higher power required that contact be maintained: "Oh, woe is her to have to hear from me again!"

I am a writer. I wear mittens. They keep me warm but make things hard to grasp. I shake the hand of my dentist, as well as the man who gives me estimates on furnaces and occasionally the dry cleaning man. I let a salesman selling plaster replicas of antiquities kiss me in the Roman forum again and again and again. I rarely wear hand coverings. I find them constricting, but if forced, in cold, I wear thin leather driving gloves that enable me to feel the wheel, and a bit of winter's bite, and something mean. I don't wish to be treated with kid gloves. I prefer a winded punch to the belly. Or so I say. The only way a gay male friend would let me touch him was to, Three Stooges–style, twist his arm in a monkey grip. Don't mind me—my people were touchers and they taught me to touch others warmly and with ease. Is there anything worse than being grabbed against one's will? Being clutched, dragged, and coiled? And then the refrain: "Please, release me, let me go." I wear gardening gloves because inevitably I get scratched in the garden and then I fear that microbes will enter my open wounds. The gloves have raised polka dots meant to help a person grip a garden tool. Eventually they get drenched with water or with sweat and I ditch them, and then the earth beneath my skin embeds so fully no soap will wash it off.

What's mysterious about contact is that it happens at all. Can contact ever become threadbare from overuse, or is its nature, its mystery, that it dissolves like candles or soap or water into air? I'm on fire with static electricity—my cat jumps back when a woolly spark accidentally ignites the touch of my finger to her sleek and lovely forehead. Don't cling to it. Attach, detach; button, unbutton; tie, otherwise you will trip on your shoelaces, or over your own words, you will become tongue-tied.

The mystery of contact has unwound. How easily we get lost, or are tossed, released from touching. I stray. Let me finger this thread, let me gather loose ends together, or pretend to.

intact

When I write, I rarely position myself as if one arm dangling out the window of a driver's seat. It's more like a process of applying oneself to a lathe, and it occasionally requires safety glasses. Preparation of materials is involved, and honing: eyes speak through the touch of pen to paper translating an internally wayward tongue. This is where play comes in. The work is quiet, and the result is rarely a cabinet but curiosities in search of one, even the dainty knob of a drawer suitable for grasping or rolling, in want of an attachment to a surface, like a chestnut across the knuckles of a palm.

Sometimes when reading, we are treated to the experience of an encounter with a perfect image. Leonardo Sciascia in *Sicily as Metaphor*, describing the extremes of hot and cold in his home town of Racalmuto, writes: "Against the cold there was a single remedy: a copper brazier full of burning charcoal. Against the heat: snow from Cammarata . . . The snow that was collected there arrived in Racalmuto in handcarts, packed between two layers of straw and salt. The salt and straw served to isolate and conserve the snow . . . We used the snow to cool wine and water, and to make *granite*: a handful of snow squirted with blackberry or red currant syrup, which the children were particularly greedy for . . . You held it in the hollow of your hand and then quickly gobbled it up before it could melt." I didn't grow up in such a place, but Sciascia's image has the capacity to stir memory till I search out analogy or difference. I do remember eating snow as a child—not to cool down in the summer but in winter—and I wonder what encouraged us to eat it: of course it asks to be eaten like a growing thing suddenly apparent, apples in an orchard, a long-awaited bounty, and it wants to be bitten into or sucked, and you enjoy watching absently a drop of melted snow brought to your mouth fall from your hand because the contact is at variance, the warmth of your body meets the cold of the snow.

Tact, unlike the poetry of Sciascia's perfect images, is a *right* use of language that is prescribed; poetry is a right use of language that no one could expect but once it has come into being strikes one as indubitable. This doesn't mean a perfect image stands still but it may transfix a reader *as well as* ecstatically transform. I do not write in order to be right: a paraphrase of Gertrude Stein. The rightness of the tactful image isn't to be found in its opposition to a wrong; it's a ripeness, and a nowness. Sciascia, in a near passage, shares memories of a restful game of tossing coins against a wall and of the yearly ritual of having his head shaved at the beginning of summer so that pistachio resin, falling from the trees to mat his hair, would not coagulate on his head: "With your head shaved, that wasn't a problem. Thus we sat down under the trees and stayed listening to the insects while the resin trickled down, drop by drop, because of the heat." The act of children put through ritual ablutions isn't always pretty in its ordering. My friend Patty didn't always brush her thick curly hair carefully enough, so that over time a knot might form stuck together with beach sand and lunchtime jelly, and it pulled her head to one side like a protuberant nest. Embarrassed, she'd go to an inexpensive hairdresser who, with a blunt razor, would cut it out. Ritual ablutions aren't always pretty in their ordering, but it's funny how they stick: eight-year-old Catholic schoolgirls and boys line up before the Holy Water font and learn to bless themselves. Like birds perched to birdbaths on a hot day, merely a touch of water only to a beak is cooling. So I loved the ritual, furtive, alone, even, of feeling water cooled in marble slightly smelling of incense touched by myself first to finger then to forehead, belly, shoulder, shoulder, pray. Even as an adult, and irreligious, I still enjoy this practice in a rare visit to a church—for tact in this case is linked to feeling *intact*, to being implicated in one's own sentience: to bless oneself with water is to stitch, feel, button self. Not that blessing at the forehead that says remember man that thou art dust and unto dust thou shalt return, but a reminder that we're nine tenths water, to enter that realization and, solidly, swim.

unfinished

Intactness might seem the opposite of awkwardness but not if we consider that awkwardness renders things tact-full: it forces an acknowledgment of weight, heft, physicality, and (im)balance. The more ordinary opposition might read intact/whole versus awkward/fragmented, but not if awkwardness is understood as an alternate arrangement of parts. I wonder about the possibility of an intactness that isn't closed, that isn't whole, that isn't finished. Is this the highest form of awkwardness, or is the breaking of what remains otherwise unbroken awkwardness's initiating stroke, each person's fall out of innocence and into awkwardness?

And what of jellyfish? At Sea World in San Diego, you can glimpse life not at sea but underwater without having to break through the surface of a wave and risk becoming breathless. You don't have to move in slow motion, peer through goggles, or wear flippers. That *unfinished* other world's underworld in all its magnificent difference, not dark as it generally appears to the creatures that live there but lit by lamps and staged with carefully chosen color backdrops is brought to our surface in the form of breathing, living aquarium art. I'm visiting the aquarium with the nephews of a friend of mine. Michael and Steven are eight and ten respectively, and they rub up against me or sidle like lazy pretty cats to ask "whatch ya lookin at" as I stand, transfixed, before the jellyfish tank. Could these be the same gooey, poisonous globs that appear washed up on the beach? Here in their faux ocean habitat they're celestial bodies moving in time to a force of gravity quite aside from the one that holds the earth and stars in place. This freefall that doesn't anticipate a ground, the way flames leap upward and across in a dance with oxygen. Was the person who invented the parachute thinking of jellyfish? Perhaps. But jellyfish as embodied parachutes can move up as well as down.

I need an oceanographer to teach me about the difference between life in the sea and life on land in terms of space, movement, gravity, ground. And light. Sun reaches through water to a certain depth and then . . . what? Just as I begin to contemplate how fish *feel*—fish sentience—I notice a tendency in each person to touch the aquarium's glass. Special signs are posted not to touch the glass of the sardine aquarium in particular, as they school in a rapid swirling motion like people on a metro rushing to work or particles spooled and fated to glide fast toward a meaning we cannot know. One tap can distract the sardine and cause a major collision among them, even a mass wounding. This glassy-eyed touching—is it a drive to get closer to the ocean or to the fish?

Is it to assure that one is on level ground?

Is it to remark a division between worlds, or to dissolve the divide?

Is it to deny a difference or summon a return?

The jellyfish isn't a formless glob after all but an immensely beautiful pulsing, like the dress of a ballerina, without the ballerina, finding its own drag and lift.

The sea is a world, and the boy, Michael, is a world.

The boy has a dream, and the boy is a dream.

"Do you think we're related to fish," I ask, and we laugh,

hard-pressed to find tails or gills even though "all life began in the ocean."

"If you could be a fish, which fish would you like to be?"

"I don't know about fish, but I sometimes think about what it might be like to be a cat," Michael says.

"I sometimes have dreams about my cat, do you?" I ask the boy.

And he proceeds to tell me a scary dream in which his cat married a cricket and they gave birth to a monster part cricket part cat, and if he didn't wake up in time he would die.

"That's quite a scary dream, that cat-cricket combo is a little grotesque."

Grotesque incongruities are fabrications of the unconscious working and re-working signifying systems, making things up and making things mean and unmean. When an extreme state finds a form, we call it grotesque. Order defiled, taboos crossed, offer up forms of grotesquerie. Monstrous extravagance and the psyche's made up fears, the grotesque roils beneath a surface waiting to emerge like a troll perched in the cranny of an unprepossessing bridge. Awkwardness engages the unconscious but is much less its manservant than grotesquerie. Michael can produce an idea of grotesqueness in his sleep, but he may not know enough yet to be awkward. Returning to the dream, the dream says, if the boy were stuck in the world in which crickets cross with cats, in which everything were wrong, he'd have to die, or at least give up selfhood as he knew it. But the boy doesn't die. He awakes intact. And remains essentially intact.

I apprehend him as a paragon of intactness. Is it his calm carriage, his thick lashes, or the fact that, frankly, he doesn't run on the soles of his feet but on his toes? The boy and his brother outline the length of our spindly and gargantuan shadows in the sand—the extent of some alien essential self sprawls before us into laughter at these spectral etchings that are us. What fairy taught the boys to do this? See how they run without an aim. Still, the older boy, having grown more, isn't less beautiful, but gangly, and therefore less apparently "intact." Michael is so compact that his body can easily, comfortably morph into now an old man shivering in his little coat, now a baby climbing into his mother's lap, now the boy again certainly staring, a tired contentment in his eyes. Here he is open, vulnerable, fragile, bare, exposed like a chick out of its nest but *unfinished* without the shiver. He is all this but *not* awkward.

Two older boys I know, fifteen-year-old Anthony and sixteen-year-old Andrew use the word "awkward" with the hip and slangy frequency that other kids use the word "cool." Andrew explains "situations are awkward when u don't know what to say or there are many silences which make people uncomfortable and their minds race. The thing that makes it awkward is u trying to keep ur cool and ur nerves are making u feel wrong." Link awkwardness with wrong and a whole cavalcade of impossibility erupts as in incorrect, in error, mistaken, out-of-joint, morally questionable, unjust. White letters on a red backdrop spelling WRONG WAY always scare me: I appear to be going the right way, but the sign is positioned just ambiguously enough on a highway entrance ramp to inject me with a split second's uncertainty and the expectation of a truck barreling toward me. There's the right way, the American way, and my way; right-of-way, the prescribed way, the only way, and one way.

Whichever way one comes eventually to move, no one arrives in the world, to begin with, whole. We undervalue brokenness, or, fetishizing it, perceive the world as a tabloid spectacle in which everyone else is broken except for ourselves, even as the ultimate goal in life is reparation. There is no reparation but only rearrangements of parts.

Intact or tactless, Michael is "just" a boy. So much is immanent in "just." Is the beautifully intact boy *not yet* broken, *not yet* divided, or *not yet* aware of it?

Are we awkward because we try to stitch ourselves but have lost the thread and can no longer tell how to match one swatch of being with another?

Or do we become awkward when told too repeatedly to mind the gap?

I wonder toward the possibility of an intactness that isn't closed, that isn't whole, that isn't finished . . .

BREACHING

mismatched

Each day on earth is at base an endless adjustment to there being too much or not enough, to there being something missing or something extra. You could trip over yourself or forget yourself. If only, if only. If you pause to ask what self suits you, if you admit the body you most resist, if you acknowledge the face or pronounce the name that you refuse to identify with, you risk awkwardness.

On a train from Providence to New York, a man drags a large brown garbage bag behind him down the center aisle. This is his job: proclaiming, "trash, trash." What image of a self must he adjust to in order to pull the bag?

A woman on a Roman streetcar has shaped her eyebrows to an arch. They arrive at a peak, and then descend to either side dramatically like the numerous arches in the city.

A woman in the apartment next to mine begins each day by yelling then follows the yelling with a prolonged period of vacuuming.

Who's to say if you're singing, you're not sinking?

Someone had chosen as his epitaph, "novità?"—as if to say, "what's new?", not death certainly, and in that act left behind a novel, unwritten.

belated

And then one day it hits you—not all at once but in waves, and who knows why this particular day is to be a wave succession or what led to it, but it hits you in a suffusing kind of way—of the time things take and of the need to live long enough to receive all the truths you weren't ready to receive, all in good time and at the right time, in readiness or shock, in openness or choosing now, marshalling your resources to throw some habit off its course; of the need to live long enough to face a desire, to make something happen and live with the happening; of the time it takes to learn about all that was good, and all the good you could do, or just to feel the ground beneath you as though it were strewn with bay leaves or egg crates, seashells, or shards; or the sense of a vanishing now at the site of what once was lush undergrowth and concrete, deep pockets of what-had-beens, a corner of the yard where a tap on the arm mingled with the smoky waft of a hot dog plumping on a grill and hydrangea was a face made of lacy stars pulling your own face toward it, or just to know it was there to hide behind, a placemarker at that juncture in the garden, like a doily dropped onto your head at church telling you you were there, you'd known this once, you'd been there before; to live long enough to become fully sentient.

Teachers are always emissaries of one sort or another. How I loved my teachers, even the bad ones. Did they know it? The way they'd bring me something or bring something forth in me, or take me somewhere and sometimes show something behind their eyes only a student could see—you spent so much searching thinking time in their presence—their eyes so fully present, so there—even if what they were saying couldn't be heard at the time, or the next day, but could only be acknowledged one day out of the blue when by some combination of readiness and a confluence of wills, or thanks to a constellation of accident, memory, and need, you went wandering and found what they meant until it meant fully for you, hitting you now. Learning's time-lag, knowing's belatedness is what makes pedagogy a fundamentally awkward affair. Teachers are always emissaries of a sort but even if they issue diplomas, they cannot be diplomats because misunderstanding is a necessary part of the game, and transgression.

undiplomatic

Awkwardness is both a force of will and an unconscious interruption. The imago, the persona "diplomat" must cultivate the disappearance of awkwardness, or use it strategically as a sign of his own humility or charm. For the most part, he at all costs avoids it by finding the perfect balance between excess and restraint.

undiplomatic   I once dated a man who was the child of diplomats—he was my
first love. He had a genuine interest in the history of nation-states
and political formations. He prided himself on completing the *New
York Times* crossword puzzle daily and on playing basketball with
boys in the 'hood even though he wasn't a boy in the 'hood. Amidst
days and nights of heated lovemaking, tangled in each other's orgas-
mic embrace—we once made out for two solid hours in his '68 VW
Bug until a coplike figure from a movie tapped on the fogged-up
glass—we never had sex.

Tactless diplomat is an oxymoron, yet, of all the book titles in
the English-speaking world that feature "awkwardness"—and there
aren't many—those related to diplomacy employ the word most:
*Awkward Dominions: American Political, Economic, and Cultural
Relations with Europe 1919–1933*; *The Awkward Embrace: One-
Party Dominion and Democracy*; *The Awkward Years: American
Foreign Relations under Garfield and Arthur*; *Awkward Partner:
Britain in the European Community*. Awkwardness in diplomacy
might be both the exception and the rule because power is at stake
in diplomatic relations, not merely friendship. Maybe awkwardness
in diplomacy is born of the rift between outward appearance, pomp,
and puppetry, the peculiar synecdoche of a person standing in for a
nation on the one hand and the real work of translation, communication, negotiation, and talk on the other.

I recently heard a radio broadcast in which political analysts
applied the word "awkward" to the war in Iraq. "It would be awkward to grant Iraqis partial sovereignty," a male voice informed an
American radio audience; "Full sovereignty," another disagreed,
"would put us in an awkward situation." Lubberly or unbecoming,
graceless or unhandy, bungling or clownish—this isn't the sense in
which "awkward" is meant; try instead, hard to manage, difficult
to reverse, embarrassing, irreparable, impossible to control. Try
awkwardness as a garishly exposing flashlight revealing American
imperialist motives.

A situation could turn "awkward" then if some truth about it
were revealed; a political situation might euphemistically be deemed
awkward if a nation-state finds itself wielding power that isn't its to
wield. Bullish interference, bombs dropped on wedding parties, bat-
talions bulldozing neighborhoods, a thousand stray bullets—it's all

rather awkward as a sign of base disregard for human life or as a *undiplomatic*
way of saying that the extremity of an act far outstrips its rationale:
violence as response to a reputation besmirched, a world power
wishing to appear muscular. Lives abruptly end as though there
were no before or after; lies used to justify war are exposed; the
emperor is naked. To describe all of this as "awkward" is to confuse international relations with a parlor game gone awry, but the
intensity of an investment in the *image* of itself that a nation projects onto an international stage looms, consequently, large as a
mushroom cloud. "Awkward," we say, because we cannot regard
ourselves self-consciously, because we cannot be held accountable
for our acts.

Our only hope, in such situations are ambassadors, not merely
figureheads but gifted communicators, diplomats of diplomats,
paragons of tact? Ambass, emboss, and ass; embarrass, adore, and
ambush; brass and sass; ambrosia and dose; boss and brash and
door; a.m., a morning man, a quietly colorful fish; eyelash, whiplash,
unabashed; embroider, embassy, ambergris, ambidextrous, ash. So
much is expected of an ambassador, it's hard to imagine him being
contained all in one suit. No doubt, a person. But when I hear the
word "ambassador" I picture the beautiful green mane and white
collar of a mallard duck. I can't begin to imagine what it would
mean to represent a nation's interests. Both the king's understudy
and a leader in his own right, an ambassador is a messenger and a
servant, a conduit and a go-between, a figure of and for something
vastly greater than himself.

I suppose an ambassador can be an eavesdropper, I suppose he
could be a spy, but the word in common usage has a halo around it,
attached as it is to peace and goodwill, graciousness and favor.
Immigrants, consider, are collapsed in the minds of the people in the
nation they emigrate to with the nation they left behind, but they
cannot be seen as ambassadors or diplomats because there is nothing
to authorize them as such, and in many cases they do not wish to
represent the country they left, the home they were coerced or forced
or driven to leave. Immigrants arrive on the international scene suffused with place, but locale isn't their only moor unmoored because
in a sense they are time travelers too. As I know from my own immigrant grandparents, immigrant bodies must learn (or not) a different

undiplomatic rhythm, they must pace themselves according to a differently calibrated day, week, month—god bless my grandfather for maintaining
his siestas. Diurnal punctuation, movements through a day, the time
reserved for eating, sleeping, work, for doing nothing, for waiting,
the time of being differs in these daily ways from region to region
across the world. But there is also the matter of time writ large where
an immigrant is concerned: stepping into future days unknown, will
he attach drowsily to a past, or reject the past like a junky amnesiac,
will he attempt to slough it off, will he, in short, be an ambassador
to the simple future, to a Mandelstamian future passive participle,
the "what ought to be," in his relations, perhaps most especially with
his "offspring"? And what language—clumsy, halting, svelte, or sub-
lime—will serve him best in this exchange, this transport?

Immigration: no structure can accommodate its layers, no one
person can hope fully to understand its numerous sides. What gets
deposited at a vanishing point of loss or painted into a corner of forgetfulness. What flourishes with more muscle now than it ever did at
home. What diminishes. What lusters, what grows, broods and fes-
ters, what blooms in the passageway, what survives transplantation.

Leonardo Sciascia explained that the people in his Sicilian town
"have always viewed America with terror, as a particularly bitter and
negative fate. Those emigrants who returned for a visit every five or
ten years, and who seemed Americanized, were regarded with con-
tempt, as if they had become stupider than before. America was
imagined as a place where no one knew how to live, where you
worked your fingers to the bone and brutalized yourself in the
process, where your senses grew dull and you dressed in a bizarre
manner: loud, garishly colored ties for the men, indescribable hats
for the women."

What will ever be comprehensible and what will remain outside
of comprehension? This is a question bequeathed me by immigration.
I sometimes observed my Italian heritage as though it were a thing
outside of us; I learned how to interpret and locate my family's
Italianness in America and which compartment to place it in amid a
universe of signs; occasionally, I was immersed in it, awash and
unknowing. What aspect of that heritage moves into the foreground
changes as I change and as the political moment in which I live tilts
the pieces of a day into a kaleidoscope of newly prioritized scenes.

Perhaps when my ancestors looked toward the borders of the *undiplomatic* United States from the inside certainly not of the prow of a boat, from inside their imaginations, they saw a spirit of continuous building, quite literally—the American tendency toward sturdy structures rocketing skyward. Perhaps they heard the lore about bottomless resources and wide expanses of land. I, on the other hand, might see a discrepancy of seemingly tragic proportions—between the island of paradisial splendor that they left—on my father's side, Sicily— and the vacancy of strip malls and derelict parking lots, of urban blight American-style, of pastries drab as cardboard, of Swiss Miss. It's possible I only apprehend American culture this way—for its blandness—because it is the culture I know: a romance by definition cannot be maintained with what is near but must attach to what is imagined as far. Still, I can't help but perceive intensity on the island: everything, from the language to the sun to the food, bites. It could be that my ancestors did not perceive the American landscape through a lens of dereliction or loss, but that, peering through a train window in New England for example, their hearts leapt at the sight of wild honeysuckle and craggy rose, of white heron, and patches of green glimpsed through mist, of piping plovers. I too might see everything anew—and in this way "for what it is"—just yesterday, the lead-edged diagram of color that sustained a stained-glass window in my neighborhood; a park at the center of a city abundant with people; the way the light turns the sides of houses platinum at dusk; a garden continuously maintained in the pretty pattern dug in the seventeen hundreds in Philadelphia.

Sometimes Americans are cast as enterprising and inventive, almost as the world's stimulant; other times, we are considered somnambulists, overworking high-consuming isolationist living dead. We are the people of the unbreakable spirit, we will not give in under pressure, which may mean we cannot be forced to speak, we cannot be tortured, we're nobody's manservant, we love our country like no other citizens of the world. At this point, imagine the immigrant confronted with the enormity of this image, never an ambassador, outside peering in, skeptical, trepidatious, convinced.

vertiginous

Scenes and priorities shift between generations, so why does it feel after three generations we are still arriving? Was it because there was no welcome wagon at Ellis Island, no ambassador of greeting other than the Statue of Liberty? I don't necessarily experience this inability to arrive, this awkwardness, as a sentimental lack. I quite enjoy cultivating in my remaindered Italianness a fly in the ointment, a resistant nub, an inassimilable raft of being, in which case I am the true American, rebellious and bellicose at heart, revolutionary without a cause. Not arrived, still close to the ground, uncertain and disbelieving, I think I feel *least* at home, most awkward, in most American shopping malls, but maybe most especially in the new mall in the city where I currently live, in Providence. I seem to prefer the ground, but everything about this mall requires ascension and suspension, punctuated as it is by "open-air" escalators that rise up like roller coasters well beyond the height of palm trees toward cubicled storefronts that face a balustrade. But there's no performance, not even a stage, only merchandise and plummets. Glass windows offer a view of the city, its canal and Early American architecture dotting what could *almost* be mistaken for an Italianate hillside if it weren't for the kitsch-carts and smell of sweetened popcorn that also define the space from which one surveys the cityscape outside. I have no desire to view the city as from a Ferris wheel. I don't wish to know it, I certainly don't feel any more at home in it given a bird's-eye view.

On one side of my family, among the men, monkish contemplators; on the other side, violent thrashers. Is this the source of instability, the incongruity that disturbs my gravity? Or maybe I haven't gotten past the fact that my great-grandmother viewed the US, and especially weekly TV westerns, through lenses bought at the Five and Ten Cent store—a visual ineptitude, a kind of Woolworth's genetic imprint, was passed down in the genes rendering heights too nebulous to be physically bearable.

ambassadorial

Numerous ambassadors have taken me to this moment; any childhood can be understood as marked by benign or malevolent, unprepossessing like thieves in the night, or insistent, confident emissaries. The nuns who taught me in Catholic grade school presented themselves as ambassadors of God, their gift his word, gagging them. Unfortunately, we only had one singing nun at our school, and she left the church for her love of a priest. Often the message of the sisters was a slap, but I enjoyed the sight of one's smooth hands, her filed fingernails, and the way she proclaimed God's word, musingly, always with a question mark, as though she were making smoke rings or playing hooky, hiding out at the far edge of a cemetery. As I think of it now, I most enjoyed delivering gifts at these ambassadors' feet when, at Christmastime, each student would walk to the front of the room and deposit her gift on the teacher's desk, and when the desk overflowed, as it always did, to crouch and place it on the floor. Why was it that the gift we gave most was a perfumed talc called "Jean Naté"? Purchased at the working-class drug store, it came in a yellow box embossed with black letters. Did the gift suggest that the nuns had a night life other than supplication to our Lord? Numerous ambassadors roamed the neighborhood—deliverers of bread and milk—they were frenetic and not TV friendly, they were a grocery store on wheels driven by a man named Butch. He signaled his arrival usually at dinnertime with a loud and repetitious blow of his horn. His truck actually was large enough to sport an aisle, a cash register, and a deli section. We only relied on him in emergencies—was it because he overcharged, or for the way he would leeringly ask "How's your mother?" All manner of sales representatives, ambassadors of companies and their cheaply made ware, appeared in the neighborhood. One succeeded in selling us an encyclopedia called Bobley's Encyclopedia, which my brother later named "the encyclopedia of the ghetto." I found it handy for school projects but remember being especially glad to find in it an entry for the word "hiccup." In the middle of a hypochondriacal phase, experiencing a bout of hiccups, I searched out *ambassadorial* information on the phenomenon and confirmed what I suspected: hiccups that don't appear to stop may be a sign of a more serious condition. Who could forget the appearance of the Fuller Brush man on those streets, wayward emissary? He had a beard that ran the length of the street, a combination Rip Van Winkle and Rapunzel, he smelled sweetly bitter of perfume—Jean Naté?—superimposed onto body odor. He appeared before us like a prophet, an existential believer in the only palpable reality—a brush bristle—and the *idea* of the brush, so many separate strands bunched in just the right proximity to clean or smooth, neaten or pleasure. How did I know as a child to think of this man as an ambassador from the land of lost souls? He never beat the door down, he aimlessly slumped through the neighborhood, he seemed both vulnerable and scary, and pseudowise. The neighborhood must have seen in him child molester, because it seems my last glimpse of him was watching him run, shielding his head from a flogging mob. In high school, ambassadors came in the form of talent scouts. A man wearing spectacles and a neat mustache matched by an even neater shirt, orange as I recall, with a white collar and a blue tie, would call the chosen out of class. Here was a visitor from another world who, if given the correct answers, we were told, could take a few of us to that better world with him.

His mission was to take us singly into a room usually reserved for interviews with the guidance counselor and subject us to hours of testing. We were told he was a psychologist, and this confused me—what relation could a psychologist have to measuring intelligence? I wore an orange leaf-colored pant suit with a built-in belt and a built-in polyester extra collar that made it appear as though an entire shirt lurked there while the psychologist with the tiny mouth—was he Italian too?—holding a stopwatch in one hand asked me to solve simple math problems, asked me basic questions about the arrangement of the planets in the Milky Way, asked me to define "recalcitrant" and spell "anomaly," but the real test, I could tell, occurred only later and consisted of mosaics made of geometric patterns. I was given a picture of an already completed mosaic along with a pile of geometric shapes made of cardboard, and the aim was to make my pile of puzzle pieces match the pattern of the one placed before me. The first few puzzles were easy—I was begin-

ning to feel insulted—but they quickly became more difficult until *ambassadorial*
the psychologist, Mr. Longo (I now remember his name), tired of
waiting, put the stopwatch on a table before him and told me to
take my time. The minutes became elongated while I fiddled with
what struck me as an utterly uncompelling Rubik's Cube, or some
other game invented by adults to get children out of their hair for
hours at a time. Soon I became more aware of Mr. Longo's presence
in the room than of the task at hand, almost as though he was the
puzzle I was really meant to solve. What did he want from me, and
why had he come? Was he himself smart, or just an evaluator of
smartness? I had guessed on some of the earlier questions and gotten them right. Could he tell? From the corner of my eye, he
appeared to be standing with one foot perched at the bottom edge
of an imaginary mantelpiece like someone out of a nineteenth-
century novel cleaning his riding boots, or like a boy made to stare
into a corner while wearing a pointy cap on which the letters were
stacked like a teetering chimney—D-U-N-C-E. I could tell by now
I had failed the test that would usher me out of the halls of the
masses and into the Gifted Program. The only person deemed such
was Robert Carrot. A teacher would assign an out-of-school project—go home and find an article in the newspaper, go home and call
as many taxidermists as you can find in the phone book—and
Robert, wiry as Ichabod Crane, would reply "we don't *have* a telephone," "we don't *have* a newspaper. We're too poor."

Other ambassadors, in time, brought me into this same room
for questioning. A burly representative from a nearly local Ivy
League college came in search of scholarship material. Here was a
regal taxi driver, a go-between, a man with a mission, who only
seemed sincere. If the Fuller Brush man had something to sell,
though one couldn't tell what, this man had something to buy,
though he pretended to bring us something. Here was a business-
man. He asked me questions aimed at calculating the measure of my
leadership skills, my curricular as well as my extracurricular interests, but at the end of the interview jokingly asked if I played
football, then offered his tactless assessment of me to the lackey
diplomat, our guidance counselor: "she's short but perky."

Whether a go-between opens a gap or closes one, his presence is
an awkward anomaly.

incomprehensible

Many years later, the invitation to visit the home of the Italian Ambassador to the United States was embossed. What system manages to print words onto paper in such a way that they appear as though they could lift off a page, as though they could salute and witness and invite you, requesting the pleasure of your company? The Ambassador had arranged a meeting of Italian/American writers to discuss the state of Italian/American letters. I was eager for the opportunity of this conversation, but stumped about how to present myself, which is to say what to wear. I had no idea what might pass as apparel appropriate to the occasion of dinner at an Ambassador's house, but I assumed, no doubt rightly, that nothing hanging in my closet of Salvation Army purchases, bright or funky—a Groucho Marx monkey jacket, a polyester dress splashed with clownish flowers in red, a sleeveless sleek Ann Taylor dress in deep blue linen—would do. Nor could I draw upon my secondary line of wardrobe: old clothes and heirlooms reserved for the demands of a character I might wish to assume at a costume party. After perusing designer dress stores in Boston and Providence, I let a clerk convince me that the finest look for my body, build, and station in life, the smartest option for my too implausibly youthful face—and given that the event would entail cocktails before and after a sit-down dinner—would be black velvet. But not black velvet alone. A black *sequined* velvet zippered jacket whose collar rose to either side of my neck like the lips of an urn, which, if pushed a tad further—say, if in place of sequins appeared encrusted jewels, if, say, the collar were to rise so dramatically as to imitate a guillotine—would risk the presentation of a self-appointed queen. The jacket came with a skirt that I had to pour myself into. The outfit was transformative in the way a fur coat might feel to a body that had only ever sported cotton, but I struggled to move naturally in it, discomfited by the feeling that it was too ostentatious, even if the black muted such a possibility, or too close to the very loudness in fact that Sciascia had described, a gaudiness made possible, somehow *produced* by Italian American peasantry's false acquisition of

finery in the United States. My worries about the dress, which simply, in the end, was *beautifying*, were mitigated by the greater
embarrassment of arriving late to the gathering. I had traveled to
the event with writer and poet, first-generation Sicilian immigrant,
and critical spokesperson for the cause of Italian/American letters,
Edvige Giunta. We had taken the train together (was it possible we
were both at the time phobic highway drivers?) and in that passageway continued to deepen a dialogue about our own shared homeland and present literary passions. We would change into our
ambassadorial dress in the train station's bathroom, we agreed. We
would wait an hour so as not, certainly, to arrive early, but we could
not have calculated the taxi driver's mistake in taking us to the
Italian Embassy rather than to the Ambassador's home. Must we
have looked like immigrants who had misplaced their passports?

No matter. Edi came to be my ambassador to Sicily as I learned
from her the details that my family never told. Sicily isn't Italy: I
learn to remember that. It is Arab and Norman, Spanish and African,
Greek and Phoenician and Swabian. It is multiply invaded but never
saved. No matter how impoverished Italians on the mainland were,
they still treated Sicilians like slaves and, the island consigned to
feudal agriculturalism, ready to exploit it. Edi took me on a literary
tour of Sicily's layers: here is the place where Persephone was
abducted, and athwart this coast, within view of Etna, the Cyclops's
rock. Sicily was, beyond a doubt, resplendent, but my Sicilian friend
explained that its lushness was uncanny because "Sicily was a land
of grief."

In Sicily, I discover, the pastries range so wide and various that
one begins to imagine a people stewing in sweets: rum baba and
ricotta cannoli, orange and zucchini marmalades, a bun overflowing with ice cream (an ice cream sandwich), pink marzipan, honey-
dipped pignoli cookies, a hard-as-a-rock cookie called "dead man's
bones." The array is infinite, the consumption daily and deep. My
father's family emigrated from there, and I've returned once, twice,
three times now as ambassador to a familial past, a familial silence.
In a pasticceria in Acireale, I ask for a dead man's bone. The proprietor hesitates—it's very hard, he says. I know, I say, I want it, I
know what I want. There is maybe no cookie so rife with longing
as a dead man's bone. These are the cookies I associate with my

father's father, a man of few words who brought a bag of dead man's bones to us every year on the day after Halloween. The cookie is mostly made of egg white and sugar—I knew that taste from meringue and longed as a child, excited by the macabre gift, to try a dead man's bone, but it is a futilely frustrating cookie: it teases you with sweetness but refuses to yield. If you take a molar or a hammer to it, it falls apart in your hands or in your mouth. Like the inside of a dead bone, there's chalk and dust. Sometimes the whiter part of the treat perches on an island that at one time must have flown lavalike as bubbly sugar but now it's so hard you need to work it with your teeth as with a file; "work it," my friend says, "like a dog biscuit." There is pleasure here on the island, I know, more readily available than in a dead man's bone. It's obvious, it's evident, it's an island of paradisial splendor, so much so that I can barely imagine how desperate my ancestors must have been to leave for points unknown.

I haven't really talked to my father since I was four, though I do remember once at a dinner table when I was twenty-one speaking the words "I hate you" then bursting into extremely hot tears. What could undo the spell of forces that kept me from knowing him— Oedipal, physical, metaphysical—cultivated daily, spooling, tightening, hardening into years and years? It was as though he had made a pact with my mother that "the children" would be hers, while he stewed in juices of unreachable rage, *intactible*. He seemed cut off from delicacy. There was no delicacy for him or about him, no rivulets, no puppies, no glorious beating of wings. Press here and feel a beautiful welling. Look there—something is joyously climbing, up, up. Can you hear it? Go there. No one had ever directed him thus. I didn't *consciously* conceive needing to get to the other side of two generations of incomprehension in order to say hello to my father, to find a place before the moment at which my immigrant forebears had become violent, bitter, and brash. To stand at the source and salute them from the site of their departure. To know. As if in order to say hello to my father, I had to get far far away, to enter another time zone, to broach a different ground for a relation. To call out from the place that they refused to look back at. But here I was; I knew this had been my plan once I lifted the black receiver of an orange telephone on a street corner in my father's parents' hometown of Belmonte Mezzagno, and felt my voice spring with *anxious* longing as if the line were made of rubberbands; I said, "I'm here"; I heard him say, "hello."

anxious

Is it possible to create more or less fitting atmosphere for talking? Some people say they feel especially moved to speak honestly on a drive, in a car. Maybe the movement soothingly rocks them and the partial distraction of driving or not makes them forget themselves enough to say what's really on their mind. In a church marquee near my home in Providence, there's a sign that always cracks me up. It reads: "Speak, Lord, your servant is listening." Behind my house in Providence, I've made a garden out of capital and imagination. I call it my "idyll"; a friend says "your secret garden"; I think "this better life." Sometimes I turn on a light on the book-lined third floor of my house and think of something ramshackle and teetering, or a whirlpool—no world can be this stable—but it is, it is, you've buffed the floor and daily, using a carpenter's plane, established a ground. Sometimes I clean the basement, brush my cat—as though she needs a human to groom her, the way I might have stroked my doll—but I was rarely into dolls, and think how memory works to bring what is distant closer as you age, while what is near cannot be recollected. Sometimes I think if you could get just slightly crazy, that would be fun, but total madness would be eternal torment. A now-famous writer of fiction for adolescents and family friend gave me a tennis lesson or two when I was ten. The racquet was my first purchase in a secondhand store—a thrift store called "Divine Sales" run by a group who taught TM, transcendental meditation, and were followers of Father Divine, in Darby, Pennsylvania. The racquet was wooden and green, and complete with press cost fifty cents. To reach back to that memory now, the store was creepy, all long fingernails and pointed beards. One day after a tennis lesson, I don't remember the context— my teacher friend explained to me, "other people can sometimes throw us off and make us lose our balance," and then, as we continued to walk, as if to counter the seriousness of his words, he said, pointing with his tennis racquet at a pile of dog shit, "That, Mary, is poop."

divided

"You're really excited," my father says whenever I return from
Sicily to tell him about it, as if to say I don't share your excitement
but I observe your excitement, and I don't know what to do with
your excitement so it might seem that I am mocking your excitement but I'm not. This time my father seems to speak a different
language upon my return. I'm describing to him the start of my garden, and trying to elicit advice on starting plants from seed. From
the corner of my eye—I'm sprawled beneath a humidifying sky,
lying atop a bed of grass—I notice how the roots of weeds cling to
their dirt even after I've pulled them; they urge toward life. And the
pansies, I notice how heartbreakingly ridiculous they look, like a
cat's, their faces are literally springing toward *what*? I'd like to
know. They insistently face a person or the sun. "You know the
most important thing for the garden," my father says. "Watering, I
guess," I say, not sure if this is a riddle or a test. "No," he laughs.
"Love," he says, "you have to love the plants. They know it when
you love them. They give back to you when you love them." My
father the banger, my father the clod—I know there is someone else
there, a child who was tactlessly handled, a clever man, a sprite, a
jaunt—my father who beat the living bejesus out of my brother and
wrung our ears with years of yelling is giving me a lesson on love.
He's reducing me to silence. I feel the urge to eat a lightning bug, to
get a new grip on nature and living things. Outside my garden walls,
my piece of paradise, the ice cream truck is playing, believe it or not,
"Who's Afraid of the Big Bad Wolf."

Returning to Sciascia, I find an intriguing paraphrase of that
other Sicilian master, Pirandello: "But let's come back to solitude.
Among us [Sicilians] the idea is deeply rooted that in order to be
yourself completely, you need to be alone; that solitude is the place
where you 'recover' yourself; that other people divide us, splinter us,
multiply us . . . that with other people you can't be a living being
but only a character; and that to earn existence as a living being,
you need to sneak away to solitude, you need to be a *uomo solo* as
Pirandello says." Sciascia doesn't agree with this position, even

though he describes it so seductively. He thinks that such an attitude *divided* toward solitude breeds complacency, an adjustment to the world as it is rather than a desire to transform it.

For some people solitude is more awkward than sociality, but it seems that, statistically, people feel more awkward among other human beings than alone. Not to try to communicate with my father could be splendid, but I opt for an ill-fitting ambassadorial cape. Maybe no emissary is as significant as the one who gives you language; for me, there have been several to witness my awkwardness but have faith in my ability to float. I don't intend to be the class clown in my first Italian language class, but this is how it goes. My partner is so overcome with laughter she could cry, so demolished by hilarity she's afraid she's going to pee as I wrack my brains to get the right pronoun, then the possessive, in the right order before a word that is torturing me, the word at the end of the sentence that would free me, the little kid word on the little kid flashcards our teacher is using to help us articulate our needs in Italian: *"orsacchiotto,"* the word for "teddy bear." The only person with an Italian surname in the class, I also appear to be the least able to shape my mouth to this language's beautiful tongue. "R-trilling is supposed to be genetic," my teacher, a Sicilian named Germana, jokes. "It should be in your blood." But the class roars with laughter at the spasmodic punch more like a series of *dahs* than a rounded *r* that issues from my mouth. When I speak Italian, one of the most beautiful languages in the world, it's agreed, I sound as though I'm gagging. Or as the teacher instructs me: "You don't have to kill it."

I remember my father's relation to a language he only partly understood and rarely spoke. He resorted to Sicilian solely for the purposes of invective, and the one word I learned from him sounded like "stew-nod," a synonym for *"stupido,"* and whose pronunciation led me to picture brains made of mush. Occasionally he would show an interest in kinship when he would ask, "Is he a 'Sidgie?'" or "Are you a 'Sidgie?'"(Sicilian), but his smile would be curled into a bitter twist or joker's grimace when he'd ask this so that I could never know if he himself liked being Sidgie or not. Sometimes his use of English had the embarrassing ring of a bad translation, like the way he called potatoes, implosively, "buhdaydahs," or how he ever referred to the bathroom as "the toilet."

My second Italian language teacher is a woman of exquisite intensity, boundless energy, and ebullient charm. I invite her to my fortieth birthday party, and she comes, but only appears a fascinated spectator of the carnival of queerness that unfolds. "Era un altro mondo"—"It was another world"—she reports to another Italian colleague on the following day while I meanwhile consider how to preserve the abundance of satin ribbon in which she has wrapped the gift she gave me. The ribbon shares an affinity with the smooth envelope, the package of documents really, that had previously ushered me into an invitation to the Ambassador's house. Now I had Dacia Maraini's *Bagheria* in my hands. My teacher was coincidentally, once again, from Sicily, the book was set there, she knew I wrote nonfiction, she offered the following inscription: "Maria Carissima, Spero che tu possa leggere presto senza problemi questa bellissima autobiografia. Tanti auguri di Buon Compleanno! Santina." Dearest Mary, I hope that you are able easily (literally, without problems) to read this beautiful autobiography soon. Best wishes for a Happy Birthday, Santina.

To read. To read without problems. Indeed. Maybe no lessons are quite as painstakingly incremental as the baby steps of language learning. Italian for me still has not deepened into a stride, but incubates. It is a distillate waiting for the right opportunity to be mixed and poured. *Bagheria* is not a difficult book, but I have not yet caught up with it. On my most recent trip to Sicily, though, I rediscovered a book my teacher had lent me years ago. At the time she gave it to me, I remember reviewing the book's photos with a kind of breezy awe. Now I glimpsed its cover on a website and wanted to see it again. What I couldn't know is that is was a cookbook— and here I had returned from Sicily determined to re-make daily the subtle pleasures of its cuisine. What I was jubilant to discover was that the book was set in a mountain town that had serendipitously arrived on our itinerary, our fingers pointing with ouija board inaccuracy at possible day trips. In the manner of a Dadaist, we could open the dictionary and point to "rocking horse" and call it poetry, or open the map and point to Regaliali and call it our destiny for that day of our lives.

I can't share the food I've been making with my father by way of diplomatic offering since most food is spoiled on him: "I feel as though it's eating away at my insides," is one of his favorite things to say about the food he's just consumed. It's true I feel like an *divided* alchemist with my Sicilian cookbooks, a concoctor, a conjurer, a chemist keen to admit a profusion from a pinch of the right herb into the dish, buoyed by the food's lightness, shocked by the bite. I notice lately how the recipes work like truth serum on respective guests. So the food of his homeland doesn't sit well with my father. Perhaps I can show him pictures instead.

I haven't visited my father in over a year, but today I am interested to learn what words in our newly discovered lexicon might follow "hello." I've posted hundreds of photographs onto a Web site where my father can see their details sprawled across a ten-by-twelve-inch screen, but when I ask him if he wants to look at them with me, he says he's seen them, not right now, he's having trouble concentrating (a symptom of Parkinson's disease), he'd rather right now watch the ball game on TV: the Philadelphia Phillies are playing the Boston Red Sox. The Parkinson's has reduced him to this, he tells me one day on the telephone: days on end of watching baseball and golf. It's an interesting misperception to blame the disease for this paring down of pleasure to the batting of balls inside a TV screen because ball games, at least, had always been my father's fancy: staring into the game for hours aside from us is nothing new.

And so I wait. Why, after all, should my father have any interest in a world so far—Sicily *or* my life, a universe away from his? Why should he respond to my demand. To people, and their endless demands? And so I ask for what I don't want to regret not knowing: what would he want to tell me if he could? Can Sicily really incite a radically different ground from which to talk to each other, can it produce a relation athwart, quite aside from legacies established in childhood of brutality and regret, desperateness, rage, and the eating away of insides? Sitting across from him on a couch, I ask him if his family ever talked about the basis of their departure, but he forgets. My mother, divorced from him, really knows more of the details of his family's past than he. "My father's sister," he brightens to recall, (her name was Mary, was she my namesake, Mary Cappello?) "had lost an eye."

"She lived to be one hundred and one," he says, "and her niece, my cousin, bought her a new eye." I knew if I stayed long enough, something would be revealed, but I'm clueless as to what to do with this outside of treating my father as an analysand who has finally unearthed the source of his own fear of knocking an eye out—a refrain we heard in childhood—or maybe it was just proof that Parkinson's had done nothing to dull a lifelong obsession. And then it happens: my father swivets slowly to lift a sheaf of papers. Documents. He explains to me that he's been trying to write a story and he asks if I will look at it. I'm eager and read parts of it aloud. It's based a bit on Rumplestiltskin, he explains, that character who falls asleep and awakes in a different land. That's Rip Van Winkle, I want to say, correcting him, but opt for tact.

"I call it 'Forty Winks to La La Land,'" he laughs and asks if I know what La La land is. He hears references to it on television and interprets it to mean Shangri-la, the perfect world, paradise. I feature it to mean oblivion, the far outpost of space cadets, but I don't correct him. The story at this point is mostly a list of bizarrely fashioned activities and settings in La La land, including performances like "cockroaches on parade." The moral, my father explains in advance, is that there is no perfect world, even La La Land is imperfect.

My favorite part so far is the delicate sentence with which the story opens: the narrator has come to the end of a day's toil in his garden and has fallen to sleep on its edge.

"What do you think of it?" my father asks.

"I think it's charming," I reply. "I think it's great you are doing this."

"Yes, but I can't really do it," he replies. "I can't write. My hands shake too much."

"Try dictating into a tape recorder, try asking your grandson to be your amanuensis," I say. "Where there's a will there's a way."

"Here are all the notes," he pushes the scraps of paper toward me, scraps that too readily resemble the bits of pieces of jotting, the anglings and inklings, the ambles and paper estuaries, the bits of fragments of traces that make the materials on my own writing desk. I still compose by hand. "Maybe you can finish it for me," my father says.

In Italy, a person in intimate conversation or in an exchange with a stranger in a store might say, emphatically, "senti"—listen, or "dimmi"—talk to me, tell me what you want—and it's not rude. "Senti, Papa, let me tell you about Sicily, senti." But my father,

mawkish as it may sound, has always been hard of hearing. "Enjoy
yourself," my father says, as if to say "because you know I'm *not*, I
can't." Senti. Here is Sicily: a stupendously pendant flower, a dessert
tray angled downward, tiny flames pointing upward from tinfoil and
wood in the shape of Arab columns. Senti. A colossus of pink black
light floats in the distance, a minutiae of blossoms, little nautilus
seedpods dot the ground, a cistern with stairs, a cave in the distance.
We emerge onto a periphery each time at a different place looking
down—a different ribbon or ledge on the margins of the tower of
Babel, the benches at each lookout only appear to be the same. The
island is anything but flat. Life is lived close to the clouds and climbing. Settling. Round a bend and pitch. Deep sway of mountain and
lift. Lush corners of flight. Rows. Poppy, geranium, broom. Olive,
fig, assume. Nothing. Poppy and fennel spring, yellow bursts amid
quiet ruins, at lunchtime, barely a soul in the cobbled narrows.
Descending here is rising, is arousing, a rose bush trained to become
a red-budded red bursting bowering towering tree. Behind a foun-
tain. Adjacent to a corner where someone has hung a slender mop
in a medieval loophole. Senti. A clutch of chamomile, a swatch of
the spindly tops of anise. Dimmi: what do you think? I met a young
man named Giorgio here. On my first visit, he was so young as to
be puppyish. On my second visit, he seemed destined for no good—
he was playing with knives. On this recent visit, he is transformed,
he's a budding botanist. How did this boy's hands go from testing
the sharpness of knives against his skin, against a block of wood,
staring woodenly toward a television set set to overloud to holding
now before us the incandescent trembling of foliage he has gathered
on an excursion to Santa Ninfa, nature preserve near Trapani, classroom to his new pursuit of botany? Each plant bears a label, like a
message set to carrier pigeon, the name of the plant deliberately
penned, lovingly applied like a band to a finger to honor a relation.
He finds for us the names of the flowers we've most liked and in
each case they carry the meaning of mouths: from bocca di leone to
bocca di lupo. Senti Papa, here is the music of Orpheus. Behold
Papa, wind and gravity. A summit beneath which sits a scooped out
maw, red copper-colored scorches to one side of the crater, black to
the other. A circus ring, or funhouse anomaly in which the room
spins and you walk its curves, this cauldron. Senti. Cattedrale fres-

coes, gardenia's live scent on a stem. Sherbet—did you know it?—is derived from Arabic sharba or sciarbat, a cold drink concocted from snow flavored with essences. Dimmi. Tell me what you think of this. We stop in a town whose name means "to wander uncertainly." A guide here walks behind rather than in front of us. What kind of guide walks behind rather than before? A kind and quiet one. Senti. Lost in another town, I meant to say to passersby, "I am lost" (perdutto), but mistakenly repeat "I am found"—what kind of person states imploringly, "I am found"?! Dimmi. What do you think of this? A man who is serving us in a restaurant in this town wants to give us something: a phone number of a friend in Cefalù named Placido, the voice of an English-speaking friend on a phone, the name of the state where some relatives live: Arkansas. Home to Clinton, better than Bush. "Bush," he says, "is worse than Hiroshima."

My father will have none of this, he simply cannot. Let me try instead brief diplomatic appeals:

In Sicily, the sun doesn't shine. It burnishes. That must explain something.

Even though you hit me, of course I'll raise my arms now to help you eat. You point out that your arm shakes most the nearer it gets to your mouth.

See, father, this is where I bleed—the deep center of a rose—a bleeding devoid of pain. I don't attach to it.

(A Sicilian cookbook writer says: "Often the most unusual and rarest of food plants are available only to the very poor, who know when and where to pick them.")

It makes no sense, I know: I spent more money than you make in a month on a dress to meet an ambassador.

My father looks up. His skin is smooth and tanned. "Do you think I have lady legs?" he asks with the same tone of appeal that he'd used to ask me if I like his story. "I think my legs are lady legs."

"Yes," I say, "they're beautiful."

It's anybody's guess what you've heard, why you've said. I must cultivate an aesthetic for the hard of hearing.

Your,

Ambassador to La La Land

tethered

When I was twelve years old, I won a medal for my performance in the fifty-yard dash. Was there any feeling quite as beautiful at that age than the force of your flat chest and barely formed ribcage breaking through the ribbon, and then to be carried on the shoulders by the one father who came to see the grade-school girls' race? He beamed for all of us, not just his own daughter. You could feel his share of happiness as if his body were tethered to the end of the ribbon pulling you up, up. A year later, I sat distracted at an end-of-the-year ceremony in the junior high auditorium. Who could hear what the amorphous bodies of middle-aged teachers wanted to say to us on the last day of school? Summer was afoot. I wore wire-rimmed aviator glasses and tried to tame my long curly hair into a barrette; tucked behind my ears, my hair fell like tufted beaver tails to either side of my face. I wore a short-sleeved shirt the color of St. Joseph aspirin for children, pink jeans that needed to be rolled into cuffs thus exposing a deeper red underside atop tan-colored earth shoes. Someone nudged me in my ribcage. "They just called your name!" they said. A man on the stage signaled with his hand for me to come. And so I rose, unsuspectingly, a little panicked to climb the stairs of the stage to collect a tiny round silver medal engraved with the words "academic excellence," my name, and the year. What was one to do with the medal? I wasn't sure. Did this mean I was smart, or that other students were extremely dumb? Because I didn't feel particularly smart. I felt obedient. I did my homework. Still something about the medal had made my mother cry. This was long ago. Perhaps I was meant to pin these tiny medals to my chest to indicate ambassador to what, I am not sure, but it's a start. Receiving medals is like being knighted, a ritual meant to help you take your place in the world usually delivered by the sweaty palm of a large putty-faced man, putting you in contact with something, saying: you are not alone.

Solitude is only awkward if something or someone led you to believe it should or would be otherwise. Before my cat attempts to scale a dresser in the bedroom that is five feet high, she meows several times, as if she is giving herself a pep talk: now she's not alone, she is herself *and* her body. She shall take her body there and not the other way around. Or perhaps she is addressing the piece of furniture whose height she attempts to conquer and in this way still she is not alone: there is herself *and* the dresser. She vanquishes her object first by letting her small meow ricochet off its corners, then by propelling her body into a physics that cannot be wholly predicted. Is it her stub of a tail that leads me to imagine her fall, or the fact that if I had the choice, I wouldn't encourage her to risk such heights?

None of us is a wholly self-governing being, but if we suspend our belief in self-governance even temporarily, we risk awkwardness. Following some short-lived terror, what might become possible if we released ourselves from the illusion of self-governance? Better not to forfeit the illusion without being prepared to deposit something in its stead.

paralyzed

Of all the biblical stories and dreamtales I was given as a child— St. Lucy's eyes falling into a plate, mutilated breasts, and limbs stretched across a rack, the compelling image of Mary Magdalene's tears, of water turned to wine and loaves to fishes, of immaculate conception, crowns of thorns, sacred carpentry, and wise men, of golden calves and lamb's wool used to disguise the identity of a son's body, of a father's knife blade set against a son's throat, of burning bushes, parting waters, and swaddling babies found among the rushes who would grow to be great men, of brother turning against brother, of returning repentant children, forgiven—the story that persists, hauntingly, is that of Lot's wife. Here's a story that still exerts a force on me, I don't know why. The lesson that our teachers told got crossed with my own need to understand it otherwise. I felt it now as I felt it as a child—a story like a boulder hurtling toward you, sure to flatten your agility or release you from the pleasure of an ankle bracelet, tethered to nothing except for play, hopping, down you go, enjoying the striped elastic give of a Chinese jump rope and the pull of another girl to whom you are happily looped. Lot's wife "looked back" and ended up with something

worse than a stiff neck. God turned her into a pillar of salt. In an *paralyzed*
instant, Lot's wife, nameless woman, was stopped dead in her tracks.

I never pictured Lot's wife dead, but worse: alive but unable to
move. Lot's wife had been paralyzed. And for what? The moral of
the tale as taught me by my teachers was obscure: her faithlessness
was her punishment. Guided by god, she was supposed to forge forward into his promise, she had to trust in something grander than
her petty attachments to past luxuries. Her ability to sacrifice her
relationship to the known and believe entirely in God's will would
have saved her. As a pilgrim of God (like a good immigrant), she
must never look back. I heard the story and was horrified: the way
I understood it, Lot's wife was paralyzed because she refused to
obey her husband's command. She was like Bluebeard's successive
wives or, further back, Pandora, a woman felled by curiosity.
Unable to fathom why I might one day be required to relinquish a
life jumping rope, an important detail lodged itself in my side, pal-
pably: Lot's wife hadn't gone back. She had merely *looked* back.
What was it, I wondered, that God and her husband did not wish
her to see? And if she saw this thing, would it have compelled her
to return?

What's worse, moving awkwardly or not being able to move at
all?

Ambassadorship is about mobility—looking out into a frozen
sea, a leader finds the figure who isn't afraid to move and names
him the ambassador. He's the one who goes on the errand, who
interprets, and delivers a message. He might be sent on a special
mission, thus rendering him an extraordinary ambassador bound to
face an extraordinary solitude. An ambassador I suppose doesn't
ever expect to be humiliated even though he may find himself somewhere he shouldn't be and doesn't belong. He can't retreat into solitude: his position requires an intimate sociality with strangers.

Returning to the homeland, I struggle with the feeling that a paralyzing fate awkwardly awaits me. I feel my limbs begin to freeze and
the air no longer air, neither clay, but putty. I return to reconfirm
there had been pleasure in the familial past. I return to a treasure
trove of pleasure. I plunge my hand deep into a steamer trunk and
retrieve a silk scarf. The fear of turning to stone but moving anyway
makes me awkward.

clueless

An ambassador could be a human telegraph, a conductor of desire, a producer of new joys, even of lexicons. I once served as a kind of ambassador between worlds that I thought would share a common ground, but the gulf of misunderstanding that truly existed between them was so wide and my position of relative invulnerability so apparent that I felt like pitching myself at the end of the meeting into the chasm that *was* the gulf.

A photographer and I had arrived in Northern Italy to document the lives of new immigrants there. We stationed ourselves in a town near Milan in the apartment of the photographer's aunt, we and her two pugs and the photographer's mild-mannered gelato-eating pit bull.

Old immigrant consciousness, by our account, would meet new immigrant consciousness. Would Italy prove to be an exception to exclusivity? Having lost so many of its own people to immigration, would it receive newcomers from South and Central America, Senegal, Morocco and Tunisia, India, China, and Ukraine with open arms? We wanted to know if Italy's borders would prove to be porous or a footfall. We would be conduits who might bring new immigrants some place they did not want to go. We would recount their stories, even if to whom and why was never one hundred percent clear.

My own experience of the Northern Italian town was stranger than I had anticipated. I felt class conscious, as though my Southern features bespoke those *other* Italians. White-haired women bicycled here, stern and strong in flowered dresses. Hand-picked bouquets pointing downward from their handlebars formed a kinship with the rabbits that hung in the local butcher shop, dreaming of cloves and garlic. One sensed a polish, even aristocracy, and then a cruelty and ennui: a bored local bar owner, I note, gets his kicks by feeding a pigeon bits of bread dipped in rum then watching the pigeon reel. One park in the town is set aside specifically for dogs while another is restricted to children. The town seems perched on an edge of new and improved, a prosperous suburb dotted with fancy shops, but tradition runs deep in the town, etched into cobbles: the local

Madonna has shed tears of blood, exorcisms are performed in the *clueless*
church, and a colorful brigade accompanies the feast of Corpus
Christi. At the town's center, an extensive public market unfurls
each week dating to the year 1000. I lose my lover, Jean, there
before a booth draped with lingerie. I had only left her for a
moment, but when I turned back to where I thought she'd been, she
wasn't there; nor was the lingerie. I wandered through a density of
color and aggressive sales in search of the telltale hanging corset,
down aisles that all seemed the same aisle, around bends that all
seemed the same bend, until we finally met up again back at
Gemma's—the photographer's—apartment. Passing as a canny
researcher, I sat like a waif on the curb in front of Gemma's aunt's
place worrying about my inability to conquer the market and find
Jean. People don't sit on curbs in this town. Or, rather, no one did
but a Senegalese vendor wearing around his neck a box filled with
African trinkets, and I. Each to his own disorientation. Buying
something from the vendor—but he has nothing that I need—is one
kind of relation; interviewing him is another. I buy something and
remember how tired I grew of the Pakistani vendors in Rome. I'd
buy one bracelet but they'd insist I buy three. I can't single-handed-
ly support the immigrant population! And then I'd consider the various forms of aggression I daily bore, without complaining, issued
by the norm, the governing principle of my world.

There is a difference of course between being a tourist and living
in a town that is foreign to one. Perhaps you notice the silverware or
feel the difference between a tiny cup close inside your fingers and a
mug bolted to your arm like a protuberant heft. Why I feel more
degrees of discomfort here than I had in the previous months spent
in Russia—such a different world to me—or Rome must have to
do with not having fully agreed upon my role here: sociologist or
documentarist, recorder or critical thinker, recipient or maker,
impressionist or realist, student or teacher, follower or leader,
ambassador or artist?

I learn idiomatic expressions and record them: "ho la luna storta"
—I have a crooked moon, or my moon is crooked—is a way of saying I'm out of sorts, in a bad mood, I got up on the wrong side of the
bed. No. It really means none of these things but refers to a specifically untranslatable Italian state of mind. My research partner's

uncle described me as *corta e malecavata*. I'm told it's a way of saying you are badly born, or born under a bad star; literally, "short and badly pulled from the uterus," you are a funny and sly person, a fun and nice person who can get along. Something doesn't square. The aunt with whom we are staying exerts a cockeyed set of demands—elaborate meals are planned in advance, prepared to perfection, and served at the same time each day. (At one point, I calculate that I have eaten fifty meals with this woman.) But much of the time she serves herself a separate non-meal: at the far end of the sumptuous table, she slices for herself a peach or stirs pastina into broda. "You should eat," I say cheerily and with gratitude, "please eat." "It's not healthy to eat if you're not hungry," she sneers. She doesn't mince words. On one occasion, she tells me my hair is lifeless. When I read in bed, she thinks I am sleeping, sleeping too much of the time. It's ninety degrees in the shade and her pugs are hyperventilating. We apply a pack of frozen peas to their jowly necks, but they attempt to gnaw through the package. An error has been made when one day I help myself to sweets, little hardened meringue puffs lightly stowed in a paper bag. "Don't eat those," she says, "those are for my dogs."

Like a good American, I sometimes wish I had a rifle. I find myself fantasizing taking potshots at the computerized bell tower that wakes me rudely every day like a hammer on an anvil at five a.m. One morning it rings for a full hour at two. The townspeople assume the Pope has died but, no, it was a glitch in the belltower's digital program.

The view from Zia Angelina's apartment is a quiet clatter of red clay roofs, mountains drawing stray lines on the horizon in the distance, and once, according to her best recollection, a bright pink UFO. On the edges of town, prostitutes from Nigeria line the road. They are mostly large women who wear short, lace-rimmed underwear to accentuate the buttocks that Italian men are said to want them for, practices they cannot perform with their wives. Recently, one woman was run over, accidentally, by a cop; they buried her without having determined her name.

I learn that the word "Albanian" refers to a "bad immigrant" no matter where the person is from; the word "Moroccan" refers to coffee with chocolate or cocoa. I'm always doing double takes here—is that a burst of small pink roses or a fist, human voices or

the wind whistling through a crevice, a man's feet passing quickly as
he turns or the flight of butterflies, a cemetery or a public vista, a
windshield or a mirror, a streetlight or the moon, a woman or a pillar of salt? Constantly taking one thing for something else, I simultaneously imagine how an immigrant receives a world of newly
imbued signs. Gemma makes a grid to help me learn to recognize
the four different kinds of Italian police: the men in the green slacks
driving the green cars are on the hunt for tax evaders, read immigrant vendors. They're the Guardia di Finanza. The Carabinieri are
actually part of the army in double-striped black uniforms and
hard-edged caps. Polizia on the other hand wear dark blue, a beret
or a hard hat. The Vigili—they're merely traffic cops. "Which kind
of hats do they wear?" I inquire. "Funny ones," Gemma replies.

Strolling along a newly paved pedestrian walkway, I'm delighted
by graffiti that resembles a marijuana leaf or an eco-positive banner
announcing Greenpeace. I come to cower in some corner of my
stomach now when I walk beneath the windows that bear this
sign. It's the logo for the Lega Nord, or Northern League, an anti-
immigration group that wants the North to secede from Italy,
reclaim all territory north of the Po, and call their nation "Padania."
An official who is a sympathizer in another nearby town recently
described new immigrants as Italy's new rapists and recommended
taking prints not just of their fingers but of their feet and of their
noses before castrating them. Zia Angelina shares her opinion with
me—it's the immigrants who are responsible for the pensioners
being without money. They are always drunk and harass the bus
drivers. It's just no good.

Still, a distinguishing feature of Italy, a reputation that attracts
immigrants, is a certain breezy attitude toward rules. A rule can bend
because people are not bent beneath its weight. They get around the
rule or outright ignore it. They don't let the rule, rule. On a visit to
a doctor in the town, not only is Jean not expected to pay him for his
service, but she leaves both with a prescription and a gift, a special
book from his library on a subject that she loves. "A problem is a
word that identifies a question." This is how a woman who volunteers at a soup kitchen to feed newly arriving immigrants responds to
the phrase, "the problem of immigration." "Thinking that the problem cannot be solved is the problem." Each person working at the

clueless shelter has a different sense of how to approach "the problem":
lower the fear because violence comes from fear; learn to identify
with immigrants; create a culture of respect based on your awareness
of their history and their culture. "Theoretically we can't feed people
who don't have papers," they tell me, "but we feed them anyway and
try to help them to get papers. If the police came here, they would
take away most of the people who came here."

One basis of the townspeople's reactions, they say, is that people in their seventies remember the southern immigration, and "that
mirror of fear keeps coming back." Reflecting on immigrant sur-
vivor rates, the volunteers admit to circumstances far beyond their
control: "some people live their clandestine life better than others."

Outside of this handful of dedicated volunteers, most of the
townspeople probably don't know that political refugees from Africa
live in a church-owned dormitory at the edge of town. The name of
the shelter is Kaleidoscope, and it has a spindly, steep, part-steel,
part-concrete winding staircase ending in barely appointed chalk-
blue rooms that seem existentially dislocated from the shelter's
name, but it's a start: it's a roof over the head, a cot in a shared bedroom, a communal kitchen in which residents can, I am told, learn
to make Italian meals. On the day on which we visit, a TV set in the
lounge is tuned to a made-for-TV drama whose white female protagonist commits suicide. A black woman at the Center is its designated cleaner; it's an industrialized task that no one person could
possibly carry out.

We chat with Kaleidoscope's director. An affable, overworked,
and patient man, he enlightens us on matters relative to immigration
policy, and by way of leavetaking, after describing our project to
him, we suggest that perhaps he could let the men currently residing
in the dorm know we are in town. If any of the men wants to talk
to us, they can tell the director, and he can contact us. "No," the
director says, enthusiastically, "I would like instead to invite you to
tell the men about your project yourself. On Tuesday nights, we
have group meetings to discuss issues the men are dealing with. We
can open this week's session with your presentation, then they will
eat cake, then they have private time together during which you will
have to leave. How does that sound?"

It didn't sound great to me, and I wasn't even sure if I understood correctly everything the director had said, even in translation, but then I remembered how *good* I was at this kind of thing—stirring up an audience, finding an unexpected language for what might seem like a predictable project, enunciating what moved us, deeply, personally, to pursue our goal, indeed, to meet these men. I was preparing to talk to the men, to deliver my ambassadorial message, not, I later realized, to lead a group discussion.

Several of the men had been victims of torture. All had outrun the long reach of the arm of a law and arrived at a point so far north that the earth to them felt perpetually hard, even in the summer. I'm sitting dressed in my sleek and sleeveless dark blue linen dress; my legs are bare. I'm telling the group that my grandparents were from Italy, and I am a third-generation immigrant interested in generational trauma. The photographer addresses the group as the "new Italy." We talk about wanting to open channels of communication between new immigrants to Italy and immigrants to the United States. I talk about wanting to compose in the most authentic poetry I can what it means to be a sojourner between cultures at the turn of the twenty-first century.

Dressed in cast-off T-shirts, shorts, and flip-flops, the group of twelve regards us forebodingly. Their postures are slack, not "up" for an evening meeting. One man sits apart from them, beside me, draped in African garb. It's about ninety degrees in the room and the mosquitoes are biting. A disaffected feeling pervades the room, while I consider what, if anything, I know about the lives these men have left, of the state they are in now, of what I am to them, of what we are doing here, of why we are here in their house. Other men trickle in, some more reluctant to sit closer to the group; one sits in the windowsill more out of the room than in.

Why do I think of the man to my left as being dressed in "African garb"? Why do my legs feel sheer and up for grabs? It's a feeling, I admit it, of phallic woundedness that scares me, this brotherhood of pain. We've been making our presentation, following our director's advice, in English and Italian. They've been letting us make it. I'm smiling, I'm serious, I'm beaming, I'm stern. I've been careful in my address and direct; the photographer, I have to assume, has been painstaking in her translation and deliberate. We're finished, are there any questions? One man raises his hand and very adamantly clueless explains that some people speak English, some Italian, but mostly French. Angrily, he reports that most people haven't understood a word that was said. "How many have not understood?" the director asks, and almost every man raises his hand. And then a riot of fear unfolds.

"What do you want from us?" one man, exhausted, pleads. "Because my life in Africa is one thing, and my life here is another. So you must tell us what you want!" Is it possible that something was ill-formed or not fully thought through in our motives? It's as if he sees us seeing him as an iconic ferryboat man, as if his purpose is to take us across waters, bridge to a world elsewhere, across waters of forgetfulness or of coerced recollection.

Another man speaks haltingly in Italian. He falters as he explains that it is very painful for him to tell his story. That each time he tells it, he re-experiences trauma. And that it was very hard for him for example when he had to write it in order to begin the process of possibly gaining political asylum here. He is looking at the director as he says this, as if to implore him not to let these interested-in-immigrant ladies require him to speak again.

"We don't want anything in particular," I try to explain in an impossible combination of English, French, Italian. "We want whatever you want to tell us. We simply came this evening to tell you that we exist and we're interested in the fact that you exist."

But nothing can be done to diminish the power of a perceived interrogation. It's happening again: what took a man to the border of his being, that instrument of torture, what took him again to the border between countries, what enabled him to pass, has arrived just now to document him.

"You must understand," a man starts up, "that it could take days before we decide to talk to you!" And another just as quickly demands, "What government do you two represent? Do you represent the Italian or the United States government?" I thought we had presented ourselves as a "type" of fellow immigrant, but we were being perceived as ambassadors; I thought we were posing as *informal* ambassadors, but I learned there is no such thing. We may as well have been torturers, border patrol agents, police.

This isn't what we intend, this isn't what we are here for. The streaks of sweat try to speak for me, seeping through and staining my dress. Here my Sicilian grandmother would diplomatically, exasperatedly blurt "cheese and crackers" in place of "shit!" She said it often, leaving me to picture a stack of crackers and block of cheddar cheese mutely arranged on a plate.

What the asylum seekers have understood is that their speaking to us is compulsory. What they've understood is that they *must* speak to us *now*.

Here my father might suggest a game of "footsy": you each lay on your back facing each other at either far end of the living room couch. You bring the soles of your feet to meet the soles of the other person's feet, then push, like pedaling a bicycle built for two.

"A large university has given us money to pursue this project," Gemma relates matter-of-factly and sincere. "For the purpose of education," I conclude her thought.

I'm sitting now in a kind of isolation booth of awkwardness, and there is absolutely nothing here to finger, speaking to the air through a kind of lunacy, saying each word separately as I remember it from French 101. "Je. Comprend. Le français. Un peu." Someone is yelling in the background, "Our photos must not be taken, our names must not appear in print."

My impulse is to bolt, but the man to my right, the man whose name I have missed in the "African garb," offers me some water. He pours the water into the enormous pink and blue ceramic mugs that make up the center's dinnerware—the cast-off donations of a local volunteer, the cups literally have faces. The cup that I drink from has a large-nosed and pallid face carved into it. The nose and droopy eyes ooze convexly out from the cup's edges, hungover and grotesque.

I thank my companion and struggle to lift what feels like a ten-pound glass of water to my lips.

"Say what you have to say quickly, in one minute, and let us think about it," the originally adamant man suggests. Surely we would do this if we could, but wasn't saying what we had to say and being understood precisely the impossibility that we struggled with?

Really, we expect nothing from them, we explain. But if they want to share anything, we're here and we'd be happy to hear their story. Anonymity, we stress, will be maintained, mistrust is understandable, we only came this evening to let you know that we are here!

The director seems satisfied that something has been communicated so he brings out our contribution to the meeting: the cake that Gemma promised, a gooey tort, made gooier by ninety-degree temperatures. They don't appear to have plates and are low on utensils, so the man in African dress begins to cut the cake and to pick up each slish-sloshing piece with the knife. I try to help him, and I urge him to use his hands. We "pour" pieces of the cake onto napkins and pass them around to the men in the group. I offer a piece to him, but he says "none for me." I also decline the treat.

I'm sweating, I'm putrefied in my dress; its linen, now bleached by my sweat, stiffens. When we're satisfied that the cake has been duly sliced and shared, we say *"buona sera," "molto grazie,"* and make a quick but dazed exit. I shake the hand of the man in African garb. We make eye contact and say goodnight, "until we meet again." The statement comforts me. We trip home as though dodging a gulf, something raw and brash and open. I think that the evening was pretty much a disaster at the level of miscommunication, and I want to blame the Director, our designated go-between, a distinct minority of one available to help these men.

Before arriving at the Kaleidoscope meeting, we'd eaten a dinner of lemon-and-egg risotto, clams, blue fish, and white wine, zucchini, and beans made by Zia Angelina, Zia Angelina's light and fluffy pound cake dusted with confectioner's sugar. It was an amazing meal. Gemma too had outdone herself, I said. And the wine—I loved the way the white wine complemented the fish. We ate the cake that Zia made. We took a brief nap before walking over to the center for the presentation.

When we returned to the apartment, *Begin the Beguine* was playing on the TV. We returned to find messages from the person who was house-sitting for me back home. There were a variety of problems she needed advice on: neighbors were complaining of what they described as a gargantuan weed that had appeared in front of the house and that they feared would overtake the neighborhood. She thinks it's beautiful—she doesn't consider it a weed—should she remove it or not? A bat had appeared in the bedroom, a bird had built a nest inside the air conditioner. On the outskirts of Milan, problems of such magnitude call for a midnight snack of cherries soaked in grappa, sweet oblivion.

Gemma isn't convinced that so much went so wrong tonight except that we terrified the men in the dorm. She'd like to show her gratitude to the director for hosting us. She knows a hardware store in town where we could purchase a fan to donate to the center. "Fine. We can do that tomorrow, first thing." It seems a suitably diplomatic gesture.

But my dress I can see is beyond repair. This is nothing a pressing and cleaning can fix. My dress, doused in the brine of my fear, disintegrates, the blue dye sputtering to white. This is the situation, this is the real: not the self but your dress turns to salt if you dare, leaving you humiliated, leaving you with nothing to wear, a condition that can be lived with, that one can move out from. Which isn't to say that I learned anything or was redeemed or that an irreversible awkwardness could be reversed or undone.

Geologists surmise that Sodom was used as a crossing point to ship salt to the Mediterranean and Egypt. Saturated soil and highly flammable bitumen may have been behind the destruction of the cities, and the Dead Sea's salt floes may have thrown up a figure resembling a female form, thus inspiring the Biblical tale.

We were only lucky that the harm we had done that night was minor. Human forces are harder to resolve than those of nature.

When I left Milan that summer, I was keen to thank Zia for all of those meals. But she paused before my hug and, looking at me, not earnestly but with her eyelids slightly drooping and her lips drawn down as well, she said something that took me off guard. "I know, I'm not a very nice person," she said. "I'm a difficult person. But it was nice to have you here, it was nice to have company in my house."

My impulse was tactfully to disagree with Zia, but I refrained; moved by her honesty, I only thanked her again, leaving out two important if perfunctory words, "*ci vediamo*"—until we meet again.

BARING

unnatural

I had a favorite awkward film, one that tutored me in the beauty of awkwardness over and against all that we took to be natural. It was a product of the New German Cinema, Rainer Werner Fassbinder's Sirk-inspired *Angst essen Seele auf*. The young Fassbinder, it is well-known, was deeply affected by an encounter with the émigré director Douglas Sirk, who fled 1930s Germany with his Jewish wife to the United States, where he arrived with no English, and later achieved success as a director of Hollywood melodramas. Sirk's signature effect was a combination of riotous color and severe control; the use of mirrors, windows, and reflective surfaces to dramatize psychic violence; deeply divided characters; and what he called "imitated lives." In the 1970s, after seeing Sirk's films and meeting the man himself, Fassbinder began to make his own brand of, some would say, dark melodramas in rapturous dialogue with the formal idiosyncrasies and psychosocial ambivalences of Sirk's aesthetic. *Angst essen Seele auf* is a newly situated version of Sirk's 1956 melodrama *All That Heaven Allows*. Like its predecessor, the film relies on thwarted energies, the awkward-because-untenable relationship between an older woman and a younger man, and on class and race as elements that muck up the machinery of love and desire.

"You can't make films about something," Fassbinder quoted Sirk, "you can only make films with something, with people, with light, with flowers, with mirrors, with blood, with all these crazy things that make it worthwhile." In 1973, Fassbinder made a film with the body of a black immigrant (Ali), the body of a white cleaning woman (Emi), with mirrors and windows and staircases, and with numerous starkly literal thresholds. "*Angst essen Seele auf*" is the Moroccan immigrant Ali's translation of an Arabic saying into ungrammatical German, "*Fear Eat Soul.*" For some reason, the film's title in English was changed to the more grammatical but also more *unnatural* awkward *Ali: Fear Eats the Soul.*

The film that issues from the culturally produced fear that eats not just the soul but more fatally Ali's stomach (by film's end he is languishing in a hospital with a bleeding ulcer like so many guest workers in Germany), *Angst essen Selle auf* is a ninety-three-minute meditation on awkwardness at its most attenuated and a film bound to produce awkwardness in its viewers.

At the center of Fassbinder's film is the cry of desire when Emi screams "Ahh-li," with emphasis on the first syllable of his name, her cry of joy of love for him, of her expectancy and his presence. "I'm in love with a Moroccan who is twenty years younger than me," Emi boldly announces to her daughter and racist son-in-law (played by Fassbinder himself) after interrupting a scene of brutal discontent between the two. (The couple seems mutually to despise one another.) While Emi and Ali dance in the Arab bar that set the scene for their first encounter, naysayers, both German and Arab, abound. Stony-faced Stepford wife bystanders to their union remark: "It's bound to go wrong," "it's unnatural, plain unnatural," "of course it won't work, how can it?"

Emi enters the Arab pub at the opening of the film because it is raining outside and, as she explains to the stern and hypersensualized blonde bar owner, she thought to herself, "Emi, better get inside that pub." Her arrival isn't entirely accidental, however, as she admits to a curiosity stirred by hearing foreign music each time she passes the pub on her way home from work. Her entry isn't accidental, but borne of a need for company. She sits awkwardly not removing her coat, she awkwardly holds her handbag in front of her with both hands. The handbag hangs below her belly like a shield to her sex. And it's awkward to hold a purse this way because it makes the purse hypervisible, or as though it announces that she expects the purse to be stolen. It's awkward because the misplacement of the purse suggests that its bearer is afraid. She had followed an impulse into the pub; what's startling is that, seeing what kind of pub it is, she doesn't turn around, or that, in a culture that is shown to hate Arabs, she felt drawn to the pub in the first place.

An Arab woman whose advances Ali shuns (he tells her that "his cock is broken"), dares him to ask Emi to dance, and he does.

unnatural   Rather than ask Emi face to face, he walks behind her, awkwardly bypassing a social convention. On the dance floor, the two of them dance in three quarter time to a piece of music scored in quarter time. The camera lights up Emi's pinky, pointing upward from Ali's shoulder as if they were a royal couple at a ball. Ali says frank and baldly revelatory, intimate things to Emi: "Germans with Arabs not good . . . Germans not same people with Arab . . . German master. Arab dog . . . Not think much: good; think much, cry much."

Awkwardness happens in a battle between what's automatic and what's willed. Something occurs on the dance floor, a conversation has ensued, but Emi and Ali walk back to the table side by side, staring straight ahead as though they are strangers on a subway platform bent, not driven, toward a destination. They are awkward in their bodies as automatons. Do Emi and Ali appear awkward because they are refusing to follow social codes for walking off of dance floors, or is awkwardness immanent because there *is* no rule or language for this, for their relation, this moment, their encounter? Or, then again, is awkwardness a sign of their adherence to the rule *not* to notice one another, confirmation of the fact that German and Arab live in different worlds?

What makes Ali figure as awkward—and his generalized awkwardness permeates the film—is the combination of a robust and ripplingly muscular body and a perfectly expressionless face. He moves through German streets with the sturdy handsomeness of a Rock Hudson, but whereas Hudson's character in Sirk's film "has nature," as Fassbinder might say, Ali has neither a correlative setting nor an oppressive symbol to attach to. Sometimes his awkwardness signals restraint, as though he moves in his body even as his body is held continuously in check. He appears in the hallways of Emi's apartment building as though he's been dropped into the scene by an invisible puppeteer. On their first night in her apartment together, Emi gives him a pair of her dead husband's pajamas to wear, awkward for the way they invoke the former inhabitant of Emi's bed but also for the way in which they instantly domesticate Ali. The domestication isn't totalized in this moment, however; their lovemaking leads each of them rather to inspect themselves in the mirror as if encountering themselves as themselves, loved, for the first time.

The physical expressions that this love can take in public are of *unnatural* course minimal, or at least they mustn't be overt. When Emi and Ali leave for their respective workplaces on the morning after their first night together in Emi's flat, they stand in front of the door to the street facing each other awkwardly as statues. Emi takes the subway, Ali takes the tram. They shake hands, then they part in opposite directions, proceed to take twelve steps or so, then turn to look back to each other as if on an abstractly Beckettian cue. Emi lifts her hand to wave, but just barely, and just barely smiles, restraining her ecstasy, suppressing her joy. Ali turns and looks as though following instructions to carry out a duel. He makes a small dash with his hand, as though to rub out a message penned on an invisible surface. Just after the two wave, the camera moves upward from the pavement on which they stand and scales the apartment building to reveal the inquiring, hateful face of one of Emi's fellow tenants. The scene is of course rendered extremely poignant by restraint, by the tension between the compulsory and the desired and desiring beings, Emi and Ali.

My students in an American university laugh at this scene, especially at what appears as an inappropriate gesture between two people who have just made love—the perfunctory handshake. Do my students find the characters, the way they are positioned, shot, and directed, awkward because ugly (*brutto*), unlike glistening post-coital Hollywood lovers; displeasing (*spiacevole*), because their gestures fail to complete an expectation about love; inconveniencing (*incomodo*), because they can't place Emi and Ali into the slot of a formfitting narrative convention for feeling; or clumsy (*goffo*), because oafish, unknowing, not as knowing as they are? I always receive this scene with a glint of a tear, which doesn't make me more sensitive than or morally superior to my students but shows Fassbinder to be manipulating awkwardness in such a way to produce contending forms of affect, even in a single viewer, and through that, the possibility for thinking about our own relation to self-alienation and disunion, while at the same time provoking a commentary on film form itself.

What *should* Emi and Ali do at the point of saying good-bye? What would better satisfy our sense of the naturalness of lovers? Should there be mewing and tonguing at the threshold into the world as their oyster? Should Ali kick the dirt and finger the brim of his hat, absentmindedly stroke the mane of his horse, say gosh and shucks a lot? It should start to rain. Emi could break open a parasol and sing a bar or two about a fella and an umbrella while waltzing down the avenue. The particles of dirt she's paid to mop could become personified before her, each dust mote a smiling star to wish upon, to stow away a little sparkling memory of Ali. And Ali could swim to work, stomping in puddles all the way, flirting with police officers, singin' in the rain.

Ali and Emi under Fassbinder's direction don't do any of the outrageous things that characterize Hollywood excess, nor do they perform any of the gestures—pat and glistening, certain and slick—that would naturalize them by Hollywood standards. Consequently they appear more awkward, which is to say, more real, and it is the reality of their bodies and the reality of the situation of their love that is not sappily tragic but heartbreaking in this scene.

"Human beings can't be alone but they can't be together either." That's Fassbinder on the human condition after watching some films by Douglas Sirk. In his own film, Emi and Ali's bodies on the dance floor, like magnets simultaneously drawn and repelled, seem to emblematize that sentence. It's awkward, the way that Emi and Ali hug each other and try to dance at the same time: stillness and movement collapse, differentiation and merger cohabit, time is out of joint with desire, and so in a later dance scene very near the end of the film, a juxtaposition of oxymoronic utterances makes an awkwardly culminating sense. Ali and Emi's love, at one time pure and perfect, has begun to erode under the influence of the corrosive invective continuously directed their way. Ali has been staying out all night, gambling, drinking, sleeping with other women until, through Emi's force of will, they reunite on the dance floor of the Arab bar where they met. "I don't want to, but always so nervous," Ali confesses to Emi the cause of his infidelities. "I know how old I am," she says, "I see myself in the mirror; but when we're together, we need to be nice to each other, otherwise life isn't worth living." "I love only you," Ali contends, and Emi replies, "I love you too." They continue to hug-dance, huddled almost, taking the shortest steps when Emi says assuringly, "together we're strong," almost immediately after which Ali drops to the floor, clutching his stomach and

screaming, not words, but deep guttural groans. "A man has collapsed," the bar owner explains matter-of-factly into a telephone
receiver.

Ali's collapse isn't in itself awkward. Its placement, though, as
an outrageous reply to Emi's affirmation of the strength of their sol-
idarity might signify a collapse of awkwardness, the failure of awkwardness and triumph of the culture, its effacement of the series of
beautiful, perverse, telling, alive, strained, and revenant awkwardnesses that this film puts into play.

irreal

Melodrama usually flattens affect and calls that entertainment,
but Fassbinder uses melodramatic form to get at something real. He
puts scare quotes around immigrant naturalization and citizen naturalness. To adapt and assimilate is to have naturalness *conferred*
upon one. No one in the film moves naturally, except maybe the
character played by Fassbinder himself, the swinish son-in-law who
seems to have settled quite comfortably into his bitterness, into his
smirk.

This lack of naturalness in favor of the production of a real is
of course a major effect of the stylizing that Fassbinder so admired
in Sirk's films. Of *All That Heaven Allows,* Fassbinder reminds us,
"the moviegoer's intense emotion doesn't come from identification
but from the montage and the music. That's why you leave these
films feeling somewhat dissatisfied." And, "The light in Douglas Sirk's
films is always as unnaturalistic as possible. Shadows where there
shouldn't be any help to render plausible emotions that you would
prefer to keep at arm's length." Just so, a moviegoer cannot expect
to be entertained by Fassbinder's film; nor can the moviegoer expect
to identify with its characters. We can only feel uncomfortable
because of their awkwardness.

Consider all that is *not* revealed when in Hollywood films the
body is presented as though its owner has a perfectly seamless and
natural relation to it. It's laughable, the labor required to make
filmic subjects appear natural. *We're* laughable, we audience members who sigh and coo, hypnotized by the fit. Fassbinder is a film-

maker who chooses instead, by foregrounding artifice, to enable something untoward to poke through. He works painstakingly to achieve awkwardness in this film, to achieve, through film form, tellingly awkward and therefore utterly illuminating arrangements as well as uncommon questions. *What would it look like,* I imagine him asking, *if we really inhabited our bodies to figure the relations we are having with each other?*

The camera is placed in an unnatural position, at unusual angles to picture as it does all four cleaning women in one shot situated on different parts of a curving staircase and landing. The door that opens out onto the landing stands glaringly in the foreground of the scene, and a crooked banister steals the show as it winds like an architectural vine around vertical copper-colored pipes and white painted columns. The camera bespeaks such relays of inside and outside—complete with woman at staircase casement, working woman on stair, woman sipping soda seated beside rung—that I'd swear Fassbinder had studied Vermeer. Emi and her fellow workers are breaking for lunch. Each is responsible for cleaning a different floor of this large building, and they meet for lunch, it appears, in the stairwell. Sitting across a table would make conversation less awkward, wouldn't it? One woman stands at the casement on the landing; Emi sits on a step several feet above her on the stair; another woman sits behind Emi on the stair; and still another stands below the landing at another far remove from Emi. They eat, sip soda, and talk. It would be hard for the women to face each other when they talk given this arrangement, but Fassbinder, having arranged the women this way, doesn't stop there in putting into motion a commentary on bodies, the illusions that accrue to them, and awkwardness.

Fassbinder shoots the conversation in such a way as to unsettle us. Emi speaks, but she's not looking at an interlocutor. Emi speaks and the camera shoots her facing the camera with the face of the woman behind her also facing the camera and just over her left shoulder. Rather than rely on shot/reverse shot conventions that naturalize conversation and the bodily positions or exchanges of gazes that are supposed to happen in conversation, Fassbinder shoots Emi as though she is talking into a void or reading an invisible (to us) script with her interlocutor awkwardly perched behind her.

When awkwardness speaks, the body assumes a real position.

Fassbinder tries to *picture* this uncanny reality. The filmmaker *irreal* makes physical, literal, and visual what is hidden by a convention of mutual looks.

We talk.

You look at me; I look at you.

We face each other.

Fassbinder's filmwork says we only *appear* to be facing each other, but we're not. If we were one of the cleaning women in Emi's world, we would stand behind each other when we talked. This positioning of our bodies would be *truer* to the relation between us since we spend a great deal of time talking behind each other's backs. The reason that Emi faces into a void rather than face her interlocutor is that she is involved in a particular kind of interview with a particular kind of authority.

Why do any of us say the things we do when we say them? Do thoughts simply occur to us to meet a situation, or have we all internalized an absent interlocutor with whom we speak even as we pretend to look into the eyes of another? Emi is confessing in this scene. She wants a reading (or maybe a whipping) from her co-workers on the subject of German women taking up with guest workers. So she tells them an immigrant man was flirting with her in the subway. The response that issues from her co-workers' mouths, with numerous variations on the theme, is that immigrant men are sex-starved pigs, and the German women who take up with them filthy whores.

Emi faces forward as she tries placing into this space a series of defenses of immigrants: perhaps they live together, she explains, because they cannot find a decent place; they're not bothersome, they do their work. Voices come at her from all directions. "No, no, no, no, Emi, you don't understand," the voices counter, and one begins to tell the story of her neighbor who must be about fifty years old and who has "got herself a young Turk," the result of which is that no one speaks to her, which "serves her right." "Maybe *he* talks with her, and she doesn't need anyone else," Emi says, reaching now for one last rope to hold her position aloft. The woman at the casement, her face sharp as a pointer, has the last word on the subject: "*No one,*" she speaks the words like a knife cutting the air, "can live without others, no one, Emi." "What can you talk about with someone like that?" the woman behind Emi adds, "Most of them don't speak a word of German!"

The scene closes with each figure scuttling back to her respective hallway, while Emi approaches and stands before the inner window, staring, her face crushed, as if to say, so this is how it is, and, what am I to do? That penultimate statement, delivered like a verdict, "No one can live without others," where others is suspended in quotation marks, forces a chilling reckoning with the alienation it predicts. But will it be the alienation of living with Ali, or the alienation of giving him up and agreeing with the women on the stairs? No one can live, the sentence could be translated, without the culture's however unsteady and ridiculous, wobbly and unreliable, stinking and petrifying but ever present scaffolding. You need to be hooked up and into the ideological network and to accept the loneliness that is its by-product. You have to stand here with us, Emi, slip-sliding in the muck of the culture, like the "swine" we identify in every other citizen, and feel good about it. No one can afford such awkwardness as Emi dares to live.

hands and eyes

The baby holds his feet in his hands until his body is a boat, brings a toe to his mouth, rocking. He points and then pokes at his face feeling the depth of his cheeks, like a plant reaching down into the soil in which it grows. He puts his fingers into his mouth. He doesn't lift things, he pats them; objects dangle from his hands, dropped by his side while he runs. He is all palm or all fingers, not yet arms, not yet kept or keeping at arm's length. He squeezes and pinches. When he cries, he runs forward with his hands raised, palms facing, hoping to find his mother in the space between. Where are his eyes in all of this? Are his eyes his hands and vice versa? A child walks toward a beloved object or person, staring, his eyes like saucers that, if they could, would touch the thing before him, but since they cannot, he learns to lift his arm to hold and have and grab and touch.

What's the point of a doctor holding a finger at her own nose and bringing it toward your nose while she watches your eyes cross? She looks into the ear of the other with her eyes. She turns off the lights and looks through an instrument into the eye. She tells me to follow her finger with my eyes but I can't do it without turning my *hands and* head, which makes her laugh. I'm always failing these tests. She *eyes* straps a band around the arm to find a pulse. Why can't the pulse be felt or found by looking in the eyes? The pulse is in the wrist. The eye is lazy, but it tells the hand what to do.

Fear Eats the Soul is all about hands and eyes. So many misplaced hands. So many stony looks. And the awkwardness of being seen, close, far, stilled, naked. The actors in this drama are rigidly fixed into the positions of seer and seen, but who is on the inside and who is on the outside is never really clear. One can never really know if one is in or out, and suddenly one's position might switch.

The most common use of the eyes here is the stare: people stare and cross their arms, they stare and prop themselves with their hands at a bar, stare and hold fast to the button on a lover's shirt, stare and let their hands droop, stare all head and no hands, they stare like window-dressing mannequins, one hand clutching a purse, hips atilt, they stare standing at the ready waiting for the command to charge, or to lift a weapon to batter or pierce. Their eerie detachment, stone cold, is unnerving as Emi and Ali appear, beautifully fluent but isolated, the only ones sitting at a bright yellow table among a vastness of such tables at an outdoor restaurant. A patch of people stands, immobile, at the door of the restaurant, wholly still, staring in their direction. Emi and Ali hold each other's hands till Ali turns to look at the starers. "Everyone is looking," he says. Emi explains envy to him and breaks down crying, happy on the one hand and not able to bear the hatred anymore on the other. "Nobody looks me in the eye anymore . . . Stop staring, you stupid swine! This is my husband, my husband," she moans (in German it sounds more poignantly like "my man, my man") and Ali strokes her head with his hand, "I love you, I love you," he quietly repeats. She answers, "I love you too."

Fassbinder's repertoire of looks and gazes in this film incorporates whoever views it into an off-putting and feeling-full space. Seemingly awkward shots disarm us, even as they call to us to draw closer, discomfited but moved. There are long shots in which we might be viewing the characters through the end of a telescope, shots reflected in mirrors, shots that frame figures in doorways, or in existential solitude: at the center of a tableau of loud, monochromatic color, Ali sits silently at the end of an expanse of bed, before the drab and drag of heavy curtains, he stares at the floor. These long shots are disarming in part because they are long both in space and time: Fassbinder holds the camera before such scenes for longer stretches than conventional cinema allows, until the space compels a viewer to want to meet the character in the beyond, to move toward him, to cross the threshold. The character is vulnerable and we are vulnerable in such moments; voyeurism gives way temporarily to identification.

When characters are kept before the camera with very little movement, this dynamic becomes most palpable: at one and the same time, people made into spectacles, absolutely; people made insistently present, alive, loveable. Fassbinder's execution of long shots creates an intimacy and softness even though the film is dark because sparse, even "seedy." Sometimes these long silent shots are laced with melancholia, making us uncomfortably aware of an unnamable absence, loss, or lack in which we feel implicated, because we don't pity Ali and Emi—they are too dignified for that, and like ourselves, fragile. (Unless, perhaps, we reside on the other side of awkwardness among the self-assured. And who are they? The most abominable current leaders of the world.)

A better title in English for this film might be "The Handshake." Or "Hands and Eyes." After Ali's first dance with Emi, he places his hands awkwardly before him on the table, head trained forward, as though waiting to be handcuffed. Expecting to be found out or, shackled, taken away. He often sits this way. After their first night together, Emi awakes partly horrified by the evidence of Ali's gorgeous body next to her in bed. She rushes to the mirror and feels her face with both her hands as if to ask, "is it still me, or someone else in this face, this body, this apartment?" She's unnerved, until he appears at the bathroom door, facing her, he says joyfully, "good morning!", and Emi gasps to embrace Ali and the impossible possibility of his presence. "I'm so happy and so afraid," she tells him, looking window-ward. "Fear isn't good. Fear eats the soul," Ali replies. She enjoys the phrase as a bit of foreign folklore, "an Arab saying," but Ali explains worldwearily, understatedly, "All Arabs speak this way."

This scene, of joy and fear, and fear of joy, this scene in which Emi finds her face with her hands while looking into a mirror works alongside an oddly companionate scene that occurs near the end of the film and that is almost impossible to watch: a scene in the men's room at the Arab bar in which Ali approaches a mirror and watches himself as he raises one hand, and then the other, to slap himself in the face again and again and again.

Handcuffs and cufflinks. Handkerchiefs and haberdasheries. Hands. What do you have in your hand? They ask this during a card game. He had a bad hand. Hands off the merchandise! Hands up! A magician performs sleight of hand. His hand fools our eyes. Hands-on was direct, unmediated, lived. "Give us a hand," could mean help us along or clap your hands for us. "I only have two hands!" a cry of exasperation when the world is asking too much of you. Hands and the various extensions outward from mere physiology. Can you handle it? Where the ability to use your hands is equated with coping, with a capacity for reception, with the ability to withstand some difficulty. "On the other hand," there always being at least two, to represent balance or opposition, choice and option, not one hand but two, hopefully a helping hand, or a hand-me-down. Head's up! Hands down! You're the winner, meaning there's no competition. If you're the type who can handle the situation, you probably didn't need a handler because you never get out of hand. Awkwardness and out-of-handedness went hand in hand. Handy and useful. Handsome and bright. "Drop the weapon and put your hands over your head," announced through a bullhorn. Handguns, and heavy-handedness, to be left holding the bag, or to discover that the left hand doesn't know what the right hand is doing. Not wanting any handouts. The hands of aunts who worked hard, how I loved their coarse and calloused fingers. The delicate hands of my mother. Whether a pair of hands suits a body or not. The fingerprint as one of a kind, a singular map for distinguishing identities. Living from hand to mouth was never good. Being head over heels was better, if untenable.

The scene in which Ali slaps himself in the face makes awkwardness seem benign and clownish and fanciful by comparison. Awkwardness inheres in the scene, yes, because the hands are not supposed to be used against the self, because the act presumes an objectification of the self by the self that is disquieting. And, yet, hands perform operations on the rest of the body all the time, from applying makeup, to putting on clothes, from feeding oneself to pleasuring oneself, from putting fingers down a throat to putting a finger up an asshole. We all scratch at and pick and prune our own bodies with our hands, whether motivated by primal urges, the need for self-comfort, by inherited standards of proper hygiene, or by unconscious drives in the form of neuroses. We all indulge, in some way or other, to some degree or other, a masochistic relationship with our bodies, via the hands or not, but such relations usually remain hidden: they are either taboo or, if culturally sanctioned, their harmfulness is denied.

The situation of Ali's self-beating is this: he is sitting in the Arab bar drinking and pissing away his wages in a card game. "Don't let them fleece you! You're gambling away a week's wages!", the German bar-owner and sometime lover of Ali scolds him. "Kif Kif!", he yells back at her, "Who cares!" He is wearing the gray suit that he married Emi in. He has been wearing it more often as if to make himself feel glad or to make himself appear less "dark." (When they first meet, Emi recommends that he'd look better, lighter, less morose in lighter colors.) He uses the urinal, then matter-of-factly approaches the mirror. He hits himself hard, then harder, fast then slowly. Because his hand seems detached from himself, because the scene makes us feel that this is not Ali's hand but the hand of some other whom he has incorporated into himself, the act seems awkward. But it reaches beyond the awkward and into the realm of the shocking. It's as though his body and his person have now slipped through an opening outside the realm of radical tension, beyond the productive tension of awkwardness. It's as though Ali has become unwound and with each slap he is trying to wind himself back up. His face looks so sweet—rather than steely and angry—it is as though he has reverted to the state of a child who is being beaten. A radical slip has occurred. And, so, one cannot help seeing, in an almost magic realist but unsentimental way, the former faces of Ali: the tender, open face that listens to Emi; the unprepossessing but frightened face apprehended through tiers and layers of distances and grates by a woman in Emi's building who seems like a concierge or building inspector; the confused face in the market where a German shop owner pretends not to understand what Ali wants; the eyes in the face cast downward when Ali pretends temporarily not to know Emi as she seeks him out at the garage where he works. His face, in other words, "reappears" in part because the slapping seems to vanquish it, and in part because the slapping seems to try to force a face into being. In a strange reversal, the slaps also seem to be a self-imposed measure to *prevent* Ali from crying. With each slap, he doesn't cry but chokes and swallows a whimper, his deep bass voice reduced to the near squeak of a withheld sob.

Not too long ago, director Shahbaz Noshir premiered his film, *Angst isst Seele auf,* a grammatically correct version of Fassbinder's title. In Noshir's short, based on a "real incident," a black actor on his way to a Berlin theater where he is scheduled to perform as Ali in a stage-play version of the film is attacked by neo-Nazis. The entire film is shot from the point of view of the black German actor in such a way that we never see his face but only his hands. Leaving us to wonder what act or effort of will or art or awkwardness could reattach the hands to the face to the voice to the body.

perverse

Awkwardness happens when something usually kept out is let in.

Sometimes awkwardness is repressive, or a sign of repression at work, and sometimes it is expressive, but it is always productive, it never fails to signify because something metamorphic or relational is always at work in its name. Roiling beneath the awkwardness of Fassbinder's film is the love that dare not speak its name. Fassbinder invites race into Sirk's class-divided melodrama, and Todd Haynes, in his stunningly beautiful and formally consummate homage to *both* Fassbinder and Sirk, *Far from Heaven,* brings the open secret of homosexuality (consider Sirk's Hudson and Fassbinder himself) into view even as he shows interracial desire to be the more awkwardly threatening relation. "Queerness" is more politically immanent in Haynes' *style* than in his content in this sense: like Fassbinder, he appropriates a form in which affect is conventionally flattened in order to make feeling happen in it. He treats Sirkian camp not as a bland 1950s signifier but as a place where alternative modes of feeling are possible.

Fassbinder never thought of his films as self-contained but, like Sirk, expected his audience to have imaginations. Beyond Sirk, he hoped that some "real" belonging to the audience would burst through the screen, or that a viewer would be driven to contemplate a real in light of his films, just as he pierced and punctured his own tableau with the real of self-mutilation and stomach ulcers. Such crossings make for unsettling awkwardnesses in art and in life. There were, however, numerous real vectors of living and loving and hating that happened among and between the people who made the film but that never made it into the film. Unbearable details threaten to perforate the surface.

Fassbinder and the actor El Hedi ben Salem were lovers, and unbeknownst to ben Salem, this film was meant as Fassbinder's parting gift to him since he intended to break up with him after shooting the film. Fassbinder died of a drug overdose at the age of 37. Ben Salem killed himself in a French prison. He was transported there after running through the streets of Berlin wielding a knife in search of Fassbinder. Allegedly he stabbed, but not fatally, two strangers. News of ben Salem's suicide was kept from Fassbinder for years. Fassbinder's own death came not long after receiving the news. His then lover, Juliane Lorenz, found Fassbinder: destroyed by a combination of cocaine and sleeping pills, he was sitting before a television set that was still turned on.

Should we use such grim and gossipy details to dismiss the power of _Ali_? It might be tempting to conclude that Fassbinder's art couldn't work as an antidote to life. Or to recast an understanding of the brilliance of ben Salem's performance as the cruel voyeurism of Fassbinder. What would it mean to have your lover appear full frontally nude on film or to stage him playing the black immigrant (who he also _is_) beating himself before a mirror just before telling him you no longer want him in your life? How can a lover of this film begin to accept or comprehend the suicide of this beautiful actor?

On a brighter side, Brigitte Mira survived well into her nineties. So brimming with life, she spoke with the greatest love and tenderness of both ben Salem and Fassbinder. She also appeared not to have known about their relationship. Of Fassbinder she reflected, "He allowed himself something that most people can't allow themselves. They can't. They simply cannot."

Fassbinder exposed a mechanics of awkwardness in order to render something sweet and possible. No filmmaker can remake the world, though with forty films at age thirty-seven, Fassbinder perhaps hoped to. We are left, nevertheless, with knowledge that we don't know what to do with. We are left to reside in an awkward age, blindfolded before a mirror. We are left to ask: what did Fassbinder allow himself that we cannot?

2

FACING

seaward

Although our interviews were chiefly confined to conversations between the brilliantly lighted drawing-room where I sat and the dusky hall just outside where she always remained, I grew very familiar with her voice, its vaguely surprised note dominant.

—MILLICENT TODD BINGHAM quoting Mabel Loomis Todd,
Dickinson's brother's lover and one of Dickinson's
first posthumous editors, *Ancestor's Brocades:
The Literary Debut of Emily Dickinson*

Fassbinder gives the lie to the body's spatialization, and so did Emily Dickinson. If social decorum made for hallucinated relations between people in space, Emily Dickinson sought to counter such fabrications with a trenchantly poetic real. Her orientation was seaward: "The shore is safer, Abiah, but I love to buffet the sea," she reports in an early letter, "I can count the bitter wrecks here in these pleasant waters, and hear the murmuring winds, but oh, I love the danger!" A letter written in the 1860s to her beloved sister-in-law and partner in composition, Susan Huntington Dickinson, admits a lifelong practice of navigating unsteadiness:

> You must let me
> go first, Sue, because
> I live in the Sea
> always and know
> the Road—
> I would have drowned
> twice to save

seaward

you sinking, dear,
If I could only
have covered your
Eyes so you wouldn't
have seen the Water—

Dickinson's orientation was seaward, and her preference was to stand inside a hallway, outside the reach of vision, when a visitor came to call. It wasn't that she lived in a beyond, frolicking in the waves of some perilous delusion that left no time for others. No. Standing unseen in a hallway was how she wished to *meet* you. To face you was both *too* much (how could two infinities hope to touch?) and *too* little (greeting occasioned a repetition of the known; proscriptive encounters were exceedingly lean). Face-to-face meetings made for the predictable awkwardness of following social form: the sentence punctuated with the proper lilt, the teacup steadied, the hands held like closed wings in the lap, the hand lifted to greet and bid good-bye, the body sitting neither too lightly nor too heavily upon the stuff of a chair. All of this *curtailed* conversation, whereas the awkward encounter with a person-out-of–sight-but-there offered the possibility of a meeting of minds, a whisper in the dark of truth, a voice listened hard for and heard.

Dickinson's awkward game is an invitation to teeter—now a floorboard squeaks; to linger—I can't rely on visual cues to take my turn to speak. For disembodiment, we must turn to contemporary culture—the telephone, the Internet—but in an encounter with Dickinson, one body feels the presence of the other on either side of the wall. Not a disembodied voice in the hallway, Dickinson's is a *differently* embodied voice. To hear her better, I look at the ceiling, I look at the floor, I look at the picture her voice draws for me, more present by being both out of sight and there. I close my eyes to take her in. Proximate, I yearn for her to speak again.

If modes of decorum prevent communication, sitting out of sight opens it up. "The precondition for all true intimacy is distance." This is how Diana Fuss summarizes one part of Dickinson's complex poetics of space. Fuss studies Dickinson's relationship to the space of her house at a time when the elite domicile was poised to become both compartmentalized and havenlike: a transitional moment in which the house was not *yet* considered a bastion of privacy but was on its way to being one. A publicness still flowed through the rooms of the Dickinson Homestead, and rooms were never wholly given over to a single or separate use. Dickinson emerges as both a novel inhabitant of shifting space and a poet-architect who *thinks*, for example, with doors and who questions repeatedly the terms by which intimacy is understood. Fuss suggests that Dickinson's strange form of colloquy was a way of training her interlocutor to perceive her as a poet. Dickinson stages the persona "poet" because of the impossibility of a radical poet finding a home in a female form.

In her efforts to perfect an awkward idiom, Dickinson relies on the slip or miss or pause; on *near* and *off* rhyme; on dashes like sudden trap doors for you to fall through; on identity mistaken. Here's the astonishing beginning of a poem on self-doubt, a poem that takes the awkwardness of not knowing if one is alive as its opener:

> I am alive—I guess—
> The Branches on my Hand
> Are full of Morning Glory—
> And at my finger's end—
>
> The Carmine—tingles warm—
> And if I hold a Glass
> Across my mouth—it blurs it—
> Physician's—proof of Breath—
>
> I am alive—because
> I am not in a Room—
> The Parlor—commonly—it is—
> So Visitors may come—

Here we might conclude that the mistake of being in a hallway tells her she's alive. To reside in the parlor is tantamount to social death (it's where socially sanctioned encounters occur) and literal death (it's where they lay the body out). It's the place where people come

And lean—and view it sidewise—
And add "How cold—it grew"—
And "Was it conscious—when it stepped
In Immortality?"

I am alive—because
I do not own a House—
Entitled to myself—precise—
And fitting no one else—

In other words, a grave.

And marked my Girlhood's name—
So Visitors may know
Which Door is mine—and not mistake—
And try another Key—

Let's hope I am mistaken, these stanzas cleverly imply, taken for someone other than the name on a grave, not easily recognized and opened: to be awkwardly encountered is to know I am alive.

How good—to be alive!
How infinite—to be
Alive—two-fold—The Birth I had—
And this—besides, in Thee!

In an erotics of reading, according to these last lines, Dickinson is born in us, if only we take her for someone else.

Dickinson doesn't cower in the dark without a clue, without a candle in her hallway habit, or in her poetry. She commands space and invites you to be discomfited along with her. When the visit is over, she tells you so by sending a servant into your space with a flower, a glass of sherry, or a verse, presumably on a tray. And here's where her awkward antics lose a little luster in the telling because if anyone remains truly disembodied in the endlessly proliferating scholarship on Emily Dickinson's life and work, it is her Irish immigrant servants. Outside of the dedicated work of Aife Murray to reconstruct their lives, readers rest content with forgetting the servants and picturing Dickinson as the individual genius, an American original, a quirk. But the body of a servant announces the end of Dickinson's peculiar form of meeting; the bodies of the servants afford space for her to make her poetry; the hands of the servant remove her slops from the room in which she sleeps and writes. They see her face to face, they nurse her when she is sick. Because art is never made in the dark, in the lone, perhaps we should refer to the poet as Emily Dickinson Maher. Maggie Maher was one of Dickinson's lifelong servants.

Maybe Dickinson didn't consider her servants personages enough to engage them in her experiments in awkwardness. What's troubling is that they were required. Maybe radical awkwardness always entails a prop, and the support, even the subservience, of others. Or maybe Dickinson employed them as cohorts and in this sense sought them out as kin: she, the awkward exile; they, the awkward immigrants. See the seven pallbearers, the Irish male immigrant servants: at her request, they are the ones who carry her tiny body in its coffin on their shoulders, according to her directions, *out the backdoor.* It's intimate and uncanny, this work she charges them with even to the end. Did her choice make for a "modest," an "unobtrusive" funeral? Or was the act a glaringly awkward statement? Or a way of saying that she, too, was a servant in the house: that the immigrants served her so that she could serve poetry? Beguiling heft. Pleasurable release.

embarrassed

Seamless interpretations aren't possible in an encounter with Emily Dickinson's work. The quest for a key to fit the lock of her verse is useless as a defense against the awkward fumbling her words incite. If we have to embrace awkwardness in order to receive her poems' unexpected gaps and turns, does this mean that her poems have the power to embarrass us? The humility of the voice, I suppose, might make us feel awkward in its presence—not exactly guilty but gangly and drawn. Drawn toward the awe that is there, at awkwardness's cresting, something breaking at a juncture of delicacy and jab. And if I blush to read her, it is for the way that she giddily strips me of my sense.

embarrassed   Dickinson stands out of sight when visitors come to call because "they talk of Hallowed Things aloud—and embarrass my Dog." A Newfoundland. Named Carlo. Whose understanding of her proved to her she could not elude others. A certain relation to language embarrasses Dickinson, but she, too, embarrasses her visitors with her intensity. Does Dickinson stand in the hallway so as not to embarrass you, no longer to embarrass Higginson, famous for his description of a rare face-to-face visit with Dickinson: "I never was with anyone who drained my nerve power so much," he wrote to his wife, "without touching her she drew from me. I am glad not to live near her."

There's a poem that begins with the line, "I was the slightest in the house." At its cresting point, in even tones that cut through the page with the poignancy of their certitude, we read, "I could not bear to live—aloud—/The Racket shamed me so—". (From a lesser writer, we might expect "alone," "for long," "anymore," "without" . . . Dickinson's "aloud" sticks, and resounds.) The poem seems to issue from embarrassment and self-abnegation, a retreating smallness sure to make a feminist reader cringe. But that's only if we take Dickinson at her word, only if we forget that Dickinson refused to announce herself in favor of announcing herself *otherwise*. Then the poem reads as one of the most divinely beautiful odes to disempowerment and sweet withdrawal. Then the poem appears ironically loud:

> I was the slightest in the House—
> I took the smallest Room—
> At night, my little Lamp, and Book—
> And one Geranium—
>
> So stationed I could catch the mint
> That never ceased to fall—
> And just my Basket—
> Let me think—I'm sure
> That this was all—
>
> I never spoke—unless addressed—
> And then, 'twas brief and low—
> I could not bear to live—aloud—
> The Racket shamed me so—

And if it had not been so far—
And any one I knew
Were going—I had often thought
How noteless—I could die—

A riotous, noisy, distracting, discordant clash of loud sounds, a jar-ring brass band of pots and pans clanging and it's not New Year's Eve. A racket. To live in the language bequeathed her by the culture, to live in the voice of a nineteenth-century American woman was embarrassing and ugly and undesirable to Dickinson. This doesn't mean that she was subdued and quiet, refined or meek or mute. The prodigious number of poems and letters that issued from her pen was anything but small or still. Dickinson pursued the *power* in ret-icence and restraint over and against empty hubbub. But there's more: the voice of her poems isn't the voice of her female accultur-ated coil—the merest in the house. The voice she wrote in was the voice as yet unheard by visitors. The voice, like a bat's navigational cry to human ears, out of range. It was a voice out of range because of the primacy placed on the eyes as reigning faculty. A voice unheard, out of range, and in search of a body.

The single lyric is that voice. Try to hear it—you can't without access to an extra sense.

The body that it finds, that Dickinson made for it, is the collec-tion of self-sewn volumes, called fascicles, the collected work.

The body that it seeks and finds is yours and mine when we read her—the reconfigured body of the reader awkwardly attuned.

faces

To be awkwardly attuned, must we face or turn away? And how does anyone know finally that she *is* looking, squarely, or turned around, not seeing at all? Maybe the truth is off to the side, and one must, like my friend following eye surgery, awkwardly point one's head toward ten o'clock for at least twenty-four hours in order to see it.

In his journals, my grandfather records one morning's deeds: drawing faces on the pages of a newspaper under a terrific heat, but the faces lack the expression he is aiming for, they fail to look for him, or at him, to see.

So much shows on your face, in a courtroom, how much or little you have to face up to; in a bedroom, how comforting or disconcerting your dreams; in a classroom, indifference or puzzlement or that glassy indecision about where to focus your gaze lest the teacher notice you. The tear withheld: young face, who has returned your gaze till now? "No one," you reply, "so much as this book, this author has." And on the street, the faces look where they are going and, if not, diminish their stride.

To save face is to conquer embarrassment or cover up an untoward act. An awkward face is one that doesn't match a situation or one that gives you away.

Faced with a difficult issue, how do you proceed? I remember at age eleven buying a book in the dollar bin at the local five-and-ten-cent store called *Creative Problem Solving*. I thought it would give me the resources I needed and lacked. That it would prepare me for high school or college.

To turn away might mean to look elsewhere, to insist on a different emphasis, to attend a margin, to highlight a fringe, to spend a day eating nothing but desserts at hourly intervals because you want to change the clock to meet a longing, to make the clockface care about you rather than pin you with its hands, your body on its wrack, winding. The face of the clock brightens with each forkful. This is awkwardness's happy off-shoot. Not that other turning away, turning as an act of tortuous refusal. Funny how rarely that brand of looking away diminishes pain. Sidestepping a pain that the mind can't meet, avoidance produces awkwardness, a life spent dodging a threat only apparent to oneself but unnamed. The sidestep *can* take the form of a graceful lilt—and there's the sadness in it—the pain *and* the awkwardness denied, like the boy Emily Dickinson cites who whistles by the graveyard to cover his fear. Sometimes when I'm afraid, I begin to skip, by which I don't mean miss a step but fly like a carefree baby on the loose or Donald O'Connor dancing up a storm and down a street.

Fear has the power to blunt other feelings, and here's where awkwardness comes in: instead of asking how you are feeling?, awkwardness asks how you are numbing. There's an ice pack on your butt when you'd like to be kissed there, no "if"s or "and"s. The place where you sit or rest, rise or fall, the hapless platitude of what it comes down to.

An organism that comes to feel it can no longer feel will continue to feel, but all it will feel is awkward.

To face equals to feel. Is that true? Or can facing occlude feeling where facing means commanding, mastering, admitting, confessing, where facing is to answer the call of one's training, numbly accepting? It seemed impossible to "face death," though each of us tried and so often in peculiarly self-immolating ways. Did you ever have that feeling that if one switch were turned off, maybe even one that's been hounding you like a switchback, that if this one were to go, so would they all? Or that a need to close up shop, if you indulged it, wouldn't induce rest but death?

Tears on a face, or tears (as in openings, breaks). Extravaganza of solitudes. Solitaires. Extravaganza of vagaries faced and made solid, given form, breathed life into, the poem's ground and sound. Intensities marshaled. Pages face, they follow, they lead, they meaningfully work; closed, they superimpose and open, disposition, dispossess one another; they regulate the contours of a book; they peel and parch and evenly blot; they kiss. Face me so I can feel your face, or should I come to it from behind with my hands open and my eyes shut? When the darkness passes, the head lifts, is lighted, can be lit again—the face half-hidden in darkness, the face asleep in the dark, the face lit by neon under erasure, the face illuminated in autumn amber light.

faceless

Emily Dickinson was an odd one, there's no doubt about it; not exactly an odd-ball, more like an odd fellow and a maker of oddments. She exploited space, margins, and gaps in her letters and her poems, often with the effect of producing an aesthetic of suspension and thresholds. She also manufactured strange envelopes which she filled with unexpected content. Consider the following letter, addressed to Susan Huntington Dickinson:

faceless

> Dear Sue—
>   Your little
> mental gallantries
> are sweet as
> Chivalry, which
> is to me a
> shining Word
> though I don't
> know its meaning—
> I sometimes re-
> member we are
> to die, and
> hasten toward
> the Heart which
> how could I woo

This part of the letter is enclosed in an envelope of sorts since, in either margin, the following menacing lines appear:

> [In margin on right side]
> in a rendezvous where there
> [In margin on left side]
> is no Face? Emily—

The letter is hard to figure in pointed and poignant ways— what's a *mental* gallantry? Why describe them as chivalrous if you don't know its meaning? Because, of course, Dickinson uses words like things, she likes the way the word shines. Then a gap is intro- duced, as though the letter's sentiment were interrupted, stopped in its tracks by thoughts of death. Longing, a hastening is announced, but the object to which the I is drawn, that Heart, seems to push and pervert the sentence that follows into a terse and inverted syntax that leaves us reeling back and forth between the acrostic "how" and "woo": "how could I woo." All of this is then framed by a cryptic envelope—a rendezvous where there is no Face. There are so many enfoldings here, and one risks, in undoing them, unraveling the poem/letter. (I often find that at the center of Dickinson's poems lurks a taut rosebud that we are not meant to force open.)

Would Susan, as lover, have been able to fill in the gaps? Would Susan have been unusually receptive to Dickinson's codes, the wholly original recipient of total understanding? I'm afraid not, because Dickinson's work neither yields to nor seeks to *fit*. This is nowhere more apparent than in the manuscript pages where, following poet Susan Howe's cue, we can heed the literal not just the immanent gaps between words. Try reading a Dickinson poem with those handwritten spaces between words restored, those gaps that are edited out by anthologizers, and you come to feel as though you are in the presence of a nineteenth-century John Cage. Dickinsonian blanks, one surmises, don't wish to be filled. Dickinson requires us to dwell in awkward silence and stir. The ear cranes after such pauses; the poem *tolls* as much as it sings; and the voice of the poems read in manuscript has less of the lilt that we associate with Dickinson's song and more of a longing. Those deliberate spaces make for a poetry of stillness and yawp, where "yawp" falls somewhere between a yawn and a yell. Each pause tempts interruption by all that language otherwise bars.

Dickinson menaces: I remain stuck at the place where she announces, on either side of a love-letter verse, "a rendezvous where there is no Face." It seems like a horrifying prospect—a meeting with Facelessness, and I don't know if it means to picture an encounter with god, faceless non-human; with the beloved, whom she cannot bear to face; or, as a friend of mine suggests, with chivalry itself, a knight's face obscured by a helmet. It seems like a horrifying prospect, but I suspect that for Dickinson it signals some possibility of bliss.

To meet without facing. Is it more awkward to face or turn away?

There is one poem by Emily Dickinson in which facing and awkwardness literally appear together. It makes me gasp, this poem, it almost makes me cry:

> If I'm lost—now—
> That I was found—
> Shall still my transport be—
> That once—on me—those Jasper Gates
> Blazed open—suddenly—

faceless

That in my awkward—gazing—face—
The Angels—softly peered—
And touched me with their fleeces,
Almost as if they cared—

I'm banished—now—you know it—
How foreign that can be—
You'll know—Sir—when the Savior's face
Turns so—away from you—

The awkward gazing face is a lost face, unfocused, without an object; the awkward gazing face is present and searching, but risks gaps and absence. The face is awkward because it knows so little and wants so much. It is awkward because it is daring to look even though meaning is beyond it. It is awkward because it's a baby face believing there is love to be found in the Face of the Maker and that the Maker can be found by it, wants to be Found by its puny self that seems to say "please?" It's Dickinson's version of Munch's *The Scream*: not a face of mutating horror unleashed but of wide-eyed vulnerability. "Once" in its life, its gaze was returned by tender Angels who not only "softly peered" but also touched the speaker with their fleeces. Who wouldn't wish for a softly peering reply to their awkwardness, and the consolation of a downy stroking by angel interlocutors?

The key word here is "Almost"—"Almost as if they cared," because this speaker doesn't believe that she really can be rescued from her awkwardness, or that angels would have any reason to single her out for saving.

In the world this poem emerges from, Dickinson's family friends, peers, and other loved ones were claiming to be "found." Religious revivals and conversion experiences abounded; "submission" to the Higher Power was the order of the day. But the movement and its fervency failed to awaken or convince Dickinson—she turned away from its consolatory power and the seductiveness of its delusions. Dickinson's refusal to "serve" the idea of the wholly comforting and possibly paralyzing returned gaze, her opting for awkwardness as a condition that one needs to learn to work with and live through is loudly announced by the seemingly tiny detail at the end of her

Jasper-gated poem where both a rhyme is refused between "be" and "you"—the match of course would be "be" and "Thee"—and, a subservience to another person, some Sir, who would claim a higher authority in being saved but whom Dickinson will not humble herself to.

What Dickinson *faced*, over and against the gaze of a reconciling god, were numerous uncanny strangers; her poems often record the effects of her looking into an abyss. It's quite possible that Dickinson found the abyss less frightening, less disarming than the face of another person.

The range of her attentions brings to mind the idea of a purview; of the limits of what a self can accommodate (which realities, which truths); and the notion of absent presences. Dickinson's poetry extends the purview of the normal range of the seen; it tests the boundaries of accommodation; and it admits and faces the absent presences in the room.

Often enough, the persona, even the "voice," produced by a Dickinson poem is accompanied by a stranger, and scores of the poems address uncanny visitors to the domestic space. "Alone, I cannot be—" one poem begins, "For Hosts—do visit me—/Recordless Company—/Who baffle Key—." The wind enters another poem, and the host is hard-pressed to welcome formlessness into the borders of her home or of her verse, but she finds a way to accommodate strange formlessness, finds a peculiar language to represent the unrepresentable when she writes:

> No Bone had He to bind Him—
> His Speech was like the Push
> Of numerous Humming Birds at once
> From a superior Bush—

The wind is accommodated in the space between the words, even the plosives, the phonemes that distinguish "Push" from "Bush." In a particularly modern piece of verse, Dickinson imagines the entry into her room of a worm, which the speaker attempts to bind with a string, but the leash only occasions a terrifying transformation of the worm into a snake, now "ringed with power." Tethers, often enough in Dickinson, never simply oppress or exert power but produce power, engender it. What grows even more startling than the bound worm's power in this poem, though, is the transformation at the level of language required to accommodate the fearsome absent presence in the room—for these poems of domesticity undone always suggest the extent to which familiarity requires a degree of pretense and denial of its other in order to be sustained and maintained. At a heightened moment of terror in the poem, the snake faces the speaker, the speaker faces the snake, and the poem turns into a highly modern Cubist piece of verse:

> I shrank—"How fair you are"!
> Propitiation's Claw—
> "Afraid he hissed
> Of me"?
> "No Cordiality"—
> He fathomed me—
> Then to a Rhythm *Slim*
> Secreted in his Form
> As Patterns swim
> Projected him.

The speaker here is *fathomed* by the thing she sought to tame, fully faced and plumbed by the uncanny other, and the result of being fathomed by the ejected strange is a radical relation to language—the poetry, the poem that the snake *becomes*.

What makes being faced awkward is the possibility that someone will see, or see through you, or, in fathoming you, vanquish you or worse, see but fail to acknowledge you, or claim to have seen nothing. Dickinson admits strange intimacies into her poems, into her purview, and so submits to awkwardness in order to produce art. But Dickinson's *presence* in light of her forays into awkwardness, her inhabitance of awkwardness, or her dance with awkwardness, is never wholly clear or true. One glance at Dickinson's life and especially at the relation she had to her work reveals a complex fort-da game with absence and presence, a many webbed dome of disclosure and secrecy.

People seemed to know and not know that Dickinson wrote poems.

The person who came to edit the first volume of her poems, Mabel Loomis Todd, never actually saw Dickinson.

Dickinson rarely left her house.

Dickinson left her house in the form of thousands of letters that she penned in her lifetime.

Dickinson eschewed print culture in favor of her hand-bound handwritten volumes.

Unlike the work of contemporary lyric poets, the aim of Dickinson's art wasn't self-expression but an exploration of self with a capital S—the production of a Self through art but also an inquiry into its conditions of possibility.

The Irish immigrant servants afforded Dickinson the degree of privacy required by her to write, but that privacy, that space within which she needed to reside in order to create, was also something that she *took*.

Writing is implicitly a public act.

Dickinson hid her poems in a trunk.

After Dickinson's departure, her poems came to light. After Dickinson's death, her poems became present.

The Dickinson persona is one of a there not-thereness. The self is ever engaged in a game with absence and presence. Each time I read a poem of Dickinson's, I think I glimpse her reappearance, and each time she reappears, on either side of an absence, a pause or a gap, she is more unexpected, more subtle, more different, more alarmingly grotesque.

This leaves me with a vexing question: why couldn't Dickinson and her poetry be present simultaneously? Why couldn't she accompany her verse into the public sphere? Why couldn't the poetry be made public until after she had disappeared? What awkwardness was she afraid would ensue? I picture Dickinson, without the protection of conversion, living life nakedly. On March 12, 1853, she wrote to Susan Huntington Dickinson: ". . . so you see when you go away, the world looks staringly and I find I need more vail." I picture Dickinson living in her body and her work without recourse to the defenses that others claimed so easily. This doesn't mean that she was helpless but that she was trying for a fuller sense of being, less relentlessly, less assuredly, less restlessly *armed*. Dickinson didn't want her verse to return to her—for us to seek *her* there, or to *be* returned to her, in the form of a package that had missed its recipient. Larger than any room or any self, it would have vanquished her. I picture Dickinson slipping out the backdoor of her own party, her own show, leaving us to wonder if what she's left us with, this abounding presence, is the stranger or the self. Leaving us to face together what she faced alone.

arms

Autumn light chooses. It doesn't douse; no swaths, no skeins of light for this season. It is particular about what it articulates. Amber, now copper, then platinum—the movement of light is slow, steady, discrete, and sudden as a finger pointing to a corner you'd never noticed before, that previously meant nothing and now means everything. For now. How the sun on such days finds a patch of earth *beneath* a tree to illuminate, I cannot know, but only that a bush burns there, now a cavern opens, chestnuts shine, or burnished fur. We're traveling one road, forward, but the light is beside and displaced, suddenly choosing matter, holding things, deliberate and whimsical, making dusty asides into tabernacles. Not the knack a cat has for finding the sole patch of light falling across a sill or a floor, usually square or oblong to nap in. Not light waiting to be found by feline sleuths or observant kittens. Light that seeks, *finds*, chooses, remaking the world. It demands nothing of us, this light—it's just a happily blessed accompaniment to forward movement on Autumn days, or is it?

I'm driving and no light touches me, but I see through my window on such days a woman who walks along the park's edge, and she is *lit*, she alone is lit, the sun has found her and it is astonishing to see a person turned essence like this. Not ghostly. Not dissolving this light, neither "shining," nor glistening, but orange-amber choosing as if to say, "this woman walks here, her hair is blonde." The sun chose her for this moment to strike and carry her, to hold and follow her. Her figure, that stunning light, reminds me of a powerful story from a childhood picture book, maybe even an image I fixated on as a child. I don't remember the tale's particulars as much as the visual image that always accompanied it. Saul had been thrown from his horse. Struck, as I understood it, not by lightning but by light. He crouches beside his horse, he looks up from the dust, and the horse seems to have grown in form to a proportion beyond his ability once to have mounted it. He holds his right arm in front of him to shield himself from this light—this light and this fall that will lead to his beginning to call himself by a different name, Paul.

I suppose autumn light is overwritten by conversion, but it needn't be understood as spiritual transformation. If a conversion is taking place on such days, it is material: we are aging and we see the world as we always have. What would have to happen for us to see differently, for our vision to be radically altered, for a sea change to occur uncorrupted by trauma, distinct.

I think I was scared for Saul, and thrilled: a light came to him that was so strong it knocked him off his horse. I think I felt sorry for Saul: he struggled to block light that was overpowering him with his hand. It's impossible to face away from certain forms of light. Contemplating the image again as an adult, I perceive Saul's hand as a woefully awkward shield, and it makes me wonder whether my hand really could be of service if a light were blinding me. Or if the better idea might be to give up one's arms, in more than one sense of that word, and let the light take you where it will—even if it floored you, even if it ground you down to ecstasy.

hands

In one of Dickinson's most famous poems, "This is my letter to the World/ That never wrote to Me—", the poet imagines her future reader not as a set of eyes, not as a face that will be struck dumb by her verse, but as a set of (unseen) hands:

> This is my letter to the World
> That never wrote to Me—
> The simple News that Nature told—
> With tender Majesty
>
> Her Message is committed
> To Hands I cannot see—
> For love of Her—Sweet—countrymen—
> Judge tenderly—of Me

Committing her poems to future readers' hands, she requests this dance; she hopes, it seems, for an intimacy in place of an awkward gawking. But a Dickinson poem is never this easy to receive, it certainly rarely holds a reader's hand, and Dickinson's figuring of hands reopens for me the awkward gulf that Fassbinder, too, explores between our very own faces and our very own hands, the face and the hand of the owner out of sync.

Fassbinder's Emi drew her hands to her face and felt her flesh—to assure herself that her happiness was real, her act of love her own. She was claiming possession and embodiment. Ali brought his hands to his face so that he might disown his fear, and with it his worthiness to love or feel or fear. "I felt my life with both my hands/ To see if it was there." In these lines, Dickinson figures a person not exactly encountering themselves with their hands in an act of self-making or undoing—in either case as a defense against awkwardness—but as a response to a fundamental question about the matter of embodiment. Dickinson doesn't locate the "life" that the hands are feeling in the body, and thus the lines' startlingly uncanny effect. I suppose we could picture this figure hugging or pinching themselves, drawing a foot up to a mouth the way they did as a baby, but the lines don't offer that closure. Instead they posit "my life" as something awkwardly poised outside of and away from the body, scarily abstracted. Dickinson didn't write—I searched my rooms for *signs* of myself to *see* if I was there, I read my poems up and down to find me loitering there. To *see* oneself may be easier and less likely even to produce awkwardness than to *feel oneself*, since the latter suggests a fundamental split that must ever be negotiated even as we might pretend it doesn't exist. That split might look like this: each one of us "has" a self or, rather, "is" a self, and each one of us can "feel" or be cognizant of that self. (The self feeling the self. The self encountering the self. At the same time that one proceeds as though one were self-same.)

The emphasis on feeling the self and being the self simultaneously doesn't edge us into the area of an observing ego, self-consciousness, or, at a pathological register, "schizophrenia." It seems more to do with the *matter* of being in some *abstract* sense (the being that inheres in an inner life) and being in an embodied sense (the being that inheres in physiology). It's not, though, the famous mind/body split that Dickinson's couplet turns us toward, but something more like the hand/matter split, the hand/life split, maybe even the hand/writing split.

People study Dickinson's hand/writing these days to uncover an aesthetic; they contemplate the folds in letters made by hands one hundred and fifty years ago to discern how cherished or troubling the letter, how often it was handled and therefore re-read. (But maybe those folds don't reveal how much a letter was read but how much it was "worried.") Readers "worry" over Dickinson's manuscripts to the point of fetishizing them—which would suggest that the absences their materiality provokes is really too anxious-making for we postmoderns.

Dickinson may have been enamored of hands—she certainly fashioned hands in her poems in delicate, bizarre, and playful ways. When she remembers finding favorite flowers, she describes mostly, in letters, not the sight of the flower—its shape, color, or scent—but her "clutch" of it. She remembers the first time she felt, gathered, handled it—or how, we might conclude, it held her since "clutch" makes possible a feel of push/pull longing. She writes into being "vacant Hands," and "Hempen Hands," "narrow," and "childish Hands." She imagines a time "when Formula, had failed . . . / And shape my Hands," and "The spider" who "holds a silver Bell/ In Unperceived Hands." This is all well and good, even a lovely celebration of hands, capitalized, hands grappling, groping, attached and detached, mysterious and feelingful. But "Hands" can never figure easily or "poetically" in Dickinson's work once a reader has encountered the image Dickinson offered of her own hands that she gave in a letter to Susan Huntington Dickinson—

> Take back that
> "Bee" and "Buttercup"—
> I have no Field
> for them, though
>   for the Woman
> whom I prefer,
> Here is Festival—
> When my Hands
> are Cut, Her
> fingers will be
> found inside—

hands

Emily Dickinson: socially awkward poet known for her brilliant sublimation of debilitating shyness into an aesthetic of reticence.

Emily Dickinson: socially awkward poet, awkward because of her inability to feign, to hide; who might come to be known for her ghoulish graphicness. Dickinson was a graphic poet, a hand/writing who answered the piercing light, glint for glint.

FALLING

bearlike

If you live in the dark, out of sync with the rest, mopish, you might feel awkward. To be the last to know something induces awkwardness because once you learn the thing that you didn't know, you're forced to see yourself for who you had all along ignorantly been, and the picture isn't blissfully innocent but sad because of your having been left out, because of the embarrassment of your not having been included and your not having known. Of course what counts as knowledge is culturally determined and time-bound, leaving me to wonder how any of us truly comes to claim the opposite of awkwardness—aplomb. Knowledges differ, sharing disparate knowledges is laborious if even possible: we're fellow gropers wandering in a dark wood, now there's a touch of color, a patch at an elbow, a nose sensing a fragrance without a name. Is to see you to feel you or to keep you at an unthreatening distance?

I remember two songs that met my ears following the "events" of September 11th. Jean and I were living and teaching in Moscow, and through the phone receiver, our six-year-old niece sang in sweetly perfect pitch, "Bonjour mes amis, bonjour," the new tune she had learned in French-immersion school. In the metro, on the 12th, a burly male accordionist opened and closed the bellows to the beat of a polka, "Roll out the barrel, we'll have a barrel of fun." These two, I won't call them innocents, were living according to their own lights—that day's lesson, the daily push to make a living. The first song made me cry; I received it as an alternative to what I thought I knew, and I wanted to reach through the telephone wire and gather Justine's small form and earnest voice to my heart so that nothing could ever harm her. The second song made me feel self-righteous: I received it as a grotesque denial of what I thought I knew, and I *bearlike* wanted to confront the mocker and yell. Ever receiving the world and other people through the limited lens of my ignorance and my knowledge, I became aware in Russia in those days of the awkward disconnect of disparate truths.

As an American, I heard certain phrases as a refrain from the lips of Russians: "he perished" and "it is not possible." Were my ears pricked to receive the stereotype of Russian subjectivity, the shroud of impossibility and death associated by the West with Eastern bloc countries? Never have I experienced such a commodious reception as I did in Russia, and a sense that, in spite of their own cramped living arrangements, our Russian acquaintances were happy for our presence and eager to "make room," to help us to fit and feel at home. Awkwardness's opposite abounded in the extent to which Russian colleagues and Russian strangers accommodated Jean and me, as though we were long lost relatives they were all the while expecting.

One day, my Russian teacher told us that she knew Americans thought of "Russians as bears." I didn't really know what she meant until the Russian writer Mikhail Epstein explained to me that awkwardness is considered a national Russian trait. He cited the work of the Russian philosopher Pavel Flovensky, who notes that Mikhails are especially subject to awkwardness. In fact, bears in Russia are called Mishas or Mikhails and vice versa. According to Epstein, there are many synonyms for awkwardness in Russian, as well as characters exemplifying it in Russian literature: Pierre Bezukhov in *War and Peace*, Epikodov in *The Cherry Orchard*, many of Dostoevsky's characters, including the author himself.

Yet I'm sure that the awkwardness thus ascribed to the Russian character sports a degree of panache. I imagine the bearlike awkwardness of which Epstein speaks to be the result of complex historical conditions, the need to huddle in cold at the same time one proudly bares one's chest, the awkwardness of bodies having survived all odds. To be American, on the other hand, anywhere in the world, was to be the most oafish inhabitant of the planet. Our ignorance of all the world's languages and modes, our screech and lumber, our capitalist waddle and tendency to grab is apparent to most of the rest of the world from miles away. But maybe American awkwardness also could be said to emerge from "complex historical conditions," the twinned legacies of the body bent for far too long before the lathe combined with the stupefying slack jaw of the body set before the television set. Americans work too hard, and when they finally look up from their work, which they rarely do, they don't recognize the world in front of them, they forget how to proceed, and flail.

Smiling gives every American away. You lumber like a donkey and yet you smile. "Don't smile," a man on the metro whose foot I had stepped on advises me, having read my smile as a badge of my nation. "Try to look normal," he says, and through his alcoholized breath and sweaty upper lip he gestures: using his hand, he pulls the corners of his mouth down into a seriously indifferent semi-purse. "Look normal," he says, and people will not bother you, people will not guess, otherwise you could be yelled at like the trio of young Fulbrighters whose smiles led a person on the metro to direct at them a tirade on the question of what there was to smile about.

ignorant

My days in Russia were made up of bands of illumination and bands of distance, part of a foot in one history (the Russian surround) but *not* in another (far from the cataclysm that newly characterized home), the known unknown. My days in Russia consisted of a perpetuity of epiphanic moments—about which I came to feel guilty. Shouldn't I be encased in gloom? Eating a berry chocolate ice cream before an illuminated cloud cluster at the Kremlin, I'm awed by the shifts of time, space, light that mark the distance between twelfth-century spiral-domed churches and the severity of art deco lines.

I experienced Russia openly and in awe.

I experienced Russia and my own country through the peepholes of an awkward mantel of dazed ignorance.

A group of beautiful children, each appointed with a colorfully flowered knapsack, had been our co-passengers on the trip from New York to Moscow. I had imagined them as Russian children on a "field trip" to New York. I later learned that they were orphans who, sponsored by an American organization, had made the trip to the U.S. and back in order to be assessed, approved, looked over, checked out. The space between what I projected onto the children and the reality of their situation gawked.

I should have felt threatened by my lack of knowledge, pure and simple, but my fears manifested instead as a false vulnerability of the "American abroad" in "times of terror."

As a lesbian, I shrank to read about a Russian poll regarding homosexuals. "How ought we to deal with homosexuals?" the poll asked. Thirty-three percent of Russians had answered, "eliminate them"; thirty percent said, "isolate them from society"; ten percent agreed to "leave them to themselves"; and ten percent hoped to "help them." Could a similar poll have appeared in the U.S.? Look, the poll was distributed in 1989. So much in Russia has changed since then! I found it menacing.

One evening, during a week-long visit to a conference in Italy in late October, we got a rare glimpse of an American TV show produced for GIs stationed in Aviano: Jay Leno and David Letterman were rehashing the previous day's events, making jokes about Arabs and their camels, pretending to show clips from Al Jazeera TV, prompting the audience to laugh and cheer uproariously at a riddle: "What's bin Laden going to be for Halloween?" "Dead!" The show was peppered with condescending public service announcements made by soldiers in uniform cheerfully reminding their countrymen to wear their reflective gear while out walking at night, or to drive safely on the Italian roads, especially when they are wet, or to be good Christians. Was this the home we thought we missed, we thought we knew?

These macabre comforts of home could be countered by the ideal Russia I was painting for myself. There were colors in my picture and creatures, cocks crowing gold-red and deep purple, and the crystalline viscosity of vodka, the earth tone of brown bread, the amber glint of a rye drink called kvass. I could sniff Russia vaguely and enter the parts I chose, of literature, music, and art, grand and magnificent, textured like nothing I had known before. I didn't have to understand the relation of parts to a whole. Stalinism could be put to one side—too horrifying, too complex. And disillusion, direness, Chernobyl, Chechnya, or the Russian and American race for anthrax. A student of mine told me about his home in the Urals,

the crumbling buildings, the people perpetually breathing in ash. *ignorant*
"Hmmm," I replied, "Hmm." "Do you want to write about it?"
"No," he replied, "it's not an appropriate theme for the classical
verses I wish to compose."

In an English-language class, where students are told they can
ask me anything they wish about the United States, one gentleman
asks if dogs are allowed to run wild in the streets. Is Russian affecting English in any way, because English is affecting Russian? Are
most Americans Mormon? Is it rude to call someone a "chatterbox"
or a "motor mouth"? When asked on an evening of dinner and
Russian movies at our teacher's house to share some "native"
American songs, all that we could think of was, "Home, Home on
the Range" and "I'm a Yankee Doodle Dandy." Why didn't we consider show tunes or gospel? Olya, our teacher's daughter, wanted to
sing a Russian hymn she had learned in school, but halfway through
her grandmother told her to stop because she wasn't singing it with
enough feeling. Our teacher wanted to sing dark songs or, according to her mother, songs to do with war. Her mother wanted to sing
songs that help with language learning, and our teacher's husband
didn't want to sing at all but to talk about Tom Cruise. The evening
ended with Olya—atheist?—and I—lapsed Catholic—offering a
duet, in English, of the Christmas carol "Oh Come All Ye Faithful."

Ivan the Terrible ordered the architect of St. Basil's to be blinded
so that this magnificent paean to the Czar could never be surpassed.
This we learned.

A man dressed in orange feathers and middle eastern silks leapt
as though from a jewel box through the frame of my binoculars; he
flitted, miniaturized; he towered over the stage; I held him in my
glass. On the way home from the ballet, in the taxi that we
"ordered" to wait for us on a nearby street corner, bypassing the
crowds, the driver played Liszt's *Hungarian Rhapsody* at top volume, and I thought how I would never be as enthralled with living
again, nor would I be able to describe the enthrallment of bass notes
and ice in tandem, the car cutting through the air like a sleigh,
whisking us.

We pet Pavlov's (stuffed) dog, his mouth agape.

We wandered through the annals of the Leningrad blockade to
find a child's diary there: November 15th, uncle died; November

20th, grandfather died; December 10th, cousin died; January 2nd, mother died. On the final page of the diary, "only Tanya left." The child was found—an aloneness beyond imagining—but died soon after of malnutrition. Rations consisted of one piece of bread per person per month and recourse to leather or glue. Nightly radio broadcasts concluded with the sound of a metronome, to mimic the heartbeat, to feed the courage to survive.

The Russian soul—so brightly somber, like bits of silver in laps of snow lipped by a beige-colored moon, so laced with intensities of darkness and light, of endurance, and devastation, of abundance and singular hope, the conviction of a country that could be a world apart, descended from gentry and serf—I pretend to try to understand it. I even think I might have a touch of it; perhaps I want it. "To hell with the Russian soul!", one of my students instructs me, "I would like to try some of that Prozac that you all take but we cannot get it here. I would like to get my hands on some of that Prozac."

drunk

In Russia, I experienced singular forms of bodily awkwardness. Around one Russian colleague in particular, I felt like a bull in a china shop. Perhaps it was her impeccable pronunciation of English, and the fluency of her ideas, but also that she moved incrementally, and out of composure, but not repression, the way she conversed and then sat comfortably in pauses. I felt cumbersomely jittery and quick around her, chatty and bloblike, so it didn't surprise but only embarrassed me when, making too broad a stroke with my hand to stress a point, I toppled a tiny crystal glass filled to the brim with cranberry vodka onto a cotton tablecloth at dinner at her house.

Sometimes I felt as though all I were was a body, and an accidental body at that, an innocent bystander. The problem of drink in Russia cannot be underestimated, and so it was inevitable that a man, drunk, would one day fall backward onto me down one of those several mile-long escalators in the metro. An escalator nightmare come true. I received his body's heaviness, its succumbing to gravity and collapse, and I fell too but eventually got out from under him as he continued his backward movement down the steps.

A body in space hurtling drunkenly backward down an escalator is *maladjusted* no fun, but I think I felt more ill at ease in my body on the one day out of one hundred when the metro stopped and we were ordered to wait for another train.

The police arrived to remove the few people who were riding the trains endlessly and to nowhere, those asleep in their drunkenness. I watched as they dropped a man from the car, his body lank, now heavy as death, reduced to flesh and muscle without movement. They dragged the man as though his body were a carcass. (Cops in all countries must be trained to "handle" bodies in certain ways.) They flopped him face up onto the marble floor, stampeded daily by a million graphite soles. After a moment, he lifted his head and only his head as though the head were detached from the body and was looking down at it, this foreigner, a new world to be contemplated. And then he peed lying down, first streams, then rivulets, and finally a sad pool of liquid gushed through his pants. Now the cops dragged him through his pee and out of the station. He didn't resist their tug. He remained, not submissive but glib.

maladjusted

I came to know men's bodies in Russia at points of thresholds crossed. I'm sure women were capable of shoulder bangs, but only men in Russia greeted me this way. Not just jostling or elbowing but a body bang was an occasional occurrence in the metro. Sometimes the contact would come from behind, sometimes from the front, but it always felt as though the assailant needed something to bang into to tell he was alive: space is not something contemporary Russians have been granted. Vast country whose people are squeezed into tiny living quarters and moving cars on wheels. Gimme space, the body banger says. It says rage. In the United States I suppose a fight would follow such forthright shows of bodily contact. In Russia it seemed like something to expect and adjust to. Nor do I imagine Americans tolerating the mechanical gate that could easily disable a person at the level of upper thigh or genitals—the metal claws that close upon you if you cross the metro's threshold without paying the fare or if, turned around, you go through it in the wrong direction *maladjusted* (as I once did) or accidentally swipe a defunct card.

I adjusted to the Russian shower in the dorm room where I lived, and I adjusted to the arm of the rector of the institute where I taught, his arm crooked in mine one sunny snowy day. I didn't adjust to inspectors making sweeps of the dorm, the out-of-the-blue six a.m. passport check in which the body is the document you hold and the inspector's conclusion in reading it, and his never telling you what he is looking for or if you're it. Ah, but the shower. On a cold day, I contemplate a way to have a bath in my shower stall. I luxuriate in this phone-booth-sized bath. I sit cross-legged in five inches of hot water at the base of the booth, and I swear it feels just as wonderful as my clawfoot tub at home. I scrub with a special scratchy sponge purchased at an outdoor market. And the rector, how he took my arm and glided. Light flakes fell before us as we spoke, and sunshine, too, lit the institute's small yard, and I told him that I found it all very beautiful.

The rector was a formidable presence on the campus of the institute where I taught. Neither simply a figurehead nor a punishing authority, his presence seemed more mercurial and all the more compelling to the students who answered to his unpredictable demands. I'd been teaching at the institute for several months and he hadn't yet spoken to me. His English wasn't good, and that he approached me at all surprised colleagues whom I told of the meeting thereafter. He asked me how I liked the institute's yard, then suggested that for my own sake I please zipper my coat. He pointed toward a window in the stucco building whose outer walls were painted yellow. I could only think of the hazardous stairs in that building—so worn down by centuries of bodies that the steps now spilled, smooth as undulating ice, menacing and Daliesque. The poet whose statue centered the yard had been born in the room behind the window to which the rector pointed. He would take me now on a tour of rooms where famous writers once lived—Mandelstam, Pasternak, Platanov. I knew that there were many great writers on the faculty, I said, but not that great spirits also hovered here. For much of the time, I was awkwardly aware of my body, encased as it was in a flaccid fake-down-filled sack that I'd purchased in the United States for six dollars at a Salvation Army before making the trip. The Fulbright guide back home had reminded us that we would be conspicuous if we wore our winter finery in Moscow; they led us to imagine that we

might be jumped in broad daylight for the hides on our backs. Better *uncoordinated*
to look "like the Russians themselves." Thus my partner and I had
dyed what a friend came aptly to call our "puffalumps," as though
they would enable us to adjust immediately to life in Russia, or to
travel in disguise, undercover. If we were lucky, we could pass for
poor people from the provinces rather than capitalist pigs.

As I strolled with the rector, nodding into his elegant asides, I was
painfully aware of the sheer ugliness of the coat I walked in, and I
imagined him pitying me for not knowing how to wear my national
identity in Russia, or for what must have appeared as an unhappy relationship to my body, or for having emerged from a culture that didn't
know how to conjoin beauty and warmth: the dye job—a shade of
green, now pistachio, now cabbage—was beginning to fade so that the
coat appeared mottled with white—a moldy display all around, and
splashed here and there with splotches of metro grime. All that I
remember of my only other meeting with the rector (a farewell dinner
in which he hoped to woo me and my partner to return to the institute) was him crawling on all fours to find the earring back that had
fallen through my partner's fingers, the result of her nervously massag-
ing her earlobe. And how we eagerly, cleverly, knowingly recommended
—we enterprising capitalist friends—that the institute could make money
by drawing tourists to the rooms where the great writers lived. Strange
that they'd never thought of that!

The rector's glide with me—it was as though we were on skates
—was neither the first nor last awkward tour that I was taken on in
Russia. I would have waltzed with him if it weren't for the puffalump,
if it weren't for my not knowing how.

uncoordinated

The situation of being paid by one group of people to take in or
consume some part of another nation's history in an afternoon is
always awkward, and, like a good tourist, I tried to play my part
well by, on the one hand, showing that I *did* know something about
Russian history and on the other hand expressing my interest in
knowing more by asking questions.

The tour of an unusual museum devoted to the life and work of

uncoordinated the Russian writer Biely was to be a special treat. In fact, no money was exchanged. Our colleague explained that the tour guide's Russian was unusually beautiful and "high," but this of course was lost on us as we trained our ears toward the all-too-rare translation of what she was saying, sentences sprinkled here and there between three, four hours of Russian. I remember how the rift between my own deafness and ignorance and the endless unwinding of her exposition made me feel as though I might swoon right smack into the middle of Biely's swaddling clothes, about which she had much to say. (Evidently he never recovered from a traumatic relation to the tight fitting swaddle.) Trying, really trying to learn something and, awkward American that I am, not used to being silent, really dumb, for such an unendurable stretch, I would try from time to time to ask the guide a question or offer a speculation based on the scattershot version of Biely that I was gleaning from the English translation. I would say something like "it sounds as if he was a sort of idealist." And she would furrow her brow, turn to one of Biely's famous homemade bio-rhythms, and say "does an idealist do this!" Why venture a guess about something you know absolutely nothing about? It's not a lesson Americans easily learn: requisite listening. Grace. Nor could I hope to understand the diligence required by our guide to have grown her hair to the length of five feet, to have intricately braided the strands, then wrapped them around and around her neck where they hung like a scarf, spilling into her lap like a lifelong pet. Was the hair a statement, hair as long as a line traced back to a czar? My own hair was a series of patchy stumps, matted by a winter hat, and the advice about fashion was all wrong: the hats the Russians wore were like secondary hairstyles, variegated and striking. They bespoke an aesthetic beyond mere expediency, whereas the hat I'd brought was hideously utilitarian and drably undistinguished, better suited to a wooden post than to a living head. Our Russian colleagues outdressed us in their color, style, and bearing every day, even if the contemporary American still pictures them as the grossest slaves to ideology, an undifferentiated uniformed mass.

Gift-giving ventures between American and Russian would seem a simple transaction, but only to a benighted, ill-informed interloper. A Fulbright brochure and sundry orientations had advised that Russians like "things from your hometown." We were told to have

plenty of American trinkets on hand for those occasions when we *uncoordinated*
might want to thank someone or if we were invited to dinner. So, in
the weeks before leaving, Jean and I combed tourist shops in
Philadelphia and British Columbia, our respective childhood homes,
and carried with us to Russia pens and pencils, shot glasses, and dish-
towels engraved with the face of Ben Franklin or First Nation art. On
one occasion, the plumber in our dorm, who had struck up many an
enthusiastic conversation with us about our families and our home,
surprised us with the small and special gift of a pin celebrating the
fiftieth anniversary of the institute where we taught. Touched by his
thoughtfulness—the gift made me feel a part of the surround and I
proudly sported it on my knapsack—I offered him a trinket from our
stash of kitsch, in this case a shot glass embossed with the Liberty Bell.
He waved his hand in front of me like a vampire to a crucifix and
said, "Thank you, but I don't drink." Later, I offered him one of my
pocket flashlights, a penlight, which he also seemed reluctant to
accept, until I forced the gadget, insisting upon its usefulness to a
plumber, into the front chest pocket of his work clothes. I don't know
what made us believe that Russians would like these things—the
graven debris of overproduction and over-consumption, American
junk food, (their own gifts to us often came in the form of music and
books), but when Russia is no longer an abstraction but a flesh-and-
blood person standing before one in relationships of friendship, possibly love, or companionate strolling through a landscape of being,
the awkwardness of the assumption is laid bare.

Our teacher, however, her mother put such items on display
when we visited them, and there was nothing more incongruous
than the Haida Indian dishcloth now spread beneath the samovar
since it was hard to know what its images, its manufacture, even its
existence as a "thing" had to do with any of us let alone as a token
or emblem of our thanks to the Russians. And thus we experienced
the awkwardness of what one might call moral uncoordination over
and against physical uncoordination. Moral uncoordination follows
an impulse that feels right at the time but whose delivery fails to
function as planned because you couldn't have had the foresight
needed. You read the book rather than inquired into the reality, you
didn't consider who the people you would be gesturing toward
might be, what they might truly want, or need.

incongruous

Incomprehension produces awkward gaps to some and an untrustworthy even fickle attention. I *think* I'm seeing, I *think* I'm hearing one thing, but then I learn that I'd been wrong and the scene suddenly shifts. I apologize, I fumble. Or failing to comprehend, I look away.

In the student cafeteria, the *stolovaya*, a silver-haired woman in a stiff dress who walks with a limp, puts her hand on the shoulder of a student and makes a stern but seemingly humorous commandment to us all. Then abruptly leaves. I turn to a student at the next table to ask if she speaks English, and if she could tell me what the woman said. "Yes, I speak English," the student sweeps around to address an annoying child, me, "but what she said does not concern you, it concerns us."

I begin to "spot" the limping woman, always dressed in gray, more and more in our vicinity. She gets off the same bus, appears in the same car in the metro, crosses the same street to our dorm. I begin to imagine that she's been "assigned" to us, to observe our doings and "report." But the awkwardness of what I cannot imagine and fail to comprehend is writ large as little by little it dawns on me that most of the people who work at the institute, administrators and faculty included, live in the dorm where I temporarily reside. Their home is a room; communal bathroom and kitchen can be had down the hall. Moscow is not a city as I understand that term and the set of diffuse relations the word implies, but a tight-knit village. I come to this realization, a life that is hard for me to grasp—living one's adult life in a dormitory room—at first through the lens of the incongruous and the macabre. Or rather, my perception, at first gothic or cold-war haunted, requires immense rewriting and dilution before it can turn real. I even jokily term my encounters with what I can't comprehend—banalities all—"Polanski moments," keeping in mind the existential and surreal xenophobia of Polanski's *The Tenant*.

Entering the dormitory kitchen alone, I come upon a sink whose spigot is turned on full force, but there is no one in the kitchen. I consider turning the spigot off and when I look down into the sink, I see a huge fish laid on its side, pelted by the stream of water, staring. The banality: a method of thawing fish. The fancy: someone is mocking me with weirdness, the horror of my displacement is staring back at me, the fish and water have no agent, they've simply appeared, deposited by a ghost.

On another occasion, I look, and look again: that figure at the end of the hallway, holding a bottle of Clorox in one hand and a clear plastic bag filled with eggs in another, could not possibly be one of the institute's administrators, but it is. Clorox and eggs made for another bizarre confusion. Why was he not at home? What assignment had they given him on the weekend to do with eggs and Clorox? The eggs were awfully white. The fellow looked as wiped out as he always did; he always looked hungover, not from alcohol but from some grappling I imagined in his soul. He and the other administrators suffered from insomnia. Was he making a decision: life by eggs or death by Clorox? He explained to me now that he, too, lived in the dorm, on the sixth floor, and he invited me to see the table tennis room. He heads a table tennis group and welcomes Jean and me to join—it's a skill, like bicycle riding, he explains, that one never forgets. The sixth floor is a world apart from our bright suite: dark hallways are lit here and there by a sheen of dull yellow oil-based paint punctuated by huge holes where plaster has fallen off the walls. Less a room than a dank shell, the table tennis room fails to light the table that wobbles and tilts like a piece of abandoned machinery. "It's a little dirty," Sergei apologizes with an emphasis on the "t," "but that's Russia."

cramped

Commodiousness the opposite of awkwardness I have said was a keynote of my six-month sojourn in Russia, but sometimes our new friends' desire to welcome us transmuted into a sense we'd have of coerced tests of strength, and attentiveness, even to the point of feeling smothered. It was never enough where our teacher was concerned to go to one museum in a day; two or three might

cramped

be adequate, followed by a six-hour meal at her house. A line began to blur between being hosted, greeted, shown the city, invited into people's lives, and being put through a set of arduous intro- duction-to-Russia paces. We finally learned to press a bit of our desire into the plans for the day but never without a degree of vis- ible discomfort on both sides of the conversation. How could it be that the space that had been made ample just for us, space that was made even to suit, could begin to feel confining? The struggle to exert our will, which could unhappily be confused with refusing an invitation, conjured images now of shoehorns, and companionate magnets turned to opposite ends. The words "but" or "we're not sure" or "how about" or "what do you say to?" emerged thick as gruel from our tubelike bodies onto a table set with flowers and crystal and caviar.

"We would like to take you out to lunch today," we say to our teacher in light of the hour-long subway ride to her house that will follow the tour of museums in freezing weather. "Oh, I am disap- pointed," she replies, "I have bought all of the food." "That's too bad," Jean is able to muster, "I wish you had called us first." I bite my lip. The plans, our plans, are agreed upon, but not with- out varying degrees of sighs all around. There are subtexts one can barely see and those that will ever remain submerged. The nearly visible wires, crossed, include the fact that Russians rarely eat out—they can't afford to, and if they are taken out by Americans, capitalist advantage is laid bare. It also strikes them as a wasteful extravagance. "Oy, Mary, please," my teacher implored, "I wish you don't tell me what you pay for a haircut." I had paid the equivalent of thirty dollars in a modest boutique in the center of the city, an amount equivalent to my teacher's salary for the month. Whether our teacher would really enjoy the meal out would be questionable, so beset the occasion would be by ideo- logical traps. She sips the soup and sighs, not the sigh of a burden lifted but a burden added, the reminder or remainder of a burden still weighing.

homeward

Sometimes, where our teacher was concerned, I had the feeling of being held. "You don't want to go back home, do you?" she would ask. "It's much safer living here now." We would chuckle, "Yes, maybe we should stay in Russia. We could teach at the institute for thirty dollars a month." Or I would look at her as if to say you can't really mean that because, safe or unsafe, I experience my country as my home, so of course I want to return. What I only learned belatedly was the fragile scaffolding of that homey notion, because once having allowed a migration in one's consciousness into another world, and once the cataclysm of 9/11 had motivated our leaders to make the kinds of volatile moves they did, I would not experience the known-ness of home ever in quite the same way. While I might not be able to claim a shattering of illusion on the scale that Russians experienced it following the collapse of the Soviet Union, I can point to my own small share of rends in the fabric of being. I'm an agnostic when it comes to believing either in the comforts of home or the contours of my citizen-subjecthood since being abroad.

The awkward rub is this: one's worldview might have been changed by life in another country, but the American landscape and the peepholes provided by America's mediating lenses go unchanged, just as one had left them before leaving. I think of a visit to the optometrist who always got a little too close to me during exams and whose breath smelled like coffee—bitter, intermingled with a harsh sweet, a sweet that couldn't mask the bitter, a peppermint candy that I would hear click-clacking inside his mouth as he'd bend toward me and ask: "Which is better; lens number one or lens number two? Is it bluuu-eh-ed—he would elongate the "u" into an "eh" or "clear-eh?" Either he had a speech impediment or a Massachusetts accent. The choice always seemed impossible to me, to the point where I began to pretend to tell the difference so that it was anybody's guess what kind of prescription I would get.

It's quite possible that the sea change in one's vision that is a consequence of having newly, differently, *lived* is just as powerful as *incommodious* the feeling one has when one is in mourning: the sense that we have when someone we love dies that the world should not go on as it always has, that it should look different to others because it looks different to us. But commensurability does not occur, or not immediately, and in either case one must consider the cost of adjustment.

incommodious

In Russia those who gave us the most also demanded the most from us. So many people we met were so caught up in living that they expected us to join the dance with as much exuberance and verve, with as much guts and presence. They expected us to be as present to them as they were to us—and why not? One person with abundant resources of presentness and pull—in the sense that to be with her was to follow her on a journey that she was in the midst of and that she insisted upon, that propelled and demanded her and that she assumed we would see the necessity of too—was an independent filmmaker in her "off" hours, but when were her "off" hours if she had to work three, four jobs to survive?

We meet Valentina at the synagogue, which is just a block from the institute where we teach, and yet another world. The security is thick, and as we enter, I expect to die here, a victim of terrorism and anti-Semitism. Valentina, as always, immediately moves to feed us. She takes us to the kitchen where we are given extra-generous portions of today's soup, direct from the cook. The inside of the synagogue is "secure," a place of identification, of ritual and worship. The inside of the synagogue is what the FBI agent who briefed Fulbrighters in DC before we left would call an "X": a none-too-moving target. His instructions to us as Americans were to be ever vigilant of our surroundings and by all means to "get off the X." But here we were being feted on an X, having a serene encounter on the X, living these moments with Valentina on the X. All of these thoughts were entering and exiting my consciousness when a man at another table appeared to be saying something friendly to Valentina. I understood that he was asking her about us, and that she was explaining who we were. He is reminding us, she says, that we must move to another table to eat, men and women don't eat at

the same table. On the Sabbath? In the synagogue? If the man is a *incommodious*
rabbi? I'm afraid the orthodox answer might be "never," but a feminist disquisition on my part wasn't forthcoming. It reminded me of
the encounter with the girl who refused to translate for me in the
stolovaya (the student cafeteria)—being told to keep to one's place,
to know it and not to stray.

We whisked, we trudged, we flew with Valentina, but we wished
to stop her long enough just once for an interview with the idea of
bringing her words and her films back to the United States. Again
we were to meet her at the synagogue at the center of Moscow, and
this time we brought a brilliant student with us to translate. The
foyer of the synagogue was freezing, and one hour gave way to two
before we discovered a comedy of miscommunications that led to a
missed appointment. Valentina did arrive but explained we would
have to trek to the Jewish Youth Center tonight, and hadn't she told
us that earlier? It was another of her jobs. There was an exhibit
there this evening on Russian Jews, and maybe Jean could speak to
the students on American cinema following a presentation Valentina
planned to give on Russian film, and I could share with them some
of my creative writing. "How about the interview?" we ask. She
asks more pressingly, "Have you eaten? We have to eat before going
out into the cold. Maybe after, we'll do the interview." And she
pulled some cans of salmon and cans of corn that had been donated
to a group of visually impaired Jews out of a box. She found plates
and utensils (and a can opener) in her office and, referring to our
translator Nadya with a fond diminutive, directed her to find a bottle of vodka and serve it to us. There was something giddily intimate
about our shared canned meal, eaten together, as we shivered
together, but it didn't quite provide the fuel needed to get to the
Youth Center, one bus and metro ride followed by a two-mile walk
on ice later.

I had been in denial about the cold and had opted for a pair of
fancy boots, purchased in Venice and maybe meant for dancing but
not for mastering Moscow sidewalks with their hidden pockets and
potholes and broad bands of translucent freeze. If you weren't careful, you could get lost looking down, you could enter a dream state,
out of which you might suddenly awake to the pain of a broken
limb, at which point the fairytale would fade and the sky would

incommodious open and close frozenly upon you, a glint, a wink of reality. By a certain point in our trek, the feeling had gone out of my feet; I thought, "the foot will have to be amputated," but it didn't, and the blood returned and even though the tea froze the instant it was poured from the pot, it helped, and we made our presentations and felt lit inside by the rosy cheeks of young people who wanted to talk frankly about September 11th and all of its untold implications. Here were fifteen ways of looking at a blackbird rather than two. There was so much substance to the students in this room. They were focused and aspiring, but one also sensed in them a range of interest and of heart. Do our eyes, and our capacity, like our literal "vision," contract and diminish with age? Not exactly "wide-eyed," the students were *capacious*. Not merely impressionable, they were able and awake.

At the end of the evening, we huddled into a taxi together—something Jean and I never did alone because of our poor command of Russian. Valentina, her daughter, Katya, Nadya, Jean, and I and the driver rode together now the two miles we had earlier walked to get back to the metro. I felt there—the car sputtering through the wet cold beneath streetlights not strong enough to merit the color beige but orblike and scudding brown patches to guide us—I felt in the ride together that we were lodged at a center, not of the world, but a center we had made together that evening. Our acts and moves and words, the range of our strides or of our smiles, the decision to try to be together come what will, the tilt and blather of communicating between cultures and languages *made* the very stuff, grain and spring, that our tushes sat upon as we drove. Collectively we moved along a sparsely populated street, at the heart of something, without heeding our being at the center of nowhere in a chaotic age.

The next morning, wondering if it was too much to ask to sleep in, we groped to answer an early morning phone call from Valentina inviting us to dinner at her apartment. Our stay was coming to a close, and she wanted to have us over for dinner before we left. Hers was the only apartment among those of our new friends that we had not yet been to.

teeth

In late December, fresh flowers could still be found in Moscow, so we brought some along with cake and wine and a treatment we had been helping Valentina translate into English, for a film she wanted to make on the relationship between Eisenstein and his teacher, Meyerholtz. We entered a room filled with the usual apologies by our hosts for its crampedness, or unkemptness, or lack of design, and in this case the fact that the apartment didn't even belong to Valentina—"so these things you see, most of them are not mine." Valentina's daughter—now child, now adult—teetered, it seemed, into the room, excited for our company and by whatever she was unsuccessfully warding off from within her late-teenaged mind. Mother and daughter had recently argued because Katya wanted to go out with her friends this evening and Valentina wanted her to stay home, and on top of this there was pressure not to reveal to us whether Katya's exams had gone well or poorly. She was aiming to be a translator, and the competition was stiff.

Valentina had prepared a small turkey for dinner and enjoined us to sit on the chairs and couch that were arranged around a tea table crammed with snacks. We made a toast and balanced our plates on our laps, while Katya sank into her chair like a piece of liquid sky, ebullient, the pupils in her eyes, I now noticed, dilated. She asked me for my most truthful opinion of Timothy Leary and of Aldous Huxley's *Doors of Perception*, on which, she said, she was doing research. What did I think about the possibility of experiencing altered states through the use of drugs? To see deeper, clearer?

"Well," I said, and as the "well" swelled upward into a condescending lilt, an avalanche's worth of feelings for both Katya and Valentina rose before me, making it almost impossible for me to finish the sentence. I felt fondly toward them and barely knew them. I felt that their longing was large and the mother/daughter dyad embattled. The child was borne alone. I couldn't imagine it for myself, this life. Was the mother in the light or in the dark of this child's life.

"Well," I chewed and cleared my throat and continued, wondering who Katya was seeing in my face through the widening pinhole of her dilated pupils, "I'm all for altered states, but I think the better challenge is achieving transformation through acts of will and mentation and creativity." (Was this going to be an I'm-high-on-life speech?) "And maybe it depends on what kind of alteration you're after. Do people really want to see things *differently* or *not at all*? I mean what does it mean to say you want to 'expand' your mind? The mind isn't a candy factory, you know, it's not made out of toffee. See, where I come from, Americans, I mean, are interested in the quick fix. I suppose I'm convinced that lasting transformation is something you have to make happen. And maybe there's an ethical dimension too—transformation doesn't happen individually but between people, like this conversation we're having could incite transformation."

Katya pondered, blinked mildly, holding her chin in her hands. She asked me to tell her more about this altered state achieved without drugs and whether I would say I was personally opposed to drugs, because talking to me would help her with her project.

Before I could answer, Valentina, who had just brought a forkful of turkey to her mouth, made a sharp sound. "Oh," she said, "oh," and bent over to collect, to our awesome, wide-eyed dismay, a large piece of her front tooth that had broken off with the bite. All of us now were turned toward the subtraction of the tooth from Valentina's mouth, from Valentina's face. I was convinced it must be painful and went into pseudo-doctor mode, asking her, as we moved together to accompany her to a mirror, if a tooth had ever simply broken off like this before. It couldn't be a good thing for a tooth to break so easily, and a front tooth at that.

The socially painful awkwardness of this moment surpassed all of the collisions that had jarred us and confusions we had navigated in Russia. Here was the awkwardness of the part that falls out of the scene, or the piece that abruptly disarranges the whole, and with it the matter of how it poises people to react or jump or shift or disappear, and the matter of how it lays bare, pulls a curtain aside, makes you *see*. Not drugs but unanticipated awkwardness had the power to induce altered states, even clarity, visibility. What it made me see was poverty—something I had read inside the lines of my immigrant grandfather's journals, pages filled with missing broken *teeth* damaged decayed teeth. I didn't perceive Valentina as impoverished, but the fact of her broken tooth made visible something fundamentally awry but otherwise hidden, a sign of a disorder of which Valentina was or wasn't aware? She never told us of her other jobs—some things you don't talk about, she said. The broken tooth was a material fact renting a hole in the evening's curtain, of grace and similitude, likemindedness and hum . . . but then the curtain was really already askew, so maybe the fact of the matter of bad teeth simply tore it right down to the floor.

Valentina's face was totally transformed by the broken tooth, making me realize how crucial teeth are to a face's arrangement, and as Valentina drew her hand to her mouth, it was partly in response to how her face must now look and partly a reflex toward the sheerly nightmarish instance of a tooth suddenly breaking. (Would it be less or more frightening for a clump of hair suddenly to come out in one's hands? One of our fellow Fulbrighters actually was losing hair, uncertain, she said, of the cause.) Valentina was most concerned that she had to attend a funeral the next day—of a twenty-year-old man, the young son of a friend who had died of a brain tumor. They had just received the news this evening, Valentina explained, of the boy's untimely death, this evening on which they did not share that news—why should they?—or show their grief but only embraced us to wish us farewell, farewell but not goodbye to Moscow and to new friends. Valentina wondered how she could possibly appear like this at the funeral, as though her disordered appearance would be an affront to the mother or would alarm when she hoped to console. I wondered if she could afford the repair and awkwardly offered to help her to pay for it if need be. In my world, there is no breakage that can't be fixed, no transformation that can't be undone by capital. I knew every day in Moscow that money was my ticket to freedom, to come, to go, to "visit," finally to leave. Valentina assured us that she could take care of it and, within minutes, recovered herself, regained her composure, and proceeded through the rest of the evening as though nothing distressing had happened at all.

afterward

If there was one constant throughout our relationships with people in Russia, it was the degree to which we lived in each other's company, unmediated, for example, by the telephone. The telephone remains rife with awkwardness and distrust in Russia—one expects to be cut off or to reach a number other than the one called, even, it seems, still to fear being overheard. Technologies meant to bridge distances haven't entirely helped us maintain contact with our Russian friends in the aftermath of our visit there. Trying to phone our teacher, I reach instead a stranger who, impatient with my poor command of Russian, yells on the other end of the line and then hangs up. Where one Russian friend has ready access to e-mail, our teacher refuses to use a computer at all, convinced that the rays it gives off might further deplete her already compromised thyroid. With Valentina, our communication is cryptic—an occasional garbled sentence might appear on our computer screens, or a brief telephone call confirms merely that each of us is "okay."

I remember now, though, that Valentina possibly relied on the phone more comfortably than our other friends in Russia. Co-workers and dormmates in Russia on the day of September 11th directed unbounded sympathy toward us, but Valentina was the only person who felt comfortable using the telephone to express immediately her response to the attack. In the weeks following, when a plane en route to the Dominican Republic appeared to have been shot down over New York, Valentina called again to express her sorrow and to see if we were all right. She invited the Fulbrighter whose hair was thinning to stay with her—a person shouldn't be alone at times like this. Remembering those phone calls from Valentina was no doubt what prompted me to call her from among all of the people we knew during the terrorist siege of a theater in Moscow in 2002. Valentina thought of us and for us, reached out to us, and yet so many aspects of who she was remained remote to me. Basic matters, like her position on Israel, for example, or her opinion of the U.S. invasion of Afghanistan, or of the war in Chechnya were never

allowed to enter our conversation. What we shared more fully was   *afterward*
the intimacy of awkwardness: the awkwardness of the mis-said, the
unsaid, the shared vulnerability of altered states.

A year has passed since our visit to Russia—or is it two?—but I
still feel unmoored. I don't always sink comfortably assured into my
homemade bed. I remember, with a degree of puzzlement, how
soundly I slept each and every night in my dorm room's Soviet-style
cot. Was my ability to sleep deeply a sign of a good set of defense
mechanisms at work, or simply the result of sheerly daily-though-
blissful exhaustion?

I've managed to get to sleep back home, when the phone rings
in the middle of the night. Valentina's voice at three a.m. is bright
and loud, she is asking how I am. I pretend wakefulness and comprehension but talk to Valentina in my sleep. I ask if everything is
okay, but I'm sure by Valentina's reaction that I am also saying
things that give away that it's the middle of the night: I speak the
language of the unconscious. Realizing that she has awakened us,
Valentina apologizes and says good-bye. I suppose it is possible to
forget the time difference between Russia and the United States, or
suddenly to figure backward rather than forward, to fail to consider how differently we are positioned on the globe. I don't know if
there was a pressing idea that Valentina was hoping to share, or if
this call was just the response to an impulse to be in each other's
company again, the way, magically, the thought will come to one to
stop the flow of a day's demands and "call," those moments we
have in which we decide to replace longing with action, and risk. To
risk awkwardness.

Awkwardness: so often it is a body that trips fast on the heels of
a surfeit of desire, to which the world can never conform, which
our bodies can barely contain, which sometimes brews to breaking
through sleep, and incipient, dream.

STALLING

tongue-tied

I felt a Cleaving in my Mind—
As if my Brain had split—
I tried to match it—Seam by Seam—
But could not make them fit—

The thought behind, I strove to join
Unto the thought before—
But Sequence ravelled out of Sound
Like Balls—upon a Floor—

—EMILY DICKINSON, #867

Ignorant, tentative, bumbling, left-handed. Crude . . . like the woman I saw in the mammoth housewares store who picked up a potted lily, tall and blooming, by its stem. She grasped its neck, lifted, then dropped it into her shopping cart where it bounced in its clutch of sandy soil and plastic. I wondered where she planned to place the plant once she got home and if the plant would continue to bloom for her or, strangulated, die. Butterfingered, fumbling, unknowing, shy. Confused at the level of categories . . . like the awkward lyrics to an Italian folksong: "Lazy Mary you'd better get up, we need the sheets for the table." Inelegant, as in a use of language. Halting.

"Being well-spoken has never been either the distinctive feature or the concern of great writers." The French philosopher, Gilles Deleuze, imagines great literature as a performative stutter, and reminds his readers of Dante, who was admired for listening to stammerers and who studied speech impediments "not only to derive speech effects from them, but in order to undertake a vast phonetic, lexical, and even syntactic creation." Creative stuttering, affirmative disjunctions: this is what distinguishes literary from other textual productions for Deleuze, and what opens literature into realms of possibility as radical as the most radical science, because it edges us into regions "far from equilibrium."

I see Emily Dickinson entering into the awkward fray that Deleuze regards so highly, because if I set myself the task of making a music that could approximate Dickinson's weird inventions with words, if I tried to conceive of a form that could truly answer to the awkward measure of her ontological project, it would begin as a stammering hymn. Dickinson, in poet, Susan Howe's words, "audaciously invented a new grammar grounded in humility and hesitation. HESITATE from the Latin, meaning to stick. Stammer." Dickinson's poetry interrupts itself, unlike Gertrude Stein's, which, like a magnificently broken record, perpetually skips. Unlike Jim Nabors, whose stutter disappeared when he sang, Dickinson's singing is an occasion for stuttering: her poetry is a stuttered song sung in church pews; the service is stalled, the prayer interrupted or endlessly deferred because of all else that needs not to be sung but silenced, whispered, or screamed.

Dickinson and Deleuze place a high premium on literature as an unarticulated middle ground of awkwardness and stammer, but many people, both writers and readers, seem to experience literature as an antidote to awkwardness. In her autobiography, Helen Keller describes literature as her "Utopia": "Here I am not disenfranchised. No barrier of the senses shuts me out from the sweet gracious discourse of my book-friends. They talk to me without embarrassment or awkwardness." Perhaps this means that characters in books are more humane than the people who write them, better fellow men than most of the people Keller encounters, because fictional characters are indifferent to her difference. Keller feels addressed without awkwardness by literature; literature is a haven that invites unmediated colloquy. In an essay on her craft, the Italian writer Natalia Ginzburg claims to feel more at home in writing than in almost any other of life's possible endeavors. "When I sit down to write, I feel supremely at ease, supremely sure of being in my own element; I use tools that are familiar and habitual and feel firm in my hands." Writing would seem to offer Ginzburg an extreme and singular comfort since any other activity, she explains, causes her pain. In fact, life's other possibilities and demands leave her in the place precisely where Keller begins: "If I do anything else, study a foreign language, say, or try to learn history or geography or stenography, if I try to speak in public or knit or travel, I'm in pain, constantly wondering how others manage those things; I always feel there must be some proper way to do them that others know and I don't. I feel deaf and blind and have a kind of deep-down nausea."

Where one set of writers values fracture, another values fluency; where one insists on mastery and command, the other opts for vulnerability, humility and what cannot be predicted. Either option— the awkward text or the graceful text, the text that stutters or the text that purrs—offers a consolation to the reader to the extent that either text confirms an alternative to the world we feel otherwise mired in, the world that can never meet our unmet longing, quell our chaos, or repair the distortions we've come to rely on to get by. This doesn't mean that reading a stuttering text will 'heal' me, but it can open a space for hearing or speaking otherwise, it can chart a breakthrough, which is altogether different from an escape, more like the birthing of a new (life) form.

I want, along with Dickinson and Deleuze, to celebrate literature as a form of stuttering, but only if literature-as-stuttering doesn't devolve into a fabulous displacement of awkwardness that might be both the cause and effect of "real" stuttering—stammering as a speech impediment—and only if literature as stutter doesn't lead us to ignore the other places in our worlds where someone *should* be stuttering but isn't.

My cousin Lou was thin, long-haired, gentle, sweet, and smart, but when he stuttered his chin would become elongated, as though reflected in a funhouse mirror, and he'd appear possessed by a demon who had suddenly tripped the button to set a maniacal jackhammer going inside his jaw. Then I'd watch him dangle across a battlefield of expression and a wild withholding, neither one a winner. Lou was three years older than I was, and a deep reader, and I remember as a child not exactly being surprised by Lou's stutter or even embarrassed for him; I did feel oddly fascinated by his problem, even rapt by the profundity of its display, but I also felt like recoiling with him because his stuttering appeared extremely painful, and occasionally I was quietly glad for how his stuttering slowed things down and cut through the family's perpetual din and jabber.   *tongue-tied*

A conversation with a stutterer requires the listener to wait a longer time than she is used to for dialogue to happen, and after waiting, if she is able, to be showered with the froth that the jaw, grinding, locked and unlocked, busily produces. A tongue pushes against the palette until, like breath gasped after a person has surfaced from underwater, a word spews. What seemed most awkward to me about my cousin's stutter was the shower of spittle that usually landed on his interlocutor's face, the exposure of his struggle (maybe especially because my greatest fear was that my own inner struggle could be laid bare), and the contortions, the virtual transformation that his face underwent in the throes of the stutter.

I remember the awkwardness of realizing at a dinner party that, in my nervousness, I'd accidentally been eating my salad with two forks rather than with a knife and fork. Awkwardness happens when something is doubled rather than balanced, this for that, right to left, forward and back, knife and fork. Was stuttering the effect of one thing blocking the other, or of two things happening at once? Would it be too silly to mention that my cousin's father's surname was "Falter"? I imagined my cousin's body overlapping with his mother's, I imagined his tongue being doubled by hers, and while I don't wish to "blame the mother," it was the case that my cousin's mother was a manic chatterer. It was as though the words she was constantly chasing as they flew from her mouth were stalled within his. He'd been called the "miracle baby," my cousin who stuttered, because my aunt had conceived him following a surgery that left her with only part of one ovary. He was her miracle baby because her first child had died suddenly of spinal meningitis at the age of two, and this led her and her husband to adopt a child, and they never conceived of the possibility of this other child, of another child born of their own bodies.

I can't speculate about the trauma that my cousin was bequeathed and that might have led him to enact a relation to loss—and what relation to loss isn't awkward?—in his mouth, with his tongue, through his face and breath, expressing and withheld, atremble—but his stutter does lead me to wonder about the circumstances of a stutter (what Deleuze might claim for the literary stutter as its "condition of possibility") and whether children born in the wake of a *tongue-tied* lost sibling are more likely candidates for stuttering.

Stuttering can suggest much more than trauma; it can speak to any number of possible cries, and it can produce, in light of its awkwardness, telling struggles.

Consider stuttering as a wish for telepathy—as a desire to bypass and short-circuit the clunky apparatus of speech, so often misconstrued.

Stuttering as a game not only with an interrupter within but with the relation of part to whole, since a stutterer tempts you to complete his sentence, even as stuttering may signify the stutterer's desire to resist your need to complete his sentences.

Stuttering as angry play, stuttering as pleasure?

A stutter says: don't make me have to say it.

A stutter says: don't leave me after I've said it. To speak is to abandon words to the air and to risk being abandoned, once said, by the person with whom you speak.

A stutter dramatizes the not-quiteness that underlies all mimicry. A stutterer is someone who is trying to imitate what he's heard, the shape of the mouth, the form of the phrase, and failing, or exaggerating the lesson to the point of grotesque imitation.

Should we deny that stutterers suffer from a biochemical neurological imbalance? Should we conclude that stuttering is really reducible to some circuitry clogged by the formation of a letter? Even if neurology plays a part, stuttering, in social contexts, *speaks*. Stuttering is productive of multiple meanings, but the awkwardness of an encounter with a stutterer, and the awkwardness of having to live with a stutter might prevent such messages from being contemplated or heard.

Some people *should* stutter but never will. Take the newscaster with upcurled lip and forward-trained eyes, glassy. She always presents triptychs of impenetrability, seamlessly sewn. This evening, for instance, in the same stream of breath, she announces without pause, that a group called "the screaming eagles," or the 47th Airborne Division has been sent to the Gulf. Continuing, intent of monotone, certitude, "we expect mass casualties on the American side should we go to war, and for the soldiers to be victims of biological and chemical weapons. Plans are already underway to perform cremations on the battlefield" since those dead will be laced with contaminants. Now she reports that five men being held pris- *tongue-tied* oner at Guantánamo Bay have tried to commit suicide. An image appears on the screen of an orange-uniformed man being carried on a stretcher by two other men. The absence of awkwardness in such uses of language is grotesque. This seamless indulgence of a non-referring use of words, this nonsense in the guise of journalism. Shouldn't she be stuttering? Shouldn't she be tongue-tied? There is no tripping up here, no break in the discourse because it is a whole. And because it is a hole.

The great writer, returning to Deleuze, "is a foreigner in his own language: he does not mix another language with his own language, he carves out a nonpreexistent foreign language within his own language. He makes the language itself scream, stutter, stammer or murmur." In the realm of great literature, "Language trembles from head to toe." Maybe what differentiates literary stuttering from real stuttering is the matter of control. Literary stuttering is manufactured stuttering, but even if it is stuttering "controlled" by an author, I am sure there is a price that must be paid by those who create such texts, aftereffects, both desirable and unpredictable, of a deliberately indulged risk. The person beset by the condition of trying to produce a word and failing, however, certainly seems less in control of the stutter. Stuttering generally isn't something one wishes to experience in his body, his relations with others, or in his world. It is something visited upon him, even if desire is operative in the creation or fact of the stutter. I once taught a text by Alice Kaplan in which she describes a French teacher of hers who also treated "immigrants with psychological trauma in their newly acquired tongue." She referred in particular to a "Vietnamese boat person" the teacher hoped to cure of a stutter. I asked my class what was at stake in curing the man of his stutter, if the stutter was a sign of provocative hesitation, of a gap pointing to that which couldn't be said but which needed to be heard. I once knew a man who was cured of his stutter and later developed an obsessive compulsive disorder. Will the people in this man's life turn toward the awkward spectacle of his running in place and respond, or turn away?

Sometimes the body insists on stalling. It requests that the show be brought to a standstill. But we appear to have no provisions available for these rebuttals against time, against flow, these attempts at interruption and breakthrough. No provisions for such intensities, such insistences, such fury, such signs of life.

If I try to stutter, I can't.

becoming

Today, instead of writing, I meticulously arranged the sundries, medicaments, slabs of soap, and types of conditioner, the tools for keeping my teeth clean, the Q-tips for swabbing wax out of a canal, the moisturizing pads for relieving hemorrhoids, and the absorbent pads for collecting menstrual blood, the nasal sprays, eye drops, nail clippers, the talcs, shower caps, sewing kits, the daily pill, and the tiny shampoo hotel samplers in my bathroom. This is what can be said for me: I neaten cabinets as a way of avoiding awkwardness, and maybe especially the awkwardness of writing. I remember my brother's rationale in refusing a game of tennis: "It only develops one arm." The same could be said for writing if, like me, you still composed with pen (just now, lead pencil) and paper. One can never really be "up" to writing because words are insurmountable. You're bound never to meet them even though you invite them daily for tea. This is what can be said for me—do you recall a parent asking, over the tops of reading glasses, "what do you have to say for yourself?" or was that only on *Leave It to Beaver*, *Dennis the Menace*, or moralizing afterschool specials in which girls wore pedal pushers but never got dirty, whose freckles were applied with makeup. Always you watched such shows on Fall early darkening afternoons, coinciding with the lessons that marked the return to school; always there was something strange in these shows like the veiny undersides of leaves fallen from trees and your own distance from your name from where you sat in a row, now spooled into yourself, coiled in a corner of the couch in red corduroys. This is what can be said for me: someday I shall suffer, and so today I arrange whatnots. I order, command, organize so that I may find the thing I am looking for rather than be made to wander. Of course, like yours, my suffering is not in my future but a condition of my being, but it's good to live as if the real catastrophe, the truly unfaceable pain is in the beyond, waiting for me, and thus, the importance now of enjoying the able-bodiedness, cognitive acumen, concentration, and precision required by putting my things in order. Amid the shifting ground and upheaval, the daily diminishment—so many lives rendered arbitrary, the untold disappearances of life—someone had carved, "Kilroy was here." So, in the bathroom, beset by the accoutrements called for by the body's upkeep, I held my ground. The conundrum that motivated such frenzied, even dogged, organizing—and don't forget the feeling of *accomplishment* that follows, even though a lover yawns, sneering, she plunks on the TV, pointing the remote, resigned, "it's only gonna get messed up again"—untouched by neatening, the conundrum was that you can't suffer and you can't not suffer.

"Did you see what I did?" I always ask Jean after these grandly neatening episodes, as if I were a martyr to our domestic happiness, because I did this for *her* too, so that she could enjoy the rightness and calm that order bespoke when really neatening was about getting her out of my way, of putting *her* in a closet in spite of my deep and eternal love for her.

What I haven't said is *how* I organized our toiletries, and this is where the true weirdness enters in, almost an undermining of the impulse to place altogether. I labeled four tin boxes purchased from Crate and Barrel (though I like to pride myself on never buying storage bins for my accumulated ware but recycling and painting the paper boxes that Stop and Shop oversized water jugs come in). I typed the words into a computer then cut them into rectangles so that they could be gained in one glance at the front of each tin box:

ALLERGY MED AND OINTMENTS

PAIN, COLD, FLU AND HEADACHE MEDICATION

FEET, EYE, FACE

STOMACH, MOUTH, AND PRESCRIPTION DRUGS

It must cross everyone's mind once, in the form of childish fascination, how the ingestion of several pills from the prescription bottle could in a flash end your life. In some dark corner of childhood memory, the news is summoned again as it was one early 1960s afternoon through the stippled speaker of a portable radio in the local hardware store. It was the era of Vietnam and Civil Rights, but I became haunted by the news that a woman had killed herself by drinking "lye" and no one could explain what lye was but that it was related to soap. So why did adults threaten to wash my mouth out with soap if I should lie? That day in my memory also bears the zinnias in my father's garden whose petals, I saw, were shaped and colored like the metal slabs of my toy xylophone. That day too was marked by the regularity with which the black tip of a shoelace attached to red shoes slapped the linoleum floor when the shoelace came undone. Such organizing principles can make no sense to others: "there's no rhyme or reason" my partner says when I show her the ordered display. Each person's obituary should describe his organizing principles and thereby his way of making art out of awkwardness, the awkwardness of being.

3

SURGING

unbecoming

A sad size a size that is not sad is blue as
every bit of blue is precocious.
—GERTRUDE STEIN, *Tender Buttons*

Children grow, so much so that they sometimes outgrow their elders. Children outgrow their parents and outgrow themselves, and sometimes, gravest awkwardness, children are old for their age, as if they have arrived in the world grown, wise beyond their years, precocious or prodigious, awkward anomalies.

A bright young Russian student tells me about her awkwardness. Julia has always been tall, and she cites her "build" as a source of ongoing discomfort: "My friends are shorter than me, and one of the most actual troubles for me is that I feel so awkward when I embrace those miniature girls. I always wanted to be small, and when I studied at the gymnasium I was very glad that there were two or three girls *much* taller than me (most boys of my generation are more or less short)." One doesn't wish to appear out of sync, physically, with one's age, and it was my fate to be one of those "minis" of whom Julia speaks, the word brilliantly indicative of her feeling of being gargantuan. I have never "looked my age," or maybe I only looked my age for one seamlessly serene year when I was eight; no, that year people probably took me for three. Which must have been why my grandfather altered his letter to me. He had decided it was time to call me Mary rather than the diminutive Mimi because, as he put it, "you are growing ~~to be a big~~ up to be a nice girl." My grandfather edited out "big," because in point of fact I wasn't big but small, always first or second in a line organized by height for the May Day procession. But of course a girl shouldn't be big—better that she grow up to be "nice"—in which case my grandfather was trying to be true to a gracious but bigoted social order.

It's almost unbearable to watch so-called "women's gymnastics" in the Olympics. Men's gymnastics features men and even seems to require adult male bodies. But women's gymnastics features girls beset by so many contradictions that the girls risk appearing more than awkward—perverse. Here are girls so greatly grown that they must also be somehow shorn or made *smaller*. The girl is strong: see her thigh muscles developed out of proportion with the rest of her body. The girl is strong: see her pull herself up to the bar, or run, surging and powerful, to vault. The girl is strong, and since you therefore might forget that she is female, she has not "dolled herself up" (because this is something a woman who can never be young again does) but made herself into a doll: her barrette and ponytail, each to a girl, not a single girl transgressing, even though the hair must affect her balance and pull her down. The girl is much stronger than you or I. In fact, she exceeds us in her self-mastery, skill, focus, balance, and command. And so the sport requires that she follow each show of strength with a grotesquely coquettish cutesy-pie flourish. The girl really *isn't* a dancer—she's an athlete—but she's been made, in between flips, to pretend to dance. Where *does* one draw the line between the circus and "women's" gymnastics? Paragons of motor coordination, why do they let their wrists go limp, their ponytail bob, suddenly for their buttocks to jut like a bustle and their chests too? Lest we forget they are *just* little girls?

What does a girl gymnast "become" in later life? What does a shotputter—strangely grunting sportsman yoked to a metal ball—dream?

The requisite out of syncness of so many girl gymnasts might make a person blink—because you can only apprehend them with awe temporarily—whereas the children who compete in spelling bees make me want to cry. An obsession with spelling can transport a child temporarily beyond circumstance. It's a great insulator for the already geeky, which is to say unadjusted-to-averageness child to develop his spelling muscle over and above everything else. The ability to spell words no one else can spell, let alone pronounce, define, or use, takes them, unfortunately, to a stage where they are charged with responsibility beyond their ken, spectacularized for their eccentric abilities, made to compete with themselves, and pressured by their parents. Often they wear braces and wire-rimmed aviator-style glasses. These are the bored kids who discover in a game of Clue that you can actually write with the lead pipe miniature murder weapon. An oddly American competition, the spelling bee can only be entered into by children because the spelling bee is all about precocity on display.

"When I am in peace with myself (unfortunately it happens not ever so often)," Julia continues, "I regard myself with a good deal of humor. When I am not in peace with myself—it seems to be my usual state—I am inclined to consider myself a pitiful nonentity. (Does not it also bear a kind of awkwardness?)" Here's a new awkwardness announced: the awkwardness of unbecoming.

precocious

There is awkwardness born of ignorance and there is awkwardness born of knowing too much. Precociousness refers to an untimely occurrence. Shakespeare's Macduff, prematurely born, was literally precocious, but the word's root, "coquere," means to cook. Figuratively, a precocious child is one *cooked too soon*. Originally, the word was only used in reference to flowers and fruits prematurely ripened. The problem with apprehending human beings this way is the attribution of appropriate knowledge, understanding, desire, and skill to a particular age: its presumption of a developmental norm.

A prodigy is a kind of precocious child, but where "precocity" as a word lends itself to nuance, "prodigy" is bound to its untold roots. In an astronomical journal of 1816, we read, "Were not comets formerly dreaded as awful prodigies intended to alarm the world?" and who can forget John Winthrop's designating the probably miscarried offspring of heretical Ann Hutchinson her "forty prodigies"? The early sources remind us that a prodigy, the word that we use to describe a child in possession of an unusually highly developed skill, talent, or aptitude, is also a portent of evil or ill: a bad sign.

Exceptionalism seems historically linked in the English language with dread.

While child "prodigies" might be celebrated, the word's unconscious suggests that the child brain or body out of bounds can't be good. Having disrupted a fundamental chronology, the prodigy comments on, even tampers with a future: who knows what's next?!

"Prodigy" and "monster" tend in the same direction: monster hails from "monere," to warn, and the prodigy, like the monster, edges into the territory of the non-human.

Jamesian

Nowhere in American letters is the affiliation of danger and precociousness, the fine line between precociousness and prodigiousness, more fully indulged than in the work of Henry James. The child prematurely initiated into knowledge is a horror. The children in *What Maisie Knew* and *The Turn of the Screw* most immediately come to mind, but the theme was to form the center of a lesser known novel titled, appropriately, *The Awkward Age*. In his 1895 notebook, James planted the seed for his tale:

> The idea of a little London girl who grows up to "sit with" the free-talking modern young mother—reaches 17, 18, etc.—comes out and, not marrying, has to "be there"—and, though the conversation is supposed to be expurgated for her, inevitably hears, overhears, guesses, follows, takes in, becomes acquainted with horrors. A real little subject in this, I think—a real little situation for a short tale— if circumstance and setting is really given it. A young man who likes her—wants to take her out of it—feeling how she's exposed, etc. . . . The young man hesitates, because he thinks she already knows too much; but all the while he hesitates she knows, and learns, more and more. He finds out somehow how much she *does* know, and, terrified of it, drops her: all of her ignorance, to his sense, is gone. . . . The type of the little girl who is conscious and aware . . .

Treating this subject was almost more than James could manage. The idea of the precocious child proved so productive and uncontrolled that the short tale morphed into a very long novel; in James's own words, the book itself grew into a "monster." "Its proposed scale was the limit of a small square canvas," but it grew, James explains in his preface to the New York Edition, out of proportion.

To the calcified adult, the idea of the not yet habituated, or unfully formed child is tantalizing. Perhaps we make a child precocious by underestimating or overestimating what a child can know. The dictionary, in other words, only tells part of precociousness's story with its emphasis on a temporal model of being when precociousness has everything to do with normative relations of power and knowledge. So in James, precocious children exert a *range* of possibility; they never fall into one and the same category. Though James was certainly interested in personalities that figure as ciphers for other people's fiendish machinations—corrupting innocence— he also fashioned children who are anything but tabula rasa to be programmed by adults, children who are clever maneuverers in their own right at the same time that they are vulnerable, sometimes to the point of extinction.

What would happen if we thought of the problem of precociousness not as one of innocence corrupted or consciousness prematurely acquired but as the condition of the child who makes vivid an original or second sight that, apprehended by adults, is not encouraged or given free play but is pressed, instead, *into the service of* a knowledge of adult "horrors"?

What is knowledge's proper time, space, body, milieu?

adolescent

The "awkward age" is generally understood as the aptest phrase for adolescence. It presumes that knowledge of (hetero) sex is the grandest, most identity-affirming knowledge that a human can gain. It supposes that sex is only fully known as an experience, or it confuses knowledge with experience of a singular consummative act. What makes adolescence awkward, we assume, is its transitional aspect, but also the varying degrees to which one feels ready— mentally, emotionally, physically—for the move into pubescence or child-bearing capability. The adolescent self is imagined to be operating simultaneously at different speeds, thus awkwardly timed and tuned: the body not yet caught up to the heart's desire; the emotional capacity still too underdeveloped to be adequate to physiological longing; the dream of a future outstripped by the reality of circumstances and the lugubriousness installed by underworked but newly activated hormones; the psyche wanting to defy gender but the culture insisting on a habituated placement; a preoccupation with death on the eve of the possibility of "generating life"; a sudden acceleration of expectation and responsibility even though you remain four feet tall.

This is the way "the awkward age" is typically construed, when the awkward age, really, is the end of experimentation and ushering into concrete.

gargantuan

Imagine pretending not to know what one knows—this is grass, this is a hand, this is what I feel. It would be impossible to live in such a state of perpetual startledness, and yet highly selective knowledge, perceptual "screening out" of stimuli, denials of the known—from the thing that defines one's most important relations with others to the daily mayhem of war—seem to be what get us through each day. I'm eating dinner at a friend's house who uses oversized dinnerware. My fork is heavy and better-suited to a weekend project involving large metal parts and hinges, maybe even a soldering mask in the garage, than the application of delicate food to a tastebud. Looking down into the immense girth of my plate makes me dizzy: a piece of spinach seems to swirl there at the center of an ever contracting vortex. Large dinnerware makes me feel awkward. Not because it fails to suit my compact frame, but for the way it denies that food will enter my gullet and bloodstream, that food will produce narratives (and gas, maybe, too), and stir memory, relax or stimulate me, fatten or sate or move me to want more, to have an appetite. Large dinnerware introduces formality into rooms where intimacy should rule. I feel in such situations that my host is trying to shield me from my food, making it unnecessarily hard for me to have it.

Awkwardness is all about what we let each other see and *gargantuan* know, what we let ourselves see and know, with the end result of figuring each other, figuring a self to others, and, as in gymnastics and spelling bees, *disfiguring* too. When the relation to knowing involves children and adults, the adults can always claim both to know more and to be better at hiding what they don't want the child to know.

Adults are always clairvoyant.

Some, like my marvelous grandmother, had a "little bird" who visited her and told her things about me that my grandmother couldn't otherwise know.

The space was quiet, spectral, and our own when, at the end of the long white tin-topped kitchen table, my grandmother, mother, and I would find ourselves alone. The space was jewel-like, the table-top pearly and then opalescent when, in receipt of a cup or saucer, of a wobbly lemon or the skin of an eggplant, a silver spoon splashed into coffee, colors fuzzy at their edges would spray the table's surface now like feathers. My grandmother had a resigned jollyness about her, my mother, the quiet desperation of a person enduring the dawn of an uncertain marriage. I had the fervency of a climber into a chair, an open-eyed interest in any word that might fall from my grandmother's bounty, and the desire to watch as if through towering bamboo shoots even though the air was clear here and perfumed with basil. In an atmosphere quiet, true, and licorice-scented, the table's cloud formation expanded like a field at the end of which leaves on a fig tree opened like hands. In those moments full with a sense of morning and the endless possibility of a day's opportunity, in those moments of having arrived together at the end of my grandmother's kitchen table, the little bird would enter.

I had ways of picturing this feathery confidante. Sometimes she was a bluebird and sometimes a robin. She was always, chest thrust forward, not exactly "bright" but distinguished, not just any bird but a bird among birds, a bird that spoke to humans, my grand-mother's familiar. Sometimes I pictured her delivering her messages to my grandmother while she hung clothes outdoors on the line. The "little bird" lands on the clothesline to peer directly into my grandmother's eyes, or she lands on her shoulder, where, interrupt-ing my grandmother's train of thought, she whispers especially *gargantuan* pressing news into her ear. The little bird isn't a carrier pigeon for every man's use but a go-between who, in addition to carrying on average bird life, exists as magical kin to my grandmother and me. In winter, the bird, I fancy, taps her beak on the kitchen window. Her tiny talons don't morph into gloved hands that she can rap with like cartoon characters I know. Being a "real" bird, she raps with her beak. I believe in the little bird and I love the idea of a bird that seeks one out with messages. I even mildly enjoy the idea of a little bird observing me without my knowing it and then reporting to my grandmother. But I'm also somewhat alarmed by my grandmother's superhuman ability to know about things that she hasn't herself witnessed. I know there is no such creature.

A little bird told me you're not eating your spinach. A little bird told me you fought with your brothers. A little bird told me you went sledding without wearing earmuffs. A little bird told me you lost a tooth. At some point I realized that my mother was my grandmother's spy, the little bird the sign of the ability of adults to tyrannize children with their own higher knowledge of them even as the little bird retained the feeling of a furry chick warmed in the hands between us. At what point does the little bird go from being a plump and highly articulate friend to a stout figure of regret and betrayal framed like a statesman or erstwhile diplomat. (There should be a place on the wall of family photos for him conferring honorary membership in the clan.)

Never has the adjective "little" done so much work as it does in describing the bird who sees all. Big Bird is clearly a bird all out of proportion to itself. Big Bird is clearly a man in clown costume, a real bird turned sluggish and dopey, a gargantuan feathered creature to look up to *and* laugh at. An alternative to real oversized creatures—adults—oversized puppets like Big Bird and Barney are benign giants. Why, then, did adults invent not just a bird but a "little" one to serve the fantasy of adult clairvoyance?

If the bird is little, the adult can dominate it; it is employed by her at the same time that it inhabits—intimately, cheerfully?—the world of the little girl. But where diminutiveness exposes the child, littleness camouflages the bird so that he can properly spy.

The little bird is the precocious creature that one never can become.

The little bird as a phantasm of fun is meant to protect the child from the too horrible knowledge that adults observe-in-order-to-shame children.

In Italian, you can make a thing or a being tinier and tinier, teenier and infinitesimally teeniest by adding pretty sounding suffixes—"ini," "issimo." As the thing or being gets smaller, it gets cuter *and* more loveable. When one is a child, a thought can grow to great proportions in one's head; a watermelon seed too can, if swallowed, grow into a watermelon inside your stomach or, worse, into a hairy watermelon vine creeping up through your esophagus and out of your mouth, only then to emit a watermelon bound to pull your tiny figure right down to the ground.

prodigious

One of my father's favorite—or more to the point, *only*—"game" was something he called "E.S.P."

"See if you know what I'm thinking. I'm thinking of a number, a color, what is it?"

E.S.P. was a power that you either had or didn't have. It had nothing to do with book learning (my father hadn't finished high school) but it could be cultivated if you were so blessed. One of my happiest memories of my father is of him smiling to hear the words orange, purple, blue streaming in correct succession out of my mouth, the very colors, one after another, that he had been thinking. Of course nothing can ever be verified in a game of E.S.P. Was my father pretending in order to please me? That wasn't his way. Usually he was a gnarled vine clinging to the couch, set before the TV, unwilling to share what he knew—of "current events" in newspapers for example. I was good with poems but had difficulty interpreting the daily news, and this was the assignment in Social Studies class. Asking my father for help required a wrench, and pruning sheers. Every now and then, he'd unexpectedly release himself. Lurching, he would lunge uncoiled toward me and yell an answer to my question about the news.

E.S.P. was something my father prided himself on ever since, as a little boy, he guessed a winning number for his grandfather in a

South Philadelphia numbers game. Twice. My great-grandfather had asked my father, "Joey, give me a number." And the number that came into my father's *four*-year-old head was *"fourfourfour."* The number won, and won so big that my father earned a new fancy 1920s Little Lord Fauntleroy suit. The next day, my great-grandfather asked his new boy partner to guess again. "444," my father said, and his grandfather replied, "Joey, is that all you can give me? The same number that you gave me yesterday?" My great-grandfather failed to play the number a second time in spite of what turned out to be another proper guess. My father never guessed a winning number for my great-grandfather thereafter, but the event offered the hope of special knowledge. And yet could this be just another instance of the misapplication of a child's second sight, the misrouting of a, so to speak, extra sense?

My father returns to that moment of magical affirmation of knowledge by "playing E.S.P." with his own children, but it's not clear to what end. Spending too much time in the world of E.S.P. makes me mistrust the real resources we have to rely on for living in and interpreting the world, as though I am being asked to reach with something other than everything I have at my disposal, to pull a rabbit out of my father's head. 444 must mean something for my father—he tells me of how the number followed him on a job site one morning and then, to his astonishment, appeared on TV as a winning number later that night. Is the number a sign that my father might be psychic if only he could follow through on his skill toward winnings? Or is it a sign that my great-grandfather is visiting—he's trying to give my father another chance to win on 444, guilty for not believing him, his child prodigy.

obscene

I love to play with children. I even feel myself opening into goofiness, giddiness, the imaginative reverb of moving in untoward directions and laughing belly laughs, feeling the weight suddenly of my adult body ecstatically breathless, feeling the feather breath of the child graze my cheek—my niece likes to whisper in my ear—or making up games without boards as my father had, games requiring words and story face to face. Games in which truth emerges in the space between what one sees and what one imagines so that banality may be transformed into a source of unexpected knowledge and of pleasure.

I delight in telling the children in my life things that aren't true: "I saw you waving to us from the garden when the plane was coming in for a landing," I tell Natasha, age six. "I looked down, and I said, 'Look, Jean, I think that little speck of purple is Natasha, and she's throwing a Frisbee!'" Natasha seems to like the fantasy of being seen from an impossible distance, and I like to find ways to say I was looking for or thinking of her. Just as often, she enjoys proving the impossible wrong: "Your cat didn't really talk to you 'cause *cats don't talk*!"

Maybe intimacy isn't forged out of what we mutually recognize but what we mutually imagine: exceeding the laws governing what we know, Natasha and I are drawn into a circle not of each other's confidence but each other's drive, desire, reach, dream. Each other's impossibility. Each other's awkwardness. Like many children, she takes a degree of pleasure in things scatological. So I offer her one day the beginnings of a vast lexicon for articulating "gas." A "silencer," I explain, is a word for a fart that makes no sound but whose aroma is deadly. The axiom "He who smelt it dealt it" could prove useful among friends when, pointing to you, a fellow asks with intent to embarrass, "Did you fart?" My friend, Arthur, Natasha's father, isn't always pleased with my lessons especially when Natasha tells him that she thinks the fart lexicon is the most important thing she has ever learned.

In a darker recess, edging into more dangerously tabooed territory, my niece Justine learns accidentally from me the word "bush." She's asked to "have a sleepover" with Jean and me at our bed and breakfast when, looking up from her blown-up mattress on the floor, she screams out loud to say she has seen between Jean's legs walking past. "I saw Jeannie, Mary, I saw her naked butt." "Did you see her bush," I ask, no chance of taking back now what I realize could read as a dirty word. When we arrive at her mother's house, Justine is still talking, to her mother's dismay, about Jean's bush, so I explain that really there are no very good words for female genitalia but that she may not want to use "bush" in public because *inappropriate* some people think it's not a nice word. The most exact appellations for the part of the anatomy she had glimpsed, I explain, are "pubis," "pudenda," or "vagina." We agree that the latter is much too technical a word for such a personal part of the body. And then Justine explains that she still prefers "bush" because of how it puns on "Bush, A-mir-ika's president" (Justine is Canadian). We had been watching the democratic convention that week, it was clear to her that Bush to our mind was an unnamable figure guilty of unnamable acts against humanity. We had also that week introduced Justine to the idea of homonyms, cousin to puns.

As a lesbian, I bear the unfortunate onus of being perceived as a potential corruptor of children, but I don't manifest as reaction formation a need to shield my small friends from dirt. What's curious to me is how I try to protect the children that I know from knowledge of my sadness. There's an undercurrent of sadness today, a blanket of darkness that I don't want the child I am playing with to see. Rather than cut it off, could I let it come out in the collage we are making together? That doesn't occur to me as an option. Is the sadness merely the ghost of the adults I observed as a child who pretended to play with me but who were distracted by their pain and who did not protect me from it? A child's brilliant inner life may not be bright. A child's wondering isn't always benign. A child is involved daily in novel combinations and assemblage. Having not learned to choose or to fend off, there's not much that a child *doesn't* see.

inappropriate

We are awkward when we are in pain because our pain cannot be part of us, *incorporate*. We are awkward because we don't trust each other to know what to do with knowledge of our pain, to know our pain and still remain in each other's company. Awkwardly, we avoid our unavoidable pain, awkwardly denying.

"Hasn't it seemed as if we really can't overcome conversational habits so thoroughly formed?" one character asks another in James' *The Awkward Age*, and I ask myself the same in the moments that form the space of what will probably be the last time I will see the face with its grizzled brightness, the hand slicking back the hair, the man still wishing he could bring something to his mouth to soothe, *inappropriate* like cigarette or booze, the coolness of a Robert Mitchum, the strong quiet type, the fixer or the gardener, the man ever on the move to the next place that would be better, the fingernails like ivory of piano keys, the nervous tic contorting his face like an accordion. To my mind, there was always something gentle and elegant about my lover's father, dying now, in spite of the years of belittling the children, his nasty harangues delivered from the far end of the kitchen table where he has always sat and sits now still like a roosting bat or white snowy owl always sure of its vantage—a lookout onto the world that he never felt more a part of than he did as a soldier stationed in Germany, a radio man in World War II, since which time he has only been able to be tired of the world, perched slightly above it looking out. But what would it mean for any of us to be part of it?

"He likes you not a whit less than he likes her . . ." a character with the diminutive name of Mitchy says to a character with the more distinguished name of Van (short for Vanderbank) in *The Awkward Age*: "Of course he wants—as I do—to treat you with a tact!" "Oh, it's all right," Vanderbank, immediately said, "Your 'tact'—yours and his—is marvelous, and Nanda's [speaking of the girl who is supposed to be most awkward] greatest of all."

James uses the word "tact" as though it were a *thing*, a wig or glove, a character armor, neurosis, or the veranda of one's being: the balcony that we don't dare step out onto but that nevertheless defines us.

I am sitting at my father-in-law's death chair. It sounds crude, I know, and disrespectful, and what right does a non–blood relative have anyway to record a dying man's physiognomy or tell a strange audience about his life? Death chair sounds too executional but it is the case that I've never seen my lover's father supine and even now, attached as he is to an oxygen machine with enough rubber tubing to enable him to go for a mile long walk if he could but he can't because breathing itself is too much of an effort let alone more elaborate movement, like walking, he insists on sitting rather than lying down. Ron was prone to long sighs and flabbergasted high-pitched sounds even before the emphysema and now cancer; since I've known him he has seemed perpetually engaged in trying to wake up, to rouse *inappropriate* himself. Sitting in his chair, Ron really hasn't gotten out of bed, and yet he importantly has because when he can't get out of bed he will truly be dying. We have sped to our places at the table, four weeks earlier than expected, because we don't want to miss the chance to talk with him before he has slipped out of consciousness, but no momentum can be spun from the momentousness of the occasion of Ron's transitioning out of life. Is our passage into death the awkwardest of all or the most "natural"?

People who are ill may be forced to do things to their bodies that appear uncouth to those who are well. Ron periodically moves the tube that has been resting inside his nostrils into his mouth. He gets more oxygen that way, but I, in the land of the breathing want to say, "Don't ya' wanna wipe that off before putting it in your mouth? Or maybe excuse yourself?" We're not living in the same world, the same body, so why should we talk to each other? We don't. We're tactful, insular even though death must be as exuberantly, as profoundly *active* as birth. As in birth, a force beyond you overtakes you, but you also have to push; a process is in motion requiring muscle and mind: it takes an effort to die.

Ron is involved in this process, novel to each of us, and common to all, and we have arrived to be with him, around him, nearby when he proceeds to tell me as if this were not an extraordinary meeting, of the origins of the phrase, "cold enough to freeze the balls off a brass monkey."

I have heard this tale numerous times in the past from Ron, though I admit never to having fully listened to all of the explanation's details. It makes me uncomfortable in the first place to have to think together out loud with my father-in-law about "balls" of any kind, be they brass or flesh. It all has something to do with a mechanism for holding cannon balls called a "monkey" (who knows why?) used on ships, and the brass in freezing weather contracting thus causing the "balls," which are made of iron and stacked pyramidally atop the monkey, to fall off of it. Now I want to know like never before what kind of "tact" it is to listen to the brass-balled monkey tale over and over and over again, never admitting to having heard it before, even to pretend to be hearing it for the first time. We are sitting in the same place we were yesterday. We haven't moved. So unchangingly stock-still are we that the palliative care

nurse laughs when she appears each day to see us sitting in the exact *inappropriate*
same places at the table, slumped into the same postures, trying to
be present. I don't know what so delights Ron about that tale—
perhaps I should have asked him. Maybe he likes the way an apparently dirty phrase takes its origin in something far removed from
prurience; or how you could never *guess* such an origin; or how we
say things never knowing what we mean. Ron tells me of brass balls
as though he were addressing an army buddy—an intimate—but I
can only hear it for what it doesn't say. How it keeps us apart from
his pain. "Not the brass balls story again!" I want to scream. "I've
heard it a thousand times. I've never understood it, and I don't
know why you tell it. Can't we instead find a way to say good-bye?"
To say what we mean to each other. To say what it means that this
is the mode of your leave-taking. To reflect together on your life?

I don't know why I should want more or different because the
brass balls story could be just a way for Ron to say "I am," and to
ask us to witness that he still *is*, the man he was yesterday. "He's in
a lot of pain, but he's putting on a good face for us," Jean's brother
concludes, thus making me wonder what is gained by the necessity
or compulsion to be tactful on one's deathbed.

Death of course is precocious: it always comes too soon; it
always knows more than we do. I remember how long it takes Ron
to tell a story. "Is that the end?" I asked Jean's mother many years
ago when she too was alive, asking her to help me find the right
reaction, to laugh at the proper junction like a good daughter-in-
law, though I wasn't yet out as such. "Not even he knows if it's the
end," she said, "and only he knows if it's meant to be funny or not."
Ron's stories are slow. Painstakingly riddled with long pauses, they
offer an alternative being in time to what he refers to as the "rat
race," making me consider that our last time together was more
significant and less protected than I feared. I remembered now how
on one of those hot, hard-to-breathe days, following my bafflement
over getting a new short-wave radio to work, he told me about the
nature of radio waves and recommended rigging an antenna with a
piece of copper wire. I remember his pausing to raise the volume on
his own radio to tell us something we never knew: how a particular
aria from *The Pearl Fishers* was one of his favorites.

Anything effortful is awkward, especially when something auto-

inappropriate nomic comes to require thought. In Ron's rooms, where breathing is laborious, sounds are raspy, sights are muffled. The extra oxygen in the room sometimes makes my eyes feel husklike and still. "I think I would panic," I say to Jean's sister, "if I had to deal with losing my breath as frequently as Ron." "No, you wouldn't," she matter-of-factly replies. "They've taught him what to do when he's short of breath. It's just a matter of learning what to do, a kind of exercise. You get used to it, and you do it." I still think I'd panic, and thus I marvel at the slow and steady control that Ron exerts over his own loss of breath, how, almost like a Zen Master, he adjusts to his sped-up breathing and rides it toward a deeper intake, a fuller outtake, until balance replaces struggle for a time.

Being around Ron now, suddenly the world seems rampant with dangerously playful forms of loss of breath. Justine holds her breath, a self-made game, whenever en route to Vancouver, we pass through a tunnel. Hayley Mills, in the movie I want to share with Justine for its outlaw girl vibe, holds her breath underwater longer than anyone could. Her eyes are crossed while a girl stands on her shoulders to make it seem to another girl whom they lure that the water she is walking toward is shallow. Who knows what occasion would prompt me as a child to pretend to stop breathing, to incite my mother's panic, attention, or concern, to trick her into noticing me. Always I performed this feat beneath the dining-room table. A bee sits panting on the windowsill, but insects evidently are lungless. Unlike humans, they breathe through tiny valves at the sides of their bodies, and they can reserve oxygen for later use. Air flow affects their buoyancy and even through some complex chemical process involving gases, governs their size; it keeps them from becoming insect-monsters.

While visiting Ron, one night I dream I have buried my own father, alive. I've buried my father alive and the voice in the dream says that I "haven't understood his work." Has he understood mine? His was a work that led to a lung disorder too—asbestosis was the resultant hazard to him and a number of fellow workers exposed. Tiny filaments the body can't eject perpetually scratch at the lungs' inner lining. Henry James's typist found his prose to be free and easy, flowing. But anyone can see how it is heavy, choked, and smothered—to turn a Jamesian phrase, "a smothered rapture."

I feel suffocated by the extent to which I won't do anything to alter *cut off*
the terms of the conversation with my father-in-law even given this
one last chance. There is no rapture there.

cut off

In any one minute of any given day, a great deal of chatter is
produced around some subjects and utter silence on others, just as
whole days themselves pass unremarked while others become lodged
not only in the memory but even in the body as hyper-significant
episodes in the narrative that composes a life. So the day on which
I last saw, not my father-in-law, but my grandfather—a day of
childhood knowing not-knowing, knowing too much too soon or
too little, a day grotesque and awkward and sad, a day not without
play, but rife, from a future vantage, with absence—is lodged but
not static, variegated but strangely unfinished, unsatisfied. It's only
a coincidence that my grandfather was dying of lung cancer too.
Nothing magical can be made of it but just the plainness of a deter-
minism: both men were smokers. My grandfather almost always
had a cigarette—filterless Camel—hanging out of his mouth. Even
when he played the mandolin or guitar the cigarette dangled
between his lips, and it was fun for us children to guess how long a
line of ash would last at the end of a diminishing butt before falling
onto the rug that my grandmother had just vacuumed, or right
smack into the hole at the center of the instrument that my grandfather strummed. If you—bored, curious—tilted the melon-shaped
mandolin and peered inside its belly, its lung, you would see a small
pile of ashes there.

I had seen my grandfather in the process of dying. I knew he
was gravely ill because his clothes no longer fit and his teeth seemed
more visible as he grimaced in pain, and he stopped eating, moved
in infinitesimally slowed-down increments, and lost his temper—
something I had never known him to do in the past. Instead of
working in the garden, he was lucky if he could sit in it now, and
one day our lessons came to an abrupt end when, failing still to play
a Haydn piece for two violins in proper time I jumped to hear my
grandfather hit rather than play the strings of his instrument.as with

cut off   a hammer. He strummed, violently producing a blunt sound, then winced as though something had broken—a bone in his shoulder?—and, rising, turned the mandolin face down on the dining room table before which our chairs and music stands were set.

He had chosen me to be his fellow mandolinist or I had responded to the call to receive some share of that almost other-worldly knowledge at age eight—music of a far off land—that he always awkwardly bore. I don't remember how I dressed myself in the week following the episode of my last lesson, the day on which we were summoned to take my grandfather away from his home, and away from us forever. We were summoned to a momentous occasion that I was not made fully to understand, leaving me to wonder now why the children were brought to the table of the occasion only to be kept from being seated at it in the end. Somehow it was decided—the inability to swallow maybe, because the radiation together with the tumor had displaced my grandfather's esophagus—that on this day he would enter the hospital and never return home.

He had shown me blights in the garden, mold on roses, and the green horned caterpillar that ate tomato plants; I knew it was a battle to keep living things alive and my grandfather was gifted in this way because he often brought other people's dead plants back to life and cultivated plants unsuited to northeastern American climes. Once he accidentally stepped on an Easter chick belonging to one of his children and, realizing he had crushed it under his shoe, spent the day supine on the couch like a depressed neurasthenic. I knew that life could crumble. I was reminded each year in church on a particular Wednesday that we were all of us "made of" dust, and on another day, kneeling amid ashen-scented incense, I felt a priest's hands bring a waxen cross, two candles tied together to form an x, up to my throat. Who knows why a bristled and burly old man should have been allowed to touch such objects to my silken neck except to fend off the prospect of forgetting how to swallow. My grandfather, it was determined, must go to the hospital because he could no longer swallow and he did not want to burden my grandmother with the bodily intrusion of his death.

That day I played a game called "horsey" with my cousin in my grandfather's shoe-repair shop as though it had been a day like any other. My cousin loved horses, and so we devised a game to suit her fancy in which one person played the horse and the other person, chasing the horse around with a pretend lasso or a stick, tried to mount her. The person who played the horse (usually my cousin) got to "neigh," and act as though she needed to be fed. I probably wasn't wearing a dress, but I remember yellow pleats unfolding like a clown collar, ankle socks, and white patent leather shoes when, readying my uncle's car for departure, my cousin accidentally closed the door, slammed it really, with my finger caught inside. I didn't know that a door could close entirely on a finger and not take the finger off, but the finger remained attached to me though it instantly grew to twice its size and throbbed to shades of reddish blue. I couldn't have been dressed as I remember because I was twelve years old that year, not six, but in my memory I was young, too young, just a baby. Really I was a tough little girl, and I accepted the pain when my grandmother pressed a cube of ice wrapped in a linen dish towel to my hand. My grandmother wasn't known for treating pain with soothing salves; she attacked you *and* the illness: in this case, it was as though she were coming at my finger with a hammer. Sitting at the end of the kitchen table while she applied the ice, I screamed for all of us, I cried not just a little but a lot, and then swallowed my tears, glad that my finger was still attached.

I heard someone say that my grandfather needed to show my uncle, my mother's brother-in-law, the suit he wanted to be laid out in. And then I remember that my grandfather needed a great deal of help getting into the car, and then blurred objects through a car window, difficulty in looking ahead because I didn't know where we were going, and seeing the back of my grandfather's head, hatted with the kind of hat no man wears anymore but all men did then—a stiff brown hat that came to two soft peaks with a dip in the middle like a buttocks or like breasts. And there the memory ends or, rather, I can't go to the end of the memory to a good-bye, a vanishing, not even a glance or a wave. As a child, though I wasn't a child but a person on the cusp of adolescence, awkwardly aged, betweentimes, I still somehow was not allowed to visit my grandfather in the hospital, a rule that pretends to protect children but that really is about keeping them out of care's way. Unprotected, instead, the child is both left and left out. What she already knows is not given the full-bodied integrity of seeing, feeling, and being near. Knowledge is left to hang like a limb without a tree. Knowledge is not allowed to arrive.

I remember a scene from a film. Though I've forgotten the film, I've always retained this scene: a man is lying in a bed breathing the labored breath of the dying. The room is bare except for a woman who attends him, not treating him exactly but sitting in a chair neither weeping with self-pity nor gripping his hand in mawkish regret, she is simply sitting with him, watching and waiting, present to the efforts of his final breaths. A young boy enters the room—a very little boy, maybe five, maybe six—looks at the man, and, frightened, asks the woman—his grandmother?—what is wrong with him. The woman takes the child into her lap and says, "Nothing is wrong with him, something very natural is happening to him, he's dying, that's all." Then the boy rests his head on the grandmother's shoulder until, watching with her, he falls asleep.

It could be said that in the name of awkwardness I had been protected from seeing my grandfather die and in another sense protected from saying good-bye. And my grandfather, he too had been protected from knowledge of my frailty, my vulnerability, my body, my humanness. Midway through the letter in which my grandfather had decided to address me with my proper, grown-up name, he added, "I shall not say anything of your wounded temple and the dark eye that was caused by an accident which I had not known . . ." thus wishing to inform me that he was not told of the accident of my fall from the diving board. The reasons, I'm sure, that parents of children keep knowledge of harm that has befallen their children from their *own* parents are many and complex, but in this case I suspect that the adults imagined they were protecting my grandfather who already had had more than his share of pain from further sorrow. If he only just learned of the accident upon seeing my bruise, however, it must have been an awkward shock. You are growing up or have grown up too quickly, the address of his letter seems to say, as though the accident had ushered me into adulthood and a new identity. No one, of course, wants to be changed by accident, but by choice. One should ever be becoming rather than finished or cut off, but becoming needn't require a continuum or a logic or a line. Leaps and bounds should be allowed, and awkward inconsistencies.

susceptible

Does access to certain knowledge violently expose a child or nurture in her an appetite for understanding? The awkward age we say is the impressionable age: "Give me a girl at an impressionable age and she is mine for life!" were Miss 's scarily tantalizing words. Still, susceptibility could be something worth cultivating rather than something worth losing, an aptitude rather than a sign of lack.

To be impressionable is to be easily influenced and seducible, not one's own person, to be easily overcome. Certain times in my life—but I cannot distinguish enough about them to name them—have seemed to ripple with just such openness, making possible magical episodes of recognition, synchronicity, the plenitude of rounding a bend to unexpected prodigiousness of sense.

I am wandering among secondhand items and homemade jewelry at an open air market in New York. I am supposed to meet an editor in an hour "for a drink" (but I barely drink, and never without food do I drink, I'm susceptible that way) and I shift between feeling up to the moment of what that might entail (just be myself!) and wary about the extent to which I have ever really sloughed off my working-class background to know how to have a drink with an editor. I'm letting my attention wander across knickknacks and old buttons in the open air market, I'm roaming, when I see a woman both from behind and in the mirror that a salesman holds before her: I see her back, lovely back, and her face, incomparable face, simultaneously. She is holding the most spectacular coat against her body, clutching it really, she regards herself in the length of a totally white lambswool winter wrap that matches her young, nearly straw-white, nearly pearly-white hair. She is slender and rare in the coat, and yet I think I know her, indeed I know her well, knew her in the fierceness of a tender age—talented writer, pulsing intellect— she wasn't *any* student, but how could this be her and this be me on the same square of sidewalk in New York seventeen years later now? She was twelve and I was twenty-two. She wasn't any student and I wasn't any teacher but one newly embarked, not settled but bubbling over and generous, certain and adrift, I was anxious, I was *susceptible* a cauldron, I was struck by the glow, then, now, of *this* student, a "stunning" ninth grader—oh, but I loved them all—and how really can a twelve-year-old be "stunning": she wasn't sweet but smart beyond her years.

"She looks good in it, doesn't she?" the salesman asks, deciding to use my staring to help make the sale. "It's obvious, the coat is meant for her," I say, and then she turns at first not expectantly, quietly now finding my face, she addresses me in a way I haven't been addressed in decades: "Miss Cappello?"

"Gillian?" I say, but there is no denying her—she's the same ninth grader seventeen years later, every detail still intact but startlingly "mature." The articulateness of her being had aroused me then and aroused me now.

"You look the same," Gillian says, "but if possible, younger."

"Of course," I say, "that's because now you are older."

Without much time to spare, we each in her turn try to find the thing most worth telling about the past seventeen years. We talk, at this ebb of the unexpected and the untimed, of desire and of writing. She is pursuing a Ph.D. in English. I have letters from her that she had written when she was twelve, did she want them? We would have to resume, if we felt moved to resume, our conversation over e-mail. Now I wonder what was more magical: the synchronicity of our being at the same place at the same time many years after the fact of our original encounter—an encounter overlaid with the intimate intensity of our respectively impressionable ages, and the gift of teaching/learning in two directions—or the fact that, thanks to a mutual susceptibility, we *recognized* each other? My father might want me to conclude that incomprehensible forces, sometimes caring, sometimes mean, put Gillian in my path, but I think it was the persistence of an impression that an adult made on a child, and a child made on an adult that engendered this recurrence of uncontainability, this co-incidence of being.

I want to believe in the extraterrestrial grace of serendipitous forces. In order to *happen upon*, one must be *open to*. I know I am in a good zone when chance encounters like this occur, because it means I am less fretful: such meetings don't confirm, but open like an envelope of risk.

Nothing is what it seems. My cat rolls onto her back and gives me her chin and belly, promising not to scratch, her paws curl *susceptible* inward as if to say, "I do no harm." I await one day her ability to produce a sound that is a word.

In my memory, the smoke that hung and billowed as a result of my grandfather's smoking wasn't a portent of pain but the atmosphere that made visible our breathing, and our moving, our surreal dancing and unreal musings, a sign of life.

A slate-colored coffee shop sign swings on its hinge while flowers push to the edge of orange anticipating an autumnal hurricane that will reconfigure the landscape toward unrecognizability and no trace of that-which-was. A lightbulb flickers, then crackles as though artificial light has been invaded by water.

"Growth" strikes one as a beautiful prospect, but not always, leaving one to wonder in what sense it may be said we grow without gaining an (awkward) protuberance? Perhaps we never grow entirely beautifully. There are always unforeseen, unaccounted for principles of growth, awkward interferences, and even what painter Emily Carr names in a painting, *A Surging New Growth* [That] *Takes Over the Old Growth*, suffocating it. I have known such woods, deep inside of which a little girl peers around a corner, passively wide-eyed and curious, looking, just looking, not looking for.

DETOURING

unnamed

I don't know of an artistic project more thoroughly soaked in awkwardness than Henry James's *The Awkward Age*: awkwardness is the book's ground and its effect; it characterizes the period in James' working life leading up to and, some would say, following its composition; it best describes the book's resulting form or style; it inheres as the book's subject, and can be enlisted as well as the aptest term for its compositional method—it was the first novel that James composed via *dictation* to a typist. Reading the novel as a kind of extended linguistic perambulation, rife with dips, valleys, bends, turns, deflections, and detours, the great Russian structuralist Tzvetan Todorov asked, "What could conceivably be more harmonious than this study of discourse carried out through the very use of discourse, this allusive manner of evoking allusion, this oblique book on obliqueness?" Todorov praises *The Awkward Age* as a neglected masterpiece that should take its place on our shelves alongside the most venerated novels in a modernist literary pantheon by "virtue of the fact that it explores in depth a path opened up by language but unknown to literature," and because it does so in more extreme and daring ways than had ever been done before or since.

Might a critical emphasis on "harmony" and its companion melodiousness, however, even by the most assiduous students of this impossible book, restore balance to its awkward enterprise? Henry James dwelled in awkwardness in the years before, inside, around, during, and after, in the moments of his thoroughly awkward undertaking. The years leading up to the composition of *The Awkward Age*, the 1890s, were so uncertain, formative, and unhappy for Henry James that biographers have since sought to name the period in various ways, as though James' life were a miniature version of the history of a world or of a nation constituted by relatively mean-

ingless or relatively significant eras, by periods of tumult followed *unnamed*
by periods of calm. James' later scriptors deemed 1890–1895 "the
treacherous years," "the Augean stable," and, yes, "the awkward
period." Currently, that period in James' life is generously designated
"the experimental phase." James himself called the eruption of failure into his writing life his "strange sacred time." It was the period
during which he tried on the suit of a different form—not fiction but
drama, and then watched as each of his plays flopped on the British
stage. James arrives in 1898, set before the idea of *The Awkward
Age*, with a condition we might now call carpel tunnel syndrome,
and the necessity, therefore, for both a typist and a radically different compositional practice. The result is a book that is its own
"awkward age"—*transitional* in every way, marking a passageway
from what James already did well in earlier novels to what he would
dare to do next in consummately self-referring vortices like *The
Sacred Fount* and *The Golden Bowl*.

In naming an age, do we keep a life or a person from bounding
forth into unnameability? Imagine living a life without being bound
by its time and all that's right for it: childhood, adolescence, adulthood, middle and old age. From 1890 to 1895, James risked difference and not knowing and gave up a certain command over his
materials. He in this way inhabited what his own character, the presumably naïve Nanda, calls *"an age without a name."* Nanda uses
this phrase retrospectively and naïvely: from her particular vantage,
you can't experience an age as nameless while you are living it but
only from the perch of another, in her case richly defined, new age.
Feeling as though she has finally entered into life and living, she
now apprehends the years of existing that preceded this moment for
her as "nameless" ones. Had Nanda previously been in a holding
pattern or a holding pen and now was launched, loosed? Had Nanda
been a child seen but not heard who now was heard because seen,
seen because heard? All of this suggests a lovely coming-into-being,
a life sketched as a series of easily demarcated manifestations of
action or dissolve. But such a free flow of calibrated stages into
bloom is contravened in James' novels by checkpoints and hedges
and the greasy fingers of other people's designs so that the most one
can hope for is life lived in a nameless age of grandly indeterminate
flux, strange, sacred, awkward, and impossible to sustain.

exposed

Just about the time that James was inhabiting his own nameless age, in the year 1895, a word was either coined, or simply overheard and for the first time recorded, by Joel Chandler Harris (author of the Uncle Remus tales and other plantation fictions) that might describe to a tee a figure like James, and if not James himself, then an aspect of his writing, and maybe most especially the style of *The Awkward Age*: "prissy." A "priss" is a prim sissy, an exacting and precise (homophobically marked) feminine man. A priss is fussy and fastidious. He cares too much about the wrong thing: that his body be portrayed in his clothes in such a way that he appear thoroughly intact. Is a priss's overly proper bearing an effect of the essential impropriety of his being? Does his hyper-propriety throw your own emphasis on a proper way to be a man or a woman, gay or straight, into high relief? You can't denigrate a priss because everything bounces off his highly polished, thoroughly collected surface. You can't efface him as you would like. His very presence makes you awkward in the way it exposes your carelessness, your slovenliness, your own numbing disregard. It shows up your natural breeziness to be a form of galumphing. But the priss is awkward too. Ill-suited to his surround, failing properly to fit.

It would be wrong, however, if, applying the idea of a prissy aesthetic to James' work, we sought out patterns of withholding or foreclosure, expression or an aggressive refusal to speak. Readers of James, then and now, often appear exasperated by a style that makes them feel that James is hiding something that he refuses to reveal. The either/or options that would expect to find truth in one place and darkness in another don't hold up inside of a Jamesian narrative. Todorov puts it well: in *The Awkward Age*, "It is as if the characters were animated by two opposing forces, and participated simultaneously in two processes with competing values: motivated on the one hand by nostalgia for a direct hold on things, they try to see through words, to get around them in order to get hold of truth; but on the other hand, the possible failure of this quest is neutralized, as it were, by the pleasure they take in not stating the truth, in condemning it forever to uncertainty."

James' prose is multi-valent and kaleidoscopic—it opens more *overcultivated* like a fan than like a shutter, suffused only by "chinks of daylight," never by a glaring spotlight or a heavenly glow.

A Jamesian aesthetic shows up and shows off.

And unfolds.

Like a geodesic rose.

overcultivated

And yet . . . one struggles to experience *The Awkward Age* this way. One struggles to experience the novel *at all*. When the novel appeared, nine out of ten reviewers dismissed it in no uncertain terms. Without using the words "prodigious" or "precocious," early reviewers exclaimed against the "overcultivation" of the book's style. "Mr. James in the overcultivation of his own special gifts seems to have lost whatever gift of narrative he may have once possessed." This assessment appeared in *The Sewanee Review*. Reviewer after reviewer dismissed the book for its obsessiveness and artificiality, its excessiveness and unnaturalness. A writer for *Critic* described the book as "clumsy and even wearisome. There is ten times too much good stuff," and, in capitulating again to the charge of the book's perversely cultivated style, "he works a delicate thing to death." In a review entitled "Mr. James Exasperates" for the 1899 edition of the *Pall Mall Gazzette*, the reader eschews the book's style on the grounds of its meta-making tendencies—"and here Mr. James has refined refinement, subtlized subtlety, and suggested suggestion to bewilderment."

Do readers experience *The Awkward Age* as a book cooked too soon or a book cooked to death? And is it really the case that James wrote a perfectly unreadable book, or a book in search of a heretofore unavailable reader? James' contemporary reviewers apprehended him, it seems, as an overly clever boy who knows something they don't know, who leads them down indescribably arduous pathways without ever revealing a buried treasure, who even if shook to death by a frustrated adult (like one of his own boy characters, Miles in *The Turn of the Screw*) won't give up his secret.

Readers are exhausted by what they perceive as *The Awkward ass-backwards* *Age*'s subterfuge, its maddening circumlocution. The book makes them feel dizzy from running or, in a different sense, smothered: "that he fails to give a complete idea of the whole proves that he has this time smothered himself with elaboration" (*Pall Mall Gazette*). And, "the atmosphere has become so artificial, partaking so little of the quality of real air, that natural healthy breathing seems almost impossible" (*Athenaeum*). I also experienced the book—the first time I read it (but why would anyone read it twice?)—as a dreadfully cramped and claustrophobic novel. James wasn't using artifice, I concluded, in a Wildean sense—as a form of camp—but in a more obviously repressive way with a resistant homophilia roiling beneath. Here was a book filled like a drawing room to bursting with a group of sniffy snuffy people who unnecessarily draw out their words and defer their meaning. The artifice was stifling, I felt, the gameplaying carried out among the characters utterly lacking the psychological drama and inner linguistic or narrative tension that makes other of James' uppercrust novels so rich. Having not yet read the reviews of James' contemporaries, I stuffed my own shirt one hundred years later, out-trumping James's cleverness or matching it with my own tacit sentences, prim as a purse and closed with a click: "This reads like a drawing room mystery—but one stifled by a replacement of who done it by who'll *do* it among a group of characters already *done in*."

This excruciation between paralysis (the already done in, the spent) and movement (the who'll *do* it)—the question of who finally will act, the question of whether all of the novel's talking palsies the ability to act or is the only muscular, desiring, fully performative act the book's humans are capable of—at once mellifluous and choked—produces the novel's *awkwardness*.

ass-backwards

So many passages in *The Awkward Age* could stand in, like a sign or a flag, for the numerous awkward problems of the novel itself, but I choose for my example a discussion between Nanda and her mother, Mrs. Brookenham, about dressmaking and dressing. Taking in the look of her daughter in a new dress—"slim and charming, feathered and ribboned, dressed in thin, fresh fabrics and *ass-backwards* faint colours," Mrs. Brookenham commands her daughter to turn around and then remarks,

> "The back's best—only she didn't do what she said she would. How they do lie!' she gently quavered.
>
> "Yes, but we lie so to *them*." Nanda had swung around again, producing evidently on her mother's part, by the admirable "hang" of her light skirts, a still deeper peace. "Do you mean the middle fold?—I knew she wouldn't. I don't want my back to be best—I don't walk backward."
>
> "Yes," Mrs. Brook resignedly mused; "you dress for yourself."
>
> "Oh, how can you say that," the girl asked, "when I never stick in a pin but what I think of *you*?"
>
> "Well," Mrs. Brook moralized, "one must always, I consider, think, as a sort of *point de repere* [a point of reference], of some one good person. Only it's best if it's a person one's afraid of. You do very well, but I'm not enough. What one really requires is a kind of salutary terror. *I* never stick in a pin without thinking of your cousin Jane. What is it that some one quotes somewhere about some one's having said that, 'Our antagonist is our helper—he prevents our being superficial?'"

Of course it is laborious (and exhilarating) to read a novel whose single passages, like this one, speak volumes. Consider, for instance, this discourse on backs-being-best as an announcement of the novel's awkward aesthetic. Here's a novel not exactly written from *behind* as readers imagine but from *within* the canvas of the *backside*. By showing us the back—the back being the "best"—James does not, as readers complain, show us his back while refusing to show us what he is seeing. It's not that the novel figures what the novelist is seeing while consigning us to a position behind him, unable to see the rich secret he describes but won't reveal. No. The novel *is* the amply rich and seductive back. It doesn't have eyes. I'm not sure it asks to be touched, however—that it wishes for us to lift a hand or touch a shoulder, to whisper, a hairsbreadth away from it, tactilely to explore its neck and valley leading down to dips and crevices. It asks, maybe, to be seen and to be read.

Who knows a person's back side? A lover perhaps. If you're fortunate enough to have one, a massage therapist. What is the back
but the site of a thrashing, or of a vulnerability, but also the finely
calibrated passageway of all of a body's feelings as well its possibilities for movement: the spine. Is it erect or crooked, cramped or
broad? How would our relations with one another be different if we
talked back to back, or front to back, back to front, awkward possibilities all.

How they *do* lie—dressmakers and novelists—promising us one
thing and producing another. But are readers any more trustworthy
or true? What part of the bargain is theirs and how do they keep
it? Customers and readers don't ever really tell the dressmaker
or writer what they want, but leave it to the writer/dressmaker
to follow their presumably truthful instruction, then blame them
for getting it wrong (as the writer/dressmaker inevitably does).
As Nanda's naïve position reveals, there really is no choice—to
dress/write for others, to dress/write for oneself. A gaze is always
operating, a reader is ever present, but the writer—now understood
as she who dresses—does not maintain a simply slavish relation to
the other, for pins and pens (mightier than swords) are involved in
the seemingly benign act of writing/dressing. Each pin is applied
with the potential to prick the reader/viewer, or to burst his bubble,
to hold him in place, to forge an aggressive mark in the name of the
complexities of, on the one hand, producing a form—a novel, a
dress—and on the other hand, acknowledging the fact that the
production is the result of a transaction in which no one admits
what one wants and in which no one is capable of being true. Mrs.
Brookenham, Nanda's mother, counsels her daughter further on this
score: not only need we admit that we dress/write for others or *in
light of their* judgment/gaze, but when we dress/write we should do
so with the idea of the person who most terrifies us in mind.
Terrified by the superficiality of a superficial readership, James
made a book in the form of a superfluously superficial back. The
superficiality holds a mirror to the reader, but the superfluity
deflects him.

Far be it for James to produce a novel (or a dress) that "suits"
us, but a novel made of displaced middles. As James explains about
his own compositional processes, try as he might to keep the mid-

dle, for example, in the middle, the center always swerves or veers. "Again and again, perversely, incurably, the center of my structure would insist on placing itself not, so to speak, in the middle. . . . I urge myself to the candid confession that in very few of my productions, to my eye, has the organic center succeeded in getting into proper position."

The Awkward Age is an improperly rendered book about propriety, and maybe the real source of readerly disturbance is the extent to which it keeps a reader from inhabiting his proper place. Forced to stare at a back, the reader wants to creep around to the front and see differently, to face and be faced. He taps James on the shoulder for his perversity, but James refuses to budge. In fact, the readerly bustle as he gets up out of his seat, his shifting and impatience, leads to no good but trips a switch that puts the book's forces in motion: now the book is a vorticist center, pulling you in and pushing you back out. Now it propels you onto an edge or a precipice—but it's not one that you hang from as in a Hollywood high-stakes-adventure movie, peering down. It's more like the sudden thrust from the front stage row to a close-to-the-ceiling perch in an ever-deepening, ever-widening amphitheater. It's not the form that does this—I've said the form is the shape of an ample and seductive back—but the action, in the form of endless conversation, that is taking place around the back. The points of interest and dynamics of desire that the book puts into play leave a reader in endlessly awkward pursuit to find and re-find a position from which to know.

inward

Maybe early readers of *The Awkward Age* struggled with the feeling that the book was a garment missing its body and hung askew on its hook. What is awkward about *The Awkward Age* is that it is one of the most *unseductive* novels ever written.

In my first reading of the novel, I sought out the particulars James had said his novel was struggling to contain, but they seemed buried or muffled. The first half of the novel read as though it were dictated by the author through a cloth soaked in ether—we feel him writhe. I reconsidered: maybe the novel requires a reader other or different from myself. Maybe my own relation to awkwardness prevents me from properly being placed by the novel. I reconsidered, because I believed in Henry James. I reconsidered, because my own turn-of-the-century circumstance and enterprise had me longing to be seduced by awkwardness. Awkwardness was to be found in this novel, and I wanted in.

In my first reading of the novel, flabbergasted, I asked myself, where is the *pleasure* of this text? Now I ask, where did my reading happen? This should always be considered in any critical accounting of a book: what were the circumstances of my taking it into my lap and peering in? I read most of the novel in a hotel room perched at an unnatural altitude high above the summit of Salt Lake City, Utah. I had never been to Utah, I had little firsthand sense of all that made the West distinctly West, and as the plane hovered above the lake for which the city was named I felt the pull of the mysticism also culturally at the city's center because I had never seen a lake *quite* display such a beguiling grid of coppery-blue shades of light, the hues that might define a rainbow on Mars. But Mars' atmosphere can't produce a rainbow. I know, I know. The point of the trip was "business"—but it wasn't my business, it was Jean's. Jean was going to attend a series of workshops planned to convene at a well-appointed conference center in Snowbird, a lushly forested ski area. Academic administrators would offer tips on troubleshooting and surviving the petty politics and numerous unanticipated problems of chairing English departments. No one trained to interpret books was trained to manage a business or negotiate intricate relations among kooky personnel, so here was a crash course in skills that, in the end, one either simply had a knack for, like winning in poker or balancing on a bike well into late middle age, or not.

I came along because hikes were promised, and the chance to see a friend who was living in Utah. He was studying, writing, being his incomparably beautiful self, and wondering how to be a gay man in a town bristling with sectarianism and its cultish offshoots. He was struggling with the feeling that overcame him now and again that the mountains that surrounded the town would melt back into glaciers and sweep everything away. He and I met at the base of a canyon where we ate crab cakes (one wondered where the crabs came from and how they got past the mountains) and drank iced tea as we teetered on plastic chairs set atop uneven terrain. He told me I seemed "serene"—or was it "at peace"?—something that meant the opposite of anxious, and I considered—perhaps he's right, or perhaps a general feeling of being anaesthetized presents as calm. We walked through gardens carved into clay paths and sandy trails that suddenly turned to brook and greenery, even to the shade of tall trees. We talked and felt splendidly aware of color, and of a man who might be cruising, and when the opportunity arrived we asked someone to take our picture together who might think we were a couple planning our wedding at the edge of swan lake, or carp pond (the fish there were plump and orange).

This was my up time at the conference, but for the rest of the time I sat in rooms in which the light seemed colored the inside of wood or just the part of a flame that is, for a flash, yellow, reading. I read furtively in the hotel room—a room that had a window that looked not out but into another part of the room, with the result that the bathroom could be seen into or out of, and which also featured a mirror that could be used to magnify a blemish or an annoying facial hair; at any rate, that anticipated self-inspection. The "real" window looked out onto a pine grove, and every now and then, peering into it, I expected Rock Hudson to appear, fresh out of *All That Heaven Allows*, inviting me to get in touch with nature, but not *my* nature, the myth of serenity at the center of the forest.

I read about Nanda—too young for the drawing room and too old for the nursery, and thought, too, it was a strange name and mused it must mean "nothing," or "nameless," in a language James had made up. I read of her mother, Mrs. Brookenham, a commanding, demanding, exquisite, impenetrable, cunning presence surrounded by male diva worshippers. Did this make her a fag hag in reverse? I met the two male principles: Mr. Longdon (a leftover from an earlier age whom James compared to Rip Van Winkle—he awakes to find the world out of joint and to find Nanda, who reminds him of her grandmother, with whom he'd been in love and whom he thinks he could love again), and Vanderbank (a man who should be interested in Nanda—he's closer in age to her than Longdon is—but can't be, and who seems the site of queer paralysis or undecidability in the text but who isn't the only vector of untoward male-male desire after all). Then there's Aggie, who is paired with Nanda as another girl who evinces the idea of the awkward age, but is distinguished from Nanda, whose cleverness ill-suits her age. "The beauty of Aggie," Nanda explains, "is that she knows nothing—but absolutely, utterly: not the least little tittle of anything." I say I was getting to know these characters, but I wasn't. In my first reading, from the vantage of Snowbird, Utah, I could not make these characters out. I could barely make out a plot, but only felt coiled by conversations as though I had happened upon a snake's nest in the desert, jittering snake language, and again, a writhing.

Sometimes I would break up my reading sessions with a walk in which I'd come upon badgers and deer and some other kind of rotund and industrious creatures that traveled in packs and weren't beavers. They hung out by a riverbed and hid among the rocks and seemed busily intent on retrieving things. The grounds were punctuated with signs warning of the first symptoms of altitude sickness, and at another juncture telling me to beware: I was entering an area where a switch might be tripped to set off explosives. I enjoyed nature, but I had never been a "happy camper." It hadn't been part of my upbringing, and I therefore failed to recognize *trails* as such. I was struck, nevertheless, by the fact that on a near stroll or attempt at a walk, I would actually see animals, and I concluded that the relative dearth of such sightings in the Northeast was a sign of western fecundity, or a more harmonious relation between the western populace and its woodland inhabitants. In the Northeast, the animals didn't dare show themselves but on a rare occasion— they might be sick or tired—or maybe there just weren't many animals left in the forest.

Midway through one of my solitary walks, breathing the serenity in deeply, expecting the leaves on the aspen literally to tinkle like the sound of silver coins in the pocket of my soul, I began to feel slightly dizzy. I'd opt then to turn back toward the confines of one of Snowbird's many gift shops. One sold extremely expensive prints, Far Eastern antiques, special clay pots from Japan for brewing tea, and, the proprietor explained as she held the piece before me to see but not touch—I had already knocked over a delicate tray perched on bamboo stilts—tiny perfume bottles that had been painted *on the inside* with brushes no thicker than an eyelash. Another store featured skiwear, and fleeces at off-season sale prices I could never expect back home, but I found my bounty in the basement of the conference center, where I bought touristy gifts for my friends at sea level: a package of salt (from the lake?), a bar of soap that mimicked the glittery inside, the veiny outcropping of a piece of native geology, a packet of seeds that probably would not thrive in Eastern soil—but so what?—and books. I bought books for myself and Jean and another colleague who also was gearing up for a new administrative post, as if to remind them that what got us all into this profession in the first place was that we loved to read.

Remembering again my own reason for being—currently to be able to read *The Awkward Age*—I returned to the hotel room and went at the novel like a journalist with a deadline. I practically harnessed myself into the wicker-back cushioned hotel chairs, hoping the tiny wheels at the base of the chair, charged with the weight of my determination, wouldn't start suddenly to spin and motor me around the room. I had brought a hot cup of something up to the room—not coffee but close enough—and slurped it between chapters. So involved in my undertaking, I turned one night to ordering room service and ate absentmindedly facing the wall, chewing really on unchewable Jamesian passages I had just read. Or, descending to the hotel restaurant, I ate without making eye contact as though I were an undercover agent in a foreign locale, intent on a mission: solitude.

Finally, I hit upon the revelation I hoped *The Awkward Age* would yield. It was only a matter of asking the book the right question and it would open. So I asked it again, where or what is the *pleasure* of this text? And I found it in Book V, Chapter XVI, in the opening paragraphs of a section entitled "The Duchess." Where is the pleasure of this text?, I asked, and this chapter replied, in the garden, the gardens that, in contradistinction to the drawing room though never clearly or simply antithetical to it, open onto a sensuality of language and relation. James prefaces Nanda's solitary wending through the labyrinthine pathways of the garden—finally to arrive at a green bench perched to provide access to an incomparable vista—with a sentence that bespeaks the opposite of awkwardness: "Nanda Brookenham, one day at the end of July, coming out to find the place unoccupied as yet by other visitors, stood there

inward awhile with an air of happy possession." This opportunity to be in
the garden alone, the revelation of the absence of others there, offers
a capaciousness that doesn't fulfill itself in the feeling of possessing
the grounds, or owning the gardens, but of owning, possessing,
being oneself. James introduces the idea of a book into her splendid
quiescence, but only as a complex placemarker—the idea of the
book as a distraction that her contentment will enable her to refuse:
"She had sunk down upon the bench almost with a sense of adventure, yet not too fluttered to wonder if it wouldn't have been happy
to bring a book; the charm of which precisely would have been in
feeling everything about her too beautiful to let her read."

I asked where was the pleasure of this text, and the book
answered with this distinct manifestation of solitude: not the solitude
of abandonment—the way James's narratives leave you hanging
from the thread of a desire unnamed but invoked. Not the solitude
of finding one's way in a narrative beset by intrigue, complicity,
interarticulation, and danger. Neither the solitude that punctuates
meetings between suitors when Vanderbank for example finds himself past bedtime, lights out, "alone in the great empty lighted bil-
liard room," or Mitchy is, "left in darkness, face to face with the
vague, quiet garden." Neither the solitude of insomnia, but the solitude of acquiescing to one's surroundings and the possibilities they
offer to the imagination to travel. Not a masturbatory and furtive
solitude—Nanda isn't *hiding out* in solitude but is splendidly, innocently (?), open—but a solitude comprised of quietude and wonder.

This solitude is not allowed to last more than an instant, however, when it is interrupted by the arrival of Vanderbank, who trips
up paths that had taken Nanda a long slow movement to achieve,
reducing a momentous egress to a game of tiddlywinks. "He bounded
up the slope, and, brushing his forehead with his handkerchief, confessing to being hot, was rejoicingly there before her . . . she made
room for him on the bench." That this solitude is broken the
moment it is achieved didn't matter to me in my first reading of *The
Awkward Age*. I was happy that, giving in no doubt to a theologi-
cal approach to pleasure in reading, having endured the labor of the
book's awkwardness, I now had found its grace. It didn't matter
what was *really* going on in the novel: I had found what I had come
for. I could even rest assured that I was experiencing one of those

novelistic tableaux vivants that James' novels eventually hit upon and are famous for: those moments where, through a coalescence of word-sounds and the placement of objects and perspectives in a space, he manages to project the stilling of a human creature awash in some highly attenuated and suddenly significant encounter with their own capacity for perception.

Ah, but what if Nanda had been left alone, left to her own devices, left to dwell at such a high vantage for more than a second? Would she be "allowed" then the experience of existential solitude, would she become confused by a false awareness of herself, would she be both terrified and elated by her own ability to step by step find her way back out of the garden's labyrinth? You can't tell what's on the other side of existential solitude until you let a character go there: it is every being's divine and necessary right, the journey toward a fullness in being. The quick fix of a sudden pleasure in the garden wasn't what this novel was about, but I rest assured in my first reading, as though in need of a surcease of its awkwardness—the very awkwardness I claimed to have been in search of—I had found its pleasure in its grace.

laborious

The second time I read *The Awkward Age* was again on a trip far from home. We were making an extended visit to Vancouver to be with Jean's father in what we thought would be his last days. Summer was the time allotted me to write, as well as numerous interstices if I could find—and if not find, invent—them, in the days in which I made my living, so I brought my work along. "You're not going to read that book *again*," my friend and writing partner, Karen, had worried. "Nnnn . . . no! Nnnn . . . no! Tell me that you're not," she demanded, almost with a smile and with emphasis when she really wanted to shout at and throttle me. "You are *so* ready to write about that book. If you read it again, it will just prevent you from finishing the writing of your own book this summer." Was this my awkwardness? Life was easy, writing was easy, being was easy, but I made it hard, laborious, so much harder than it ever had to be. "Well, the last time I read the novel was a year ago," I *laborious* defended myself. "Uh-huh," Karen agreed, "and you have that pile o' notes to rely on." She pointed to a folder bulging at the seams with writing spilled like blood onto yellow legal pads. Think of Ginger Rogers, I wanted to say, all those trips back up the staircase with her feet bleeding until she got it right, so that we could enjoy the resulting illusion of ease, of grace. Maybe the more interesting musical would consist of those trials—the multiple takes, the falls, the bloody bandages.

I read the book again and realized that the first time I hadn't understood much of it at all. I read it this time in the hours of waiting purchased in my sister-in-law's backyard. The sun was scorching and I never wore sunglasses. Alongside me, perpetually, sounded the articulations of my autistic nephew, Casey, and the therapist assigned to him that hour in a day's endless round of at-home Lovaas therapy. Here were two forms of excruciation juxtaposed: the repetitive Pavlovian commands and questions met occasionally by Casey's correct reply and the same exclamations of praise—a high-pitched "Good boy Casey!"—over and over and over again, alongside the difficult, seemingly meaningless utterances of Henry James. In the background of this novel, a novel made up entirely of conversations between people who seem either beyond the ken of the very language they call their own, or unable to hear each other, or beset by the impossibility of desire in language, or struggling with a tangle of words that won't be undone, or engulfed by the vacuity at the center of words, or awkwardly enslaved by the disconnect between words and acts, I heard the innocent chirpings of my nephew, making sounds only meaningful to him, surrounded by therapists intent on making his language meaningful to them too.

"I hope we're not bothering you," the therapist asked between rounds as Casey raced toward the trampoline, his playtime reward for all of his work. "No," I said, "I grew up in a noisy and chaotic household. I'm well trained to be able to read with all kinds of activity going on around me." Did this prove I was on the far other end of autism, or that precisely a degree of autism was required for anyone to concentrate, and particularly to read a book that demanded and refused one's attention by turns in an overstimulating environment. (I had learned from an early age how to tune things out.) My sister-in-law got angry, however, whenever I wanted to suggest that Casey's autism was on a continuum with a norm. "Look at him!" she would *laborious* beseech me, at a rare low ebb (usually she was up to the minute-by-minute challenge of her son's condition). "Do you really think that your brain and his brain have anything in common? When he underwent tests, they showed that his brainwaves are all messed up. They move at different speeds and intensities that just aren't normal. And somehow he has to function with that. He has to live in the world."

"Hi, Mary," Casey recognizes me, but the word retains a degree of vacancy and lack of full conviction. "Hi, Casey," I reply. "Bye-bye," with an upward lilt on the last syllable, he offers, and the therapist and I mutually confirm how much progress he's been making in the past year, how amazing it is that he can recognize people now, say their names, and almost interact. "Your work is so important," I say. "Well, I just love working with him," she says. "I'd be daunted by doing something like reading that book all these hours like you've been doing. I just wouldn't have the patience."

Each of us, if we're lucky, gets to choose our struggle and then convince ourselves that the other person's is harder. Would Casey, presumably without selfconsciousness, never feel awkward? Here he is frustrated, restless. He hugs me suddenly around my knees, then runs again and cries, there's no telling why. Is there a way I could help with the therapy today? Why don't I consider it and ask? I have a richly intimate relationship with my niece, Casey's sister. Why don't I make the effort to be a presence to Casey as well? I have this work to do, that's why! I have the chance to explore the awkwardness cast across the pages of a novel by a writer about whose work I feel more than fond, and whom I fantasize as "fellow." It isn't easy. It's hard, and it's a choice. I cross my legs and continue to swelter beneath a burning sun. I can feel myself burning, but don't apply lotion. Sweating, I experience the reading as that much less fun, but if I have to read, I want to read outdoors. Turning back to James' page, I *finally* begin to understand what he was up to in each awkward phrase. Or so I say.

wrong

If wrong was a synonym for awkward, what was right? Jean has spent the hours from four o'clock in the morning to one o'clock the next afternoon in an emergency ward after being struck in the middle of the night with severe stomach pains. In twenty years, I have never seen her in such unremitting pain, pain so out-of-the-blue and indecipherable that we become convinced this is destiny working: this will be the blow ever after which our world will cease to be the same. Lines of intravenous have been introduced, a clock face set to 6:40 whose hands never move, a small error that sends Jean's blood pressure plummeting, tests and speculations, urine and blood, and my hovering so close that a male nurse turns toward Jean's now heavily medicated face to say "she's really protective of you." To which I reply, "Well, we've been together for twenty years. We take care of each other!" In the end, there was—happily?—nothing "wrong" but pain, and nothing to do but go home and wait it out.

Why, I want to know, did I give into an impulse to fold the rumpled sheets that Jean had writhed in rather than leave them bunched in a ball, gathered as they would be anyhow as so much mess and then thrust into a laundry chute along with other people's muck and sweat and "chunks" (in the cubicle next to ours, a nurse spoke to a man's having produced *less* large chunks than in the past in his urine, and explained how to use the take-home catheter) and oozings (in the cubicle next to ours, a cocktail waitress described the suppurating globule that had appeared just above her belly button). I felt wiped out, spent, dazed, but I thought that I should fold the sheets neatly. For one sheet, I reserved a special place: after folding it, I hung it from the railing that straddled the gurney as if I'd spent the past twenty-four hours luxuriating in a fancy hotel room rather than in a hospital ward. I could give in to the miserable lousiness of the situation, the implicit squalor, or I could neaten as if to deny the mess, or to show gratitude for the nurses who, though they couldn't help, did care. It didn't seem right simply to leave. I imagined the nurse returning, never before to such neatness, and musing that one of us must have suffered from OCD.

And yet, and yet, after we walked to the car and Jean had vom- *wrong*
ited a cocktail of narcotics—none of which had reached the pain—
into a basin, I found myself of necessity dumping the contents of the
basin onto the parking lot's asphalt. I did consider: better not to
dump it into the nearby earth, it wouldn't be good for that young
sapling. And if she had a virus? Mightn't I be unleashing a plague
on Providence? I imagined that a bird might fly by and, wafting the
fumes, be instantly felled. Should I have walked back into the hospital with the vomit-filled basin, displayed it to a receptionist, and
asked, "is there a place for this?" I dumped it even though it seemed
so wrong, as though I were in a hurry to exit the scene of an already
committed crime and one more violation wouldn't matter. Neatening
was wrong and so was soiling. What would have been right? The
only option was "awkward."

We only pretend toward acts that naturally suit a situation.
Why had no one told us that our goal in life *shouldn't* be to aim
toward what was right, that we shouldn't try to *meet* a situation,
but to transform it?

The awkwardness of *The Awkward Age* I now considered was
tantamount to so many forms of "wrong": of a mother and a
daughter loving the same man; of the incest that hovers in James'
narratives; of the daughter coming, by the end of the narrative, to
feel the need to protect *the mother*, whom she now perceives as "so
fearfully young"; of men who cry, who produce enough tears to
produce more oxygen all around; the gaffe of no one ever staying in
their place; last but not least, the poignant wrongness of intergener-
ational desire. Here the love that dare not speak its name isn't a love
between men but an erotic alliance between young and old, a line of
force, a draw, a drive, a pull toward, in some sense, not so much a
consummation as a preservation of each person's sad and singular
solitude.

Mrs. Brookenham, anxious about the alliance and eager cleverly
to undermine any sign of serious attachment between her daughter
and Longdon, jokingly asks Nanda if Longdon wishes to "adopt" her,
and then explains that she and her father don't intend to give Nanda
up. By this account, Longdon can only be a father figure to Nanda;
together, they can only remain within the confines of a properly
oppressive familial relation. In a wonderful move, however, Nanda,

refusing to be infantilized by the suggestion, invents a new meaning of the word, "because what it comes to seem to be that I'm really what you may call adopting *him*," she says. Having reversed the chronology as well as the assumed relations of power that usually attend the word "adopt," Nanda goes on to explain that by "adopt" she means not taking him in or taking him on but helping him to *adapt* to her as she is, which is to say a girl who will never marry, not him, not anyone.

What I love about the exchange in which James reworks the terms of "adoption" is how it inaugurates a relation for which there is no word but which Nanda insists she will, in concert with Longdon, actively invent. Nanda *to the end* is awkward in the sense that she is "the horrible impossible" who has "covered everything else with [her] own impossibility." By the end, she is, "a very much older person than her friend." She had earlier made explicit to Longdon that "I shall be at the end . . . one of those who haven't married . . . I shall be one of the people who don't." Because Longdon himself is one such, he misreads her pronouncement in conventional terms. He replies, that is to say, mournfully to Nanda's pronouncement:

> "No, my child," he returned gravely—"you shall never be any-thing so sad."
> "Why not—if *you've* been?" she wants to know. He looked at her a little, quietly; then, putting out his hand, passed her own into his arm. "Exactly because I have."

What Longdon doesn't grasp is that this is how Nanda will show her love for him: not by remaining virginal because they can't have each other, not as sacrifice, neither by way of identification, but by inventing a relationship defined by two people's being, in concert, singularly wrong.

Awkwardness isn't something to grow out of but to grow into. Awkward is something, by this account, one might hope to main-tain against all odds; in the end, to become.

wayward

In order truly to comprehend awkwardness, each person might have to answer for himself the question of the moment he gave up his capacity for *squirm*. Where did it go, we each might ask ourselves, our particular forms of polymorphous movement, a banging of forks and spoons onto tables into bowls, a sudden drop to the floor mid-meal to crawl, the emission of a squeal or pleasing repetition of a nonsense phoneme—like *ough, ough, ough* or *eep, eep, eep*—while the adults are "talking," the necessity suddenly to twirl like a top before dessert arrives. What had to be deleted from a libido embodied to make possible the rigid posture I now assume? Each person's awkwardness must be equivalent to that nascent, forgotten, unplumbable, haunted space between a body's numerous forms of egress—the space between our hopping like a bird or tiptoeing because twilight twinkles, between clapping hands for no reason but the sound or the contact, or the necessity, because candy is on the tongue, suddenly to walk exaggeratedly heel to toe, heel to toe, or scuffing, skimming, skipping—and the agreement now for the rest of one's years only ever *to walk*.

Only an adult, you might say, could truly feel nostalgic for a child body out of bounds, beyond its own control, only an adult who enjoys self-control or whose body hasn't fallen prey to illness. Maybe there was never a time when the body wasn't awkward, and to deny that, we invent self-control. What's sad is the admission that the only form of resistance to bodily decorum and sublimely achieved composure that we can imagine might be to fantasize jumping out of our seat at a dinner party and walking rather than sitting while we talk. Or at least this is the feeble sign of life that James' characters in *The Awkward Age* indulge.

Late in the novel, Nanda asks at a tense moment (but are there anything but tense moments in the narrative?) for the permission to walk while she talks to Longdon: "Do you mind if I don't sit down?" she asks, and he replies that he doesn't really care what she does with her body, she could stand on her head, he says, for all he cares. She assures him she won't do anything so trying of his patience as that but only that she doesn't want him to "worry" if she "walks about a little." She doesn't want for him, we might assume (only lending the most obvious reading to the lines) to interpret her movement as a sign of agitation, uncertainty, or nerves, as though this break with decorum could only be read as the body's needing to find an outlet for the excess energy that passionate thoughts induce. James submits that, quite unlike Nanda, "Mr. Longdon, without a movement, kept his posture," after which Longdon then gives his permission to Nanda to *dance* on him if she wishes, given, he says, the passive thing she has made of him. And here the language of postures rightly or awkwardly assumed thickens:

> 'Well, what I have had from Mitchy,' [Nanda] cheerfully responded, 'is practically a lesson in dancing; by which I perhaps mean rather a lesson in sitting, myself, as I want you to do while *I* talk, as still as a mouse! They take,' she declared, 'while *they* talk, an amount of exercise!'

Is it a degree of ellipsis in talking or a sliding of syntax like a staccatoed glissando that makes it hard to keep track of a referent here, of who is sitting and who is standing, who is dancing and who is watching, of whether sitting is the same as or different from dancing? Do Mitchy and his kind exercise *while* talking, or does listening to them require a degree of exercise on the part of their presumed interlocutor? This much is clear: conversation is never a free and easy exchange of thoughts and words between equals but always an occasion for one person to perform while the other watches. Conversation is a matter of tentative permissions and measured allowances. Talking is a disciplined and highly structured contretemps whereby one person gets to move while the other remains still, in which one strays while the other stays in place. Nanda never merely imitates the lessons she learns, however, and I like to imagine her wish here to walk while she talks as her requesting an oh-so-infinitesimal release into polymorphous possibility, *not* in the name of taming an excess, but in the hope of altering the terms of a relation, embodied.

physical

And then there is James . . . walking, or is it *pacing*, while he writes, which is to say when he *dictates The Awkward Age* to his typist, William MacAlpine. Writing is a still and solitary activity, you say, in which case Emily Dickinson was no more "reclusive" than the next great writer/philosopher since the activity of writing and thinking seems to require any author to give an exorbitant amount of time over to a well-chosen interior, not always cork-lined. But dictation introduces another person and a machine into the room, thus freeing if not requiring the writing body to move. Do you mind if I don't sit down? Do you mind if I walk while I talk, Nanda asks Longdon, and in another sense, then, she becomes Henry James: a writer whose writerly effort demands a motor, and who, in time, so driven by the typewriter, by the fact of dictation, to continue to produce more and more text, begins to confuse talking with writing. Another of James' typists, Theodora Bosanquet, describes in her book about her work with James how "his own speech assisted by the practice of dictating, had by that time become so inveterately characteristic that his questions to a railway clerk about a ticket or to a fishmonger about a lobster, might easily be recognized as coined in the same mint as his addresses to the Academic Committee of the Royal Society of Literature." No longer confining the creation of a special use of language (writing), the inhabiting of one's language like a foreigner, to the room in which he wrote, James becomes a weirdly awkward figure: a writer-in-public.

When I first tried to imagine writing-as-dictation, it occurred to me that James' *The Awkward Age* was so awkwardly rendered because the act of dictation introduced an encumbrance, by way of a physical relation, into the writing process. Now it occurred to me that a different physical relation was at issue, but not one simply of a bar or block.

In writing-as-dictation, the tactile is replaced by the spoken, the hand by the tongue.

Writing as vibration rather than mark.

To write, then, is to voice rather than to indent, to scratch, to rub.

I try to imagine the typewriter: the earliest typewriters, I consider, must have been heavy: they must have not lilted but made thudding sounds. (In the computer age, we've refined keyboard technology to mimic the sound of tiny teeth chattering, gnawing at word-chips). Here's James' voice, rising and falling, emphasizing and pausing, breathing and growling, murmuring and speeding, rounding and playing like an orchestra. Here's the typewriter thudding and sputtering, pounding, like a boxer, letters into the tough surface of a page, returning to the striking of a bell another round before each sentence is through. How did this not introduce a certain insanity into the writing scene?

"The click of a Remington machine acted as a positive spur," according to Bosanquet, and James "found it impossibly disconcerting to speak to something that made no responsive sound at all" — another, quieter typewriter. Talk-writing seemed easier: "'It all seems,' he once explained, 'to be so much more effectively and unceasingly pulled out of me in speech than in writing. . . .'" But all of this begs the question of the presence of another *person* in the room in which one writes. Is the other person a column, an obstruction to the "flow," or a conduit, a medium, a skin through which the writing becomes apparent?

For James, the thud of the machine seems to have been preferable to the presence of the person doing the typing, who, as other commentators (Thurschwell, Seltzer) have reminded us, was also called the "typewriter." One concludes after reading Pamela Thurschwell's illuminating biographical account of Bosanquet that Bosanquet never really materialized in the room with Henry James. She remained, to the end, and after, no more than an abject transcriber of the great writer's words. Even on his deathbed, he calls to her to dictate phrases to her; as the story goes, he suffers less from the condition of his stroke than from a feeling of not being able to find the proper word for his feeling—"paralysis" won't do. After his death, Bosanquet tries to write herself, but by spirit-channeling James as though to seek his approval and affirm her word *in* him, issuing from him. The relation with him appears to have produced a bizarre form of surrogation. In the book that she wrote about James, she assumes that in their first meeting he found her "harm-

less" while she found him "overwhelming." "If the interview was
overwhelming," she goes on, "it had none of the usual awkwardness of such curious conversations. Instead of critical angles and disconcerting silences, there were only benign curves and ample reas-
surances. There was encouraging gaiety in an expanse of bright
check waistcoat." Bosanquet wants us to believe what we cannot—
that this encounter wasn't awkward, that they were in accord, at
one—only, I think, in order to permit herself to write such a char-
acteristically Jamesian sentence.

Could all of those places where ends don't match up, where
word fails to meet meaning, where gaps and gulfs and silences glare
in *The Awkward Age* be a sign of the ghost of the body of the typist? Would it matter that the original body of that ghost was male
(the probably gay MacAlpine) rather than female (the probably
lesbian Bosanquet)? Did James write or imagine his typists *into* his
fiction? It's hard to say, but somehow I think not. No doubt, given
the surplus of activity that was the writing—James's endlessly paced
oratory—he expected his typists never to move, possibly to pose,
certainly to remain in place.

hands

What does writing become if it is no longer a form of handi-
work? James claimed that "manual labor," the hand writing, was an
aid to "brevity." Conversely, dictation, or the freeing of the hands
in favor of the vocal cords, apparently led to more compositional
ease, but the end result may have been a more laborious prose.

In the computer age, I still compose by hand, which isn't an
eccentric boast but an admission of a refusal to break a physical
(and probably cognitive, mental, compositional) habit. I write by
hand . . . words that only I can read before I type them. Maybe what
James loved about dictation—what made it seem "easier" to write
this way—was that it pressed his prose immediately into *print*, even
if that step still was intermediate to publication. It must have *felt* as
though one could bypass the authorial stamp and closure of the editor, press, and printer: it was an immediate making public of the
text. My words are only readable by me, not for any cryptic, crazy,

hands   spiritual, or superstitious reason, but because my "penmanship" has eroded over time, as though my hand can't move at the same speed as my thought. The hand always lags behind the brain. Even if you whistle high and with the promise of an offering, the body won't follow but, ear to the ground, sluggish and dumb, remain behind.

Penmanship, in the form I learned it from the Sisters of the Immaculate Heart in the early 1960s, was a synonym for citizenship: it was a sign, the nuns would have us believe without quite saying it outright, of character, intelligence, and art. It proved your responsibility to a form, your ability to imitate the loop-de-loops of angels, as if to suggest that if you worked at it hard enough, if you gave your handwriting enough care, you might someday become transcribers of the word of God. But what if it was your own words that you wished to transcribe? What if you wished to treat the page as a mystic writing pad, uncertain of which words would appear, what words would follow your hand?

If some people do achieve perfect penmanship it must mean forfeiting their own bodies in the course of making letters, because sooner or later in spite of the best teachers modeling the finest technique, one's "own" handwriting emerges.

Realizing this, I enjoyed, on the cusp of adolescence, tracing the letters of other people's handwriting. Not in order to have them, but because I thought that by doing this I might be able to know what it was physically to *be* them. I didn't want to imitate their script (though the idea of forgery did tantalize for awhile) but to feel for a fleeting instant the life and movement of another.

Writing is both a remembering and forgetting of the body of the other.

4

DELVING

inconsistent

Awkwardness is supposed to be inimical to diplomacy, but the current president of the United States is admittedly crude. What is vexing about this is that his opponent in the presidential race for 2004, John Kerry, lost the election on the basis of his awkwardness. According to the rhetoric that ushered Bush into the oval office for a second term, the two candidates offered the choice of a contrasting *ontological* presence, and what Americans were voting for, then, wasn't a distinct set of moral principles reflective of the American way (no matter what blue and red states hoped to figure), but something imagined as transparency or opacity in *being*. A picture was projected to figure an irresolvable crisis in the American imagination: on one side, awkwardness, and on the other side, certitude. George W. Bush won the presidency in spite of the acknowledgment of how little he knew about the world because of a conviction that he had a thorough knowledge of something much more important: himself.

We voted for what we could read; we voted for coherence even if the pieces that constituted president-as-assemblage spelled out doom and dunce: that the pieces fit into place is what mattered, the hat fit securely on its bearer's head.

Where Kerry was painted as an awkward emblem of agonizing indecision, Bush was loved for the word he seemed to coin following the attacks of September 11th: "resolve." Resolve might be a euphemism for bull-headed arrogance—"just do it!"—in which case, Kerry could only *dis*solve into the haze of awkward hesitator, a thinker over and against an actor. American consciousness at the turn of the 21st century petrified the distinction between the two. We might ask why.

irresolute   Malinger, malign, misalign, missile, reassign, resign, misalliance, miscellaneous, pusillanimous, animosity, monstrosity, range.

irresolute

Am I anxious today, awkward, ill at ease because of the test I must submit to at noon, because of the hormones that will wreak havoc in my body by four, because of the childhood trauma that pulses in snakelike patterns as a reminder of repressed memories of something that happened in the long ago and faraway when the clock struck six? Or because, daily I live the disconnect between what I know to be true but am forced to deny, between what I intuit as real and what I am daily told is real. Awkwardness might be a form of (healthy) cognitive dissonance.

Does this mean we must give up the desire or possibility ever to be met? To be met is splendid, not as in *Meet Me in St. Louis*, though that might also be perfectly fine as bubbles in a beer glass. I was met one afternoon because of what I was told by someone else about me. The speaker was a poet of some renown, open to experiment and play, the author of a book-length poem built out of letters as an address to family members lost in the Holocaust. I was hosting the poet at a public reading. Before and afterward, I offered her something to drink, sparkling water followed by wine. I asked the poet questions about her work, and she seemed to enjoy them. She said to me, almost reaching for me with her hand, smiling broadly slowly wisely assuredly she said, looking straight at me—"you have a [FILL IN THE BLANK] mind." The adjective she used to describe my quality of mind I have since forgotten, but the adjective was so unusual, precise, and *right*, that I felt exquisitely met. Maybe that was what she said—"you have an exquisite mind." I knew she hadn't said I had a sassy mind, a sterling mind, an exuberant mind, an exorbitant mind, or a chilling mind. She said the word that was *right* for me, that gladdened me, that made me feel suddenly okay, affirmative, there. She said, smiling, looking into me, "You have a _____ mind," and I said, smiling back at her, "thank you, but it helps to have a book as fine as yours to shape fine questions." Suddenly, I was the epitome of grateful graciousness. That night, still moved by her generosity, I reported the sentence to a friend I could trust, who accepted that though I appeared narcissistic, like everyone, I wanted to be loved.

That night, I repeated the sentence to myself as a lullaby I might drift securely on to sleep. The next day, in between the turning of a page, in the pause between the steps that took me to my office and to work, I felt the urge to have the sentence again, to whisper it, just to know it was there like a mandarin hidden in a pocket, like **my** thumb circling a button while waiting for a train, like a cat rubbing her head against my ankle, suddenly warm. But the next day, the next night, I forgot the word. It was as though a piece of stolen bubblegum stowed in my pocket and whose juicy chomp I anticipated was nowhere to be found when I searched for it—it had fallen through a hole in the dirty little ragged little pocket of my coat. I wasn't sure what was more ridiculous, embarrassing, awkward: that at forty-four, I should treat a single sentence haphazardly pronounced by a stranger as a newfound raft of being, or that by way of some pathetic perversion—Catholic guilt and the necessity for selflessness?—I could no longer remember the word—the *perfect* word *for me*. I tried to brainstorm: had she said "splendid"? No. "Sartorial?" No. "Humpbacked?" No. "Beautiful?" No, that appellation was forever doomed now to be associated with a bad film about schizophrenia.

When my cat loses a toy mouse behind a chair, I sometimes get out the broom and swish its long handle back and forth across a mound of dust beneath the piece of furniture until the mouse appears again in view. My cat cowers before the broom—a sign I always assume of some previous owner's terrorizing act—then looks surprised and happy when the mouse appears. There is no handle long enough it seems to find this word. It was delightedly I should suppose *for* that instant, the instant of that relation and nothing more. Where there's a will to awkwardness, there's a way. To remember such an agreeable word would be to cease to be awkward . . . or to be awkward because embarrassed by such a bald and exacting regard. The word, come to think of it, cut, through my hide, like a knife, like a knife through butter.

groping

The indigo box being safely tucked beneath her arm permitted a somewhat awkward handling of her domestic chores. . . . She poured [sic] over the little box on the floor before her and pondered its fate. She could not help but feel that she possessed something very special, for her whole being was being drawn toward it. Her mind was beginning to devise ways of opening it and expose the hidden treasures of knowledge, but she cringed at the thought of damaging it. She felt a deep inexplicable obligation of reverence for this mysterious indigo box. She decided then and there that cutting or breaking it open was out of the question. . . . So she stood firm in her decision to leave her precious indigo box intact.

—from "The Mysterious Indigo Box," Joseph Cappello

In his infamous *Letters to His Son,* a book that became a kind of eighteenth-century etiquette manual, imitated and parodied by turns, one Lord Chesterfield goes to great lengths both to exemplify awkwardness and to guide his son in the fine art of its avoidance. Awkwardness, Chesterfield warns, is messy. Not only does the awkward man unnecessarily incite the attention of others but his awkward ways can terribly affect the company in the room, even to the point of spreading contagion. Awkwardness implicates others in one's physicality. It makes demands, is non-normative, it produces displeasure in others. Altogether, awkwardness requires an audience in order for it to exist. But what of awkwardness furtive and solitary, witnessed by no one but ourselves?

My father, I discovered, wrote a story about a girl left alone with a mysterious indigo box. Stella Brite, the story's protagonist, is "bright" and yet has so much still to learn. She finds the box in the recesses of her high school guidance counselor's office in a room filled with similar boxes awaiting a quester. Most of the story is taken up with Stella's fascination with the box and how exactly she will let it yield the promise of knowledge it holds out without violating it, which is to say without handling it awkwardly. Stella is patient, and the reward for her patience is revelation in the form

of a beam of light that guides her eyes across the writing in her *groping*
copybook, the pages of which the beam of light also turns, illuminating errors like a magic wand without fixing them but without
punishing Stella for them either. The force inside the box even takes
her, later in the story, toward a kind of out-of-body experience
through which she becomes one with the heavens, that magnificent
play of lights.

The story ends with a poignant conceit: no one had really
bestowed such a box on Stella; the box as benign ghost-teacher and
conduit to starry beyond never really existed. The story we read *is*
the box filled with the content of Stella's daydream, a daydream she
was indulging while sitting in a classroom. The classroom wasn't
adequate to the relation to knowledge Stella wished to have, thus
leading Stella to invent her own escape hatch into knowledge, but
she had also been daydreaming when she should have been writing.
At the story's end, Stella is "awakened" by a nudge in the shoulder
from a fellow student and a yell of her name from the teacher asking her to recite her homework from the night before—a composition—but Stella, having forgotten to do her composition homework, has no composition to read. Only pretending to read words
on the page, she recites, instead, her daydream. As if to ward off
impending embarrassment, "nevertheless, Stella Brite's eyes stayed
riveted to the blank pages in the open book," my father wrote.
"Mark Egdelwonk, aiming to dispel Stella's hesitancy, laid a hand
on her shoulder and said, 'Now Stella, let us begin with your title.'
Stella Brite smiled, took in a deep breath and with a sharp clear
voice said, "The title of my story is. . . 'The Mysterious Indigo Box.'"

I wonder what was the quality of solitude out of which my
father penned this story? And if he had fancied Stella as a figure for
himself—he who dreamed rather than composed, who gave into a
flight of fancy when he should have been listening, who was more
interested in escape than the paltry summons life held out to him.
For a man who had no patience and who continually broke things,
for a man in whose presence nothing ever remained whole, it is
interesting to find the projection of an ideal of patience in Stella.
Because she does not awkwardly force the box open but gracefully
waits for what she needs, she learns what she needs to know.

untutored

Labor Day is supposed to be a day on which labor ceases, but I don't know if the dog days of summer ever were laborless for me. I loved the sound of a distant hammer on such days: the feint assuredness of a tapping into wood. It starts out slowly then grows slightly louder, faster, turns back to slow, then fades. I like the sound of someone working early in the morning on a weekend, as though something is in the process of being made that isn't compulsory. On one such summer day, my grandfather lifted the lid of the piano in his dining room and bid me to peer inside. I gasped to learn that, like a body, the piano was made of a webwork of strings that you couldn't see from the outside, but what was more astonishing was the simple realization that the sound the piano produced wasn't intrinsic to the keys. The keys were levers attached to tiny hammers that struck the strings. On the days that formed late summer in my childhood, it seemed lucky for me to hear as I often did hear not both at once or even in unison but playing in a separate distance the sounds of a solitudinous making: one person hammers, and another person hammers too but we call it playing the piano. It was Labor Day, I recall, the day on which I applied myself to The Frog. Kites may have sailed that day, drums probably rolled, and the brass bellies blaring in a local parade probably made some girl feel her heart in her chest in her stomach in her chest. She probably stood wide-eyed on the sidelines untethered as a giddy balloon dreaming of an afternoon made of cotton candy flounces and hotdog stripes. I, however, was in the basement of our row home applying myself to The Frog.

My older brothers spent summer days immersed in science projects. Together they poured over Edmund catalogs, the scientific supplier for young men. They built and flew wooden rockets, they made and drove motorized go-carts. They established an observatory with a timed telescope in our backyard, thus making the narrowness of working-class alleyways open into the significance of a speck that was part of a vast and beguiling universe. Some days of the week they enrolled in seminars at the local science museum, The Franklin

Institute. Fingering a rock collection dusty with disuse—but then   *untutored*
how does one *use* a rock collection, I imagined my brothers getting
to experience (not just watch) the kind of experiments a 4-H club
might carry out on TV. I recalled that the Institute had a static electricity ball and I pictured my brothers giggling "oh my!" as they
applied their fingers to the ball and felt the tips of their crew cuts
stand upright, then returned to their notebooks seriously to record
what they observed. One day, "dissecting kits" appeared in the house
and, along with them, specimens.

I don't know if this technical, hands-on venture into biology
was linked to the classes at the Franklin Institute, if Edmund was
having a special that week on dissecting kits, or if the peculiar box
of instruments came into our house through the door of an unusual
"hobby" shop in downtown Darby, PA. The store had sprung up
overnight in an abandoned and otherwise boarded-up hut on the
edges of downtown. The new owner installed one window where a
board had been and applied the words in uneven large block letters:
AL'S PET AND HOBBY. Al, a slightly grimy, slightly mad, extremely
hirsute and beer-bellied man stood at an elevated height behind the
counter just before the shelves on which the specimens also stood
floating in formaldehyde-filled jars. The only live animals to be
found in the store—possibilities for pets—were a forlorn bird, a
small pack of mewing kittens, and a reptile of undescribed origin
that for some reason had a tiny label wrapped around its ankle
which it occasionally gnawed. Though there wasn't room in the
store for a bathroom, it smelled nevertheless as though a toilet had
recently overflowed, or that the hut were the leftover flotsam of a
serious storm, and Al tried to tamp down that smell with the aroma
of a weak-bodied marijuana. Wanting "in" on the adventure into
the unknown that was my brothers', I gathered nickels and pennies
from a variety of hiding places and, picking among them, counting,
I cupped into a hand enough money to buy a specimen of my own.

Requesting a specimen from Al was terrifying, worse somehow
than buying condoms or liquor before my time. It was clear I was
too young and too female to be purchasing "specimens." On the
day that I'd determined to make my purchase, Al was low on sam-
ples. He glowered at me from behind the counter as though I were an
infant insistent on the purchase of a fat cigar, then, as if to present me

untutored with an even more fitting analogy, he slapped onto the counter like a bartender in a wild west saloon the specimen that was within my means to purchase: a large clam. Needless to say, the clam was an enormous disappointment as a specimen for dissection. Back home, I withdrew the clam from its jar with tweezers and inspected it. With so little to inspect, I quickly got down to "dissecting" the clam. Even though a stick had been forcibly jabbed into it before it had been dumped into its jar, it resisted opening. It sputtered beneath my hands, its slickness stubbornly eluding my grasp. What use the tools could be with the clam, I didn't know. Failing to pry it open, I finally succeeded by smashing it with a hammer, then picked the bits of shell out of the wholly unsatisfying prize—a yellowish, snotty-looking globule. During the procedure, some of the solution that the clam had been floating in accidentally splashed up into my mouth. I immediately rinsed out my mouth but had already swallowed some droplets.

I needed a frog, but I knew it was off-limits. I wanted to delve deeper, I wanted what I knew was disallowed. Picture a nine-year-old pixie offering to mow people's lawns for a quarter, to shine my father's shoes for less, to sell door to door nylon potholders that I had woven on a plastic Woolworth's loom. Cash in hand, I returned to Al's the day before Labor Day. He shot me a look like a dealer who recognizes a junkie but who is willing to compromise any ethic he might harbor for the sake of a sale. "I'll take the frog, please," I tilted my head and felt suddenly that it might be a bobbin that could easily be loosed from its spindle, or that if Al wanted to he could by means of a single stroke snap my head off my body as if it were a doll's. He did no such thing but gave me the bottled frog, this time in a brown paper bag as if to acknowledge that a girl and a frog specimen should not appear in plain view. I told no one of my plan. I couldn't ask for my brothers' guidance. Opening the kit with its gleaming tools, I began furtively to work beneath a dim light at a crude table in the basement. I went at the frog with the kit, first pinning its limbs onto the piece of wood that came with the kit for such purposes. I wasn't sure what all of the instruments were for, but I recognized the scalpel and cut a line beginning at the frog's neck and piercing down past and into its abdomen and intestines. I "opened" the area with the other instrument and looked inside to an even graver disappointment: the frog seemed to consist of nothing so   *untutored* much as veins and goo. I didn't know what I was looking for or why. I panicked to observe that I had somehow defiled an otherwise whole, even though no longer living, creature. I was making a mess of this intact figure in the name of the power and pleasure of the scientific investigations that my brothers must enjoy. Becoming more fierce, more determined that the frog must yield something to me, I considered what the application of a different instrument might enable or reveal. Though the effect of this instrument was ghoulish—a slender metal handle at the end of which protruded something like a bent needle—I didn't clutch and apply it furiously like a figure out of Poe, but exactingly, I applied it to the frog's eye.

I was learning in these moments how profoundly awkward it was to unleash oneself from an instructor, to delve, and to fail. Even as I tried to make the experience come out right, even to be delicate with the frog, I was all fists, and pushing the needle into the frog's eye I jumped with a giddy kind of recklessness when, to my part horror part unexpected glee, the eye popped directly out of its socket, forever lost to the debris that crowded the basement floor.

How does any child reckon with the suspicion that gaining knowledge is a matter of entering realms not of the sacred but of the profane, not of piecing together but taking apart? That knowing comes with a degree of violation? The awkwardness of the situation wasn't to be found in my sense that I might have been silly or stupid to dissect a frog without instruction, but in the guilt I afterward felt over what I knew was an act of violence and desecration. It was as though I really did want to reach into something and force it open, to tear something limb from limb, to exact chaos where order claimed to reign, secretly to force an eye out from its socket and regard the gaping hole. I wonder if I felt as a little girl that this in so many untold ways had been done to me, or if, unmotivated by harm or by revenge, I simply was passionate to know more about the awkward ways any body is poised at thresholds without the elasticity required to cross them, the ways any body is required to stretch toward and beyond its own edges, to grow, resignedly, unknowingly, Gumby-like, to be poked, prodded, examined, kept in place or released, hugged and slapped, stroked and jarred, rattled sometimes by the voice and hands of other beings, and sometimes simply because of physics, untoward propulsions, or the tendency of sharp or hard, cold metal to accompany the swings in the playground that enabled one to fly.

fumbling

Awkwardness could be an effect of the rough handling of reality over which one has no control, or it could be an audacity only humans seem capable of. Each person's way of navigating the essential incompatibilities that are the stuff of life determines the peculiar shape of his awkwardness, and his alone.

"Awkward" could name the situation of being left holding what one has broken, the breakages carried out in private, in the rooms in which we try and fail in front of no one but ourselves.

To be awkward is to be left alone inside a vale of experimentation, left with nothing more than deeply wrought tributaries of desire.

I was in my late twenties, and Jean and I were both on the cusp of completing our doctoral dissertations at the graduate school where we had met. I was writing my way through a history of early American letters, a century-long trajectory of representations of illness and health. Jean was writing a book-length study of both the obscure and better-known works of Samuel Beckett entitled "Expression as Extortion." A disorder for which I had been misdiagnosed for years required me finally to "go beneath the knife." Not long thereafter, still feeling shorn and somewhat physiologically shredded, I accompanied Jean on a four-week whirlwind tour to revisit her numerous friends, in some cases former lovers, who were scattered across several European countries. We were on the cusp, too, of monogamy, and the trip seemed partly an attempt on Jean's part to reassure herself that none of her former lovers was the missed or better choice.

We were very young, and soon after our return home and newfound decision to live together, Jean received news that her mother had been diagnosed with an aggressive form of uterine cancer. Jean moved herself and her dissertation from Buffalo to Vancouver, where, in the shortening periods of her mother's naps, she finished her work on Beckett at the tiny tables and diminutive chairs afforded her at

the local library of a Vancouver suburb. I was to visit around the   *fumbling*
winter holidays.

Meeting Jean's mother for the first time and in the moment of
her illness was worse than awkward. It was sad, and I imagined
myself poised before her, carrying neither a spray of roses nor a bas-
ket of fruit, but the picture on my face that was the story of the love
I felt from and for her daughter.

Jean came out to her mother and then felt guilty for giving her
more incomprehensible information to bear. I wrote Jean's mother a
letter, even though I was there, to tell her how much I cherished
Jean. I tried not to be too visible in my visit; I glanced at Jean's
mother to find Jean in her; I tried not to seem to stare as she became
more ill and more reliant on the invasions of her body, the introduc-
tion of perforations, the abomination of tubes. Still, there had been
whole days of wellness shared together, and a particularly pleasant
afternoon spent talking, wandering, then sitting before the aquari-
ums of the Vancouver maritime museum.

One special item I had stowed in my knapsack, otherwise crammed
with books and a few pieces of clothes, was a thirty-five-millimeter
camera that my mother's new partner, Sidney, hearing of my trip,
had let me have. He called it his "Mickey Mouse" camera, as if to
suggest that it was the least sophisticated version of a thirty-five-
millimeter camera a person could own, but he explained the light
meter no longer worked. The moves required to adjust the camera
properly toward the prospect of crisp pictures in spite of the broken
meter struck me as anything but "Mickey Mouse," but I knew I could
rely on Jean to figure it out since she was a schooled photographer.

Across the space of our days in Vancouver together, I filled the
camera with twenty-four well chosen scenes, cognizant of the weight
of the act: that these might constitute, in some incomprehensible
way, "last pictures." Then I traveled what seemed like an endless
journey across bare and arctic tundra back to Buffalo alone, the
Buffalo winter still ahead of me as well as the last chapter of my
dissertation. I was eager for abundance and for a recognition of the
time I had just spent with Jean and with her family in Vancouver.
Like a post-holiday gift, the photographs would have meaning for
us, like a scarf spun out of an encounter that you wish to keep close,
the photos as record and as lifeline.

Never having worked a thirty-five-millimeter camera—and yet on the verge of claiming a Ph.D.—I didn't know how to open it to retrieve the film. I tried doing something with a crank. I pushed hidden buttons that seemed lost inside the body of the seemingly simple machine. I fumbled much as I had with the clam, with the frog. I knew I should wait and ask someone who knew, but I just was so eager to get at so as to develop the film. At the same time, I knew I was breaking rather than finding something, courting irreparability. The back of the camera popped open, the film unwound, exposed. Rather than try to save the film if possible by closing the camera again, I ripped it from the inside and watched it stream, completely ruined.

Was the film the camera's guts or the camera's eye? Its memory? I guess it was none of these, but an element like paper—but not paper, celluloid—that receives an impression of the world without interpreting it, perhaps, closest, physiologically, to just one part of the eye, the retina.

I want to say this series of oafish acts was accidental, but I'm afraid it wasn't, unless the convergence of competing feelings, the ever unbridgeable crosshatch of knowledge and desire can be forgiven and dismissed as accident, which it cannot.

It was hideous to have forced the camera open, but like all awkward acts it left its indelible mark. I found myself, in the days that followed, left, as if it were imprinted on my retina, with the saturated outlines of the last photo I had glimpsed through the viewfinder: it was of Jean's mother, wearing a blue winter coat, smiling, standing before the dolphin sculpture at the front of Vancouver's aquarama. The coat was so blue it verged on turquoise, so bright it seemed incongruous against the grades of onyx the dolphins, stilled, midflight, were sunk in, the grains of gray that made up the winter sky. When I took the photo, I remember thinking what a wonderful photo it would be, how grateful Jean's family would be to have it.

How vain my effort in so many senses was, how heavy with meaning, too heavy with meaning for any representation to bear. I could say I didn't *break* the camera open. I could say it exploded.

ecstatic

There are grooves to which one might return, spaces, silences remembered where no exasperation may be found. The reading room on the tiny campus of the Gorky Literary Institute in Moscow has become such a place for me. A librarian nods through bifocals. Bent, she files magazines into consoling rows. I claim a rectangular patch to be the surface upon which I am to place and replace the pages I will read. I feel thin and tall as I sink into my place, straightening only to adjust my lamp, its button tender as the book of the same name from which I read. The snow falls in windless sheets, piling like drifts of paper through the window. In between reading or before, I might step lightly, inconspicuously into an adjacent building to use the bathroom. The room is so filled with smoke it smells of cooked tobacco. The students hang out here, drying wet and matted wool across the heaters. The doors of the stalls don't quite close, and I'm con-vinced my students can observe me shitting or, if they can't, one of them will accidentally burst through the wobbly door and find me not invisible but there. What would be the correct Russian word to apply to the situation? A simple "Nyet!"? Before using the toilet, I must, I find, lift the broken wooden seat from off the floor. I clean it, then adjust it precariously into place. I don't use the book-sized mirror while I wash my hands to neaten tousled hair, but glide somehow nodding past the students who, though they tilt their heads cockily while they smoke and sigh, part the waters of the mass of them to make a path for me. Wherefore pure joy of feeling *not* at home, that's what I'd call it, not awk-wardness but bliss, or bliss of awkwardness. Was it a bliss born of having had to work to surmount the challenge of a dirty toilet seat? Or was it the rightness of the plastic indoor flowers against through-the-window snow that made me glad? Inimitable per-plexity: the hills of live blooms available in winter at periodic overflowing stalls?

My father's story bears re-reading, I surmise. I realize I don't want him to die before someone has read his story and also told him

ecstatic

so. "You can do whatever you want with it," he's said to me. He'd said it when I spoke so fondly of "The Mysterious Indigo Box." Here's Stella skipping on high at the prospect of how the box will lighten her, mellifluous. The contents of the box will enter and transform her, at the very least *bestow*, but the people around her perceive the box as a "paperweight." Sometimes struggling with her impatience—"with an exasperated sigh, she rested it on her stomach"—other times groping for, not finding it, mourning its inevitable absence, she finds she's sitting right on top of it. Seek, and ye shall find, beneath your rump.

Few and far between, but to each person there must be had a taste of sudden romance, when the forces of nature conspire to bless a space of lovers' being in the world. Jean and I share the last warm day of Autumn; we gather, and we kick. It's a rare day off of nothing but pleasure in walking in New York. We're seated at a table lit by lanterns in a patio in the middle of the city but tucked away from the street. The food is Thai in this open-to-the-night-sky enclave. Leaves from a towering lime tree fall onto the table while we eat, sometimes right into our food, and the one that has fallen just between us, I decide I want to save. Before I can reach it, and still mulling in my fantasy, the waiter passes by, and with an abrupt jerk of the long arm of a waitering machine, as if his job were to trim the excess and excise the out-of-place, he snatches the leaf from the table and it disappears. The awkwardness of the moment is shocking, and ripe. More memorable and live than the act of completion I would have exerted in pressing it.

Sometimes a breast must be made to do what it resists in order for it to be pictured. No one's flesh moves the way it needs to in order to achieve a mammogram because a breast is attached to a body. The technician attempts to lift my breast as if it were a baby orange with legs and arms onto a platter. I want to give her *more* breast, assuming the relative smallness of my breasts (I'm not complaining) is making it hard for her to grasp enough unyielding dough to *place* onto her plastic slab. As the machine begins to *press* the breast between two plates, I clutch the bar she has instructed me to hold, and then it's *me* who is mocked, not this process, this machine, or its inventor. "You don't have to hold on for dear life," she says, "Relax your grip. This isn't the dentist!"

ecstatic

Let me exert my own recalcitrance, I want to say, this awkward pas de deux.

One afternoon not even morning I awoke to discover that the leaves disappeared overnight. The trees' nakedness, I found, appalled me. I could not say exactly of what I was afraid.

In a windowless restaurant mid-November, in a backroom banquet reception hall, my seven-year-old niece, Justine, sketches my portrait broadly on the back of a placemat. As always, she has picked up on an awkward circumstance. Call it the technicality of queer relatives at your rehearsal dinner, or structured absences for which there are no words, a situation that is nobody's fault. We're leaving, we've survived the first part of a family member's wedding, when I notice Justine carefully placing the drawing of me on the table as if she means to leave it there. "Let's leave it, Mary, and have somebody find it," she says, "like the people who work here." "We can't leave *me* behind!" I protest. "Don't be afraid," she pets my hand, then interlards the thought, staring up at me like a little philosopher god, she asserts, "You're yourself!"

An exotic insect had disturbed Thanksgiving dinner, and when I told a learned friend about it, hoping to get an entomological read of what it might be, he reported what he'd learned about insects on TV: scientists have determined that if we weighed all the insects in the world, we'd discover the collective mass outweighed that of all the humans in the world. You're making me rethink my world, I want to say. I want to say, awkwardness inheres: we are so much lighter, so much heavier than we suppose.

"She didn't say, did she, 'supple' mind?" I ask my friend Karen at our newfound favorite diner even if the hash browned potatoes taste like plastic and the pancakes resist rather than absorb their syrup, and the owner wraps the silverware with a paper band that one must break like those strange paper bands strung across the seats one sometimes finds in public bathrooms that seem symbolically to announce that defecation or using the toilet is *banned*, but that are meant to say "these premises are clean." Sensitive, splendid, savory, enthusiastic, keen, rare. No. "Didn't she say, 'incandescent'?" Karen says, convinced as a loving friend who is a poet in prose. Let's fantasize together. Incandescent is a wonderful word. But no. That word is reserved *ecstatic*   for a rose. Is a rose is a rose. "Psychedelic," I say, enjoying the thin fringed leather coat and sunglasses that Karen is wearing on this, the coldest day of the year.

Let's enjoy the certainty of what she *hadn't* said—Awkward—"you, my dear, have such an awkward mind!" Certainly she hadn't said that, no one would ever say *that*.

ACKNOWLEDGMENTS

A fellowship from the U.S. Fulbright Program enabled me to teach and study at the Gorky Literary Institute, Moscow, Russia, in the Fall of 2001, and the Dorothea Lange–Paul Taylor Prize from the Center for Documentary Studies, Duke University, enabled me to reside in Italy and Sicily in Spring of 2002 in order to document the lives of new immigrants to Italy from an array of nations across the world. Significant portions of this manuscript draw from my experiences in Russia and in Italy.

Scholarship on the life and work of Emily Dickinson is vast. I cite here only those scholars to whose work I am most particularly indebted in the pages of this book. These include Sharon Cameron on an aesthetic of "choosing not choosing"; Diana Fuss on Dickinson, space, and the architecture of the Homestead; Ellen Louise Hart and Martha Nell Smith on the letter poems that passed from Emily Dickinson to her sister-in-law and companion author, Susan Huntington Dickinson; Susan Howe on the manuscript space of the poems; Aife Murray on Dickinson's servants and her relationships with them, especially with Maggie Maher, as well as the detailed contours of keeping a New England house in the mid-nineteenth century; and numerous biographies of Dickinson not least of which include Cynthia Griffin Wolff's magisterial study of Dickinson's life in the context of the Second Great Awakening. All citations to poems refer to *The Poems of Emily Dickinson: Reading Edition* (Massachusetts: the Belknap Press of Harvard University Press, 1999), edited by R.W. Franklin. Letters to Susan are drawn from *Open Me Carefully: Emily Dickinson's Intimate Letters to Susan Huntington Dickinson* (Massachusetts: Paris Press, 1998), edited by Smith and Hart, and extracts appear here from letters 113, 242, 16, and 102, respectively.

Quoted matter relative to Dickinson's life, work and letters in the order in which it appears in this manuscript are drawn from the following sources: Millicent Todd Bingham quoting Mabel Loomis Todd, Dickinson's brother's lover, and one of Dickinson's first posthumous editors, in her *Ancestor's Brocades: The Literary Debut of Emily Dickinson*, (New York: Harper and Brothers, 1945); Cynthia Griffin Wolff, *Emily Dickinson* (New York: Alfred A. Knopf, 1986); Maryanne M. Garbowsky, *The House Without the Door: A Study of Emily Dickinson and the Illness of Agoraphobia* (New Jersey: Fairleigh Dickinson University Press, 1989); and Diana Fuss, "Interior Chambers: The Emily Dickinson Homestead," *differences: A Journal of Feminist Cultural Studies* 10 (Fall 1998).

My thinking on Henry James' *The Awkward Age* was aided by the writing and scholarship of David McWhirter, Eve Kosofsky Sedgwick, Tzvetan Todorov, Keven J. Hayes—editor of *Henry James: The Contemporary Reviews* (New York: Cambridge University Press, 1996), from which I quote in these pages; Merle A. Williams, Barbara Hochman, Mark Seltzer, and Lawrence Rainey on dictation and modernist aesthetic impulses. Pamela Thurschwell's tremendously interesting work on the typewriter, especially on James' typist Theodora Bosanquet, and on notions of dictation and telepathy that figured in early psychoanalytic theory and practice, were distinctly provocative and informative. Theodora Bosanquet's *Henry James at Work* (a reprint of the 1924 edition published by Leonard and Virginia Woolf at the Hogarth Press, London, which was issued as volume three of the Hogarth essays) was an indispensable resource. All references to the novel proper refer to the 1987 Penguin edition of *The Awkward Age*, edited and introduced by Ronald Blythe. The excerpt from James' notebook appears on page 312 of the Penguin edition. Todorov's commentary on *The Awkward Age* from which I quote appears in *Genres in Discourse*, translated by Catherine Porter (New York: Cambridge University Press, 1990).

Lynn Sharon Schwartz' essay on the telephone in *Tolstoy's Dictaphone: Technology and the Muse*, edited by Sven Birkerts (Graywolf Press, 1996) provided a stirring intertext early in my thinking about awkward silences. Natalia Ginzburg's essays, in particular "My Craft," from which I quote and which appears in *A Place to Live and Other Selected Essays of Natalia Ginzburg*, chosen and translated by Lynne Sharon Schwartz (New York: Seven

Stories Press, 2002), Helen Keller's autobiography, *The Story of My Life* (New York: Houghton Mifflin, 1928) from which I quote, Alane Salierno Mason's translation of Elio Vittorini's *Conversations in Sicily* (New York: New Directions, 2000), Leonardo Sciascia's *Sicily as Metaphor*, conversations presented by Marcelle Padovani translated by James Marcus (Marlboro, VT: Marlboro Press, 1994), from which I quote, Anna Tasca Lanza's books on Sicilian cuisine—I quote from page 53 of *The Heart of Sicily: Recipes and Reminiscences of Regaleali, A Country Estate* (New York: Clarkson Potter, 1993) as well as the beautifully rendered *Bitter Almonds*, co-authored by Mary Taylor Simeti and Maria Grammatico, were sources of indescribable guidance and inspiration.

I refer to Gertrude Stein, *Tender Buttons* (New York: Dover Publications, 1997).

Some of the theorists whose voices I had hoped to sing in concert with in these pages include Roland Barthes on *The Pleasure of the Text* (translated by Richard Miller, New York: Hill and Wang, 1975), Gilles Deleuze "On Stuttering" (in *Essays Critical and Clinical*, University of Minnesota Press, 1997), and Avital Ronell on stupidity in her book, *Stupidity* (Chicago: University of Illinois Press, 2002).

Mikhail Epstein's published and unpublished, translated and untranslated masterpieces, especially for these pages his essay "Econopoeia, or The Poetry of Business" were a source of conversation and ongoing dialogical thought.

I owe a special thanks to Christopher Mayo, who informed me that at least half of Lord Chesterfield's (1694–1733) *Letters to His Son* treat the subject of awkwardness, and for his generosity in sharing choice examples from that vast body of work.

Alice Yaeger Kaplan's, "On Language Memoir," from which I quote, appears in *Displacements: Cultural Identities in Question*, (Bloomington: Indiana University Press, 1994), edited by Angelika Bammer. Bruno Schulz' "Treatise on the Tailor's Dummies or The Second Book of Genesis" appears in *The Street of Crocodiles*, translated by Celina Wieniewska and introduced by Jerzy Ficowski (New York: Penguin Books, 1977).

No poem that I know speaks as succinctly and directly to a conceptual center of my book than Laura Riding's "The World and I," which appears in her *Selected Poems in Five Sets* (New York: W. W. Norton, 1973). Amy Hoffman's *Hospital Time* taught me invaluable lessons about the politics of tact and tactlessness in the age of AIDS.

I relied on Christian Braad Thomsen's *Fassbinder: The Life and Work of a Provocative Genius* (University of Minnesota Press, 2004), for biographical material on Rainer Werner Fassbinder. Quotations derive from "Imitation of Life: On the Films of Douglas Sirk, An Illustrated Essay by filmmaker Rainer Werner Fassbinder," and excerpts from *Behind the Mirror: A Profile of Douglas Sirk*, a 1979 BBC documentary featuring interview footage with the director, both of which appear as special features on the Criterion Collection DVD of Douglas Sirk's *All That Heaven Allows* (Universal, 1955, 1983, 2001). Further invaluable source material, including an interview with Brigitte Mira and the short film *Angst isst Seele auf* directed by Shahbaz Noshir, is available on the Criterion Collection DVD of Rainer Werner Fassbinder's *Ali: Fear Eats the Soul* (Rainer Werner Fassbinder Foundation, The Criterion Collection, 2003).

I gratefully acknowledge the editors of the journals in which excerpts of this manuscript appear: Barry Weller, Willard Spiegelman, Christopher Arigo, Miranda Mellis, Kate Schatz, and Tisa Bryant, editors at *Western Humanities Review*, *Southwest Review*, *Interim*, and *Encyclopedia*, respectively.

Innumerable co-authors and readers brought *Awkward* into being. These include my students, graduate and undergraduate, at the University of Rhode Island, whose creative elaborations, voices, and hard work often inspired my own. Two seminars in particular provoked the call to which this book responded: "Immigrant Subjectivity and Documentary Discourse" and "Literature and Medicine: An Ethics of Care."

Special thanks to Agata Stepien and Ted Williams for reading suggestions, and for the encouraging and critical engagement of my colleagues, whose own challenging and original work is in many ways a model for my own: Stephen Barber, Carolyn Betensky, Naomi Mandel, Nancy Cook, Valerie Karno, Amity Gaige, Talvi Ansel, Bob Leuci, and especially Don Kunz, whose generous responses to my work over a number of years were inestimable. My colleagues, students, and new friends in Russia and in Italy introduced me to new worlds daily and were immensely patient both with my ignorance and with my awkwardness. One could not find better fellow journeyers and guides than Yaroslava Muratova, Tatiana Orlova, Julia Lapteva, Nadia Koncha, Helen Vorontsova, Irina Shishkova, Galina and Anya Evtushenko, and Sergey Tolkachov. I am especially indebted to the immigrants to Italy—Ecuadoran tailor Lourdes Mariana Veintimilla Casiddas and Syrian tailor Maher DiBalle—who shared their stories with me, and the political activists and writers— Senegalese immigrants to Italy Dieng Daouda, Pap Khouma, and Saidou Moussa Ba—who introduced to me a productive gap between the idea of Italy bequeathed me by my immigrant family and Italy's contemporary competing realities.

This writing would not have been possible without the intellectual companionship and friendship of Arthur Riss and Nina Markov, Jennifer Manlowe, Russell Potter, and Penelope Cray. I have been fortunate to have in my agent, Malaga Baldi, a reader who gives me back my work in her own words, who understands what I'm up to, and keeps the faith. My editor, Erika Goldman, gave the manuscript scrupulous attention and care and helped to smooth its jaggedness while maintaining its awkward byways. Her inspired sense of juxtaposition and structure helped to make *Awkward* a better book.

James Morrison, my writing guru, is present to all that I compose, and my friend and writing partner Karen Carr read or listened to each new incarnation of this project (several times). Karen's readerly acuity and writerly rapture opened a space of permissibility and the unexpected. *Awkward* is dedicated to our on-going dialogues. Jeannie Walton, she "from whom I never run away," my partner in adventure, makes possible what seems impossible; including the adventures that instigated this book. The example of my mother, Rosemary Petracca Cappello's life and of her writing, its risks and passionate heights, graces this composition, and so much more.

INDEX

About the Author

Jean Walton

Mary Cappello is a poet, essayist, and the author of *Night Bloom*. Professor of English at the University of Rhode Island, she lives in Providence, Rhode Island and Lucerne-in-Maine, Maine.

For more information about the author, visit her website at www.awkwardness.org